A
BITCH
IS BORN

A BITCH

IS BORN

BY
ROBERTA GREGORY

FANTAGRAPHICS BOOKS

Other Books in this series

As Naughty as She Wants to be
At Work and At Play with Bitchy Bitch

FANTAGRAPHICS BOOKS

7563 Lake City Way NE
Seattle, WA 98115

Editorial Consultation by Kim Thompson
Design and Art Direction by Roberta Gregory and Patrick Moriarity
Color Separations by Jamison Services
Gary Groth and Kim Thompson, Publishers

The material in this collection originally appeared in Naughty Bits #3, 4, 6, 7, and 8 with the exception of "Weekend Condition."

First Fantagraphics Books edition: May, 1994
Second Fantagraphics Books edition: June, 1996
PRINTED IN CANADA
ISBN: 156097-156-6

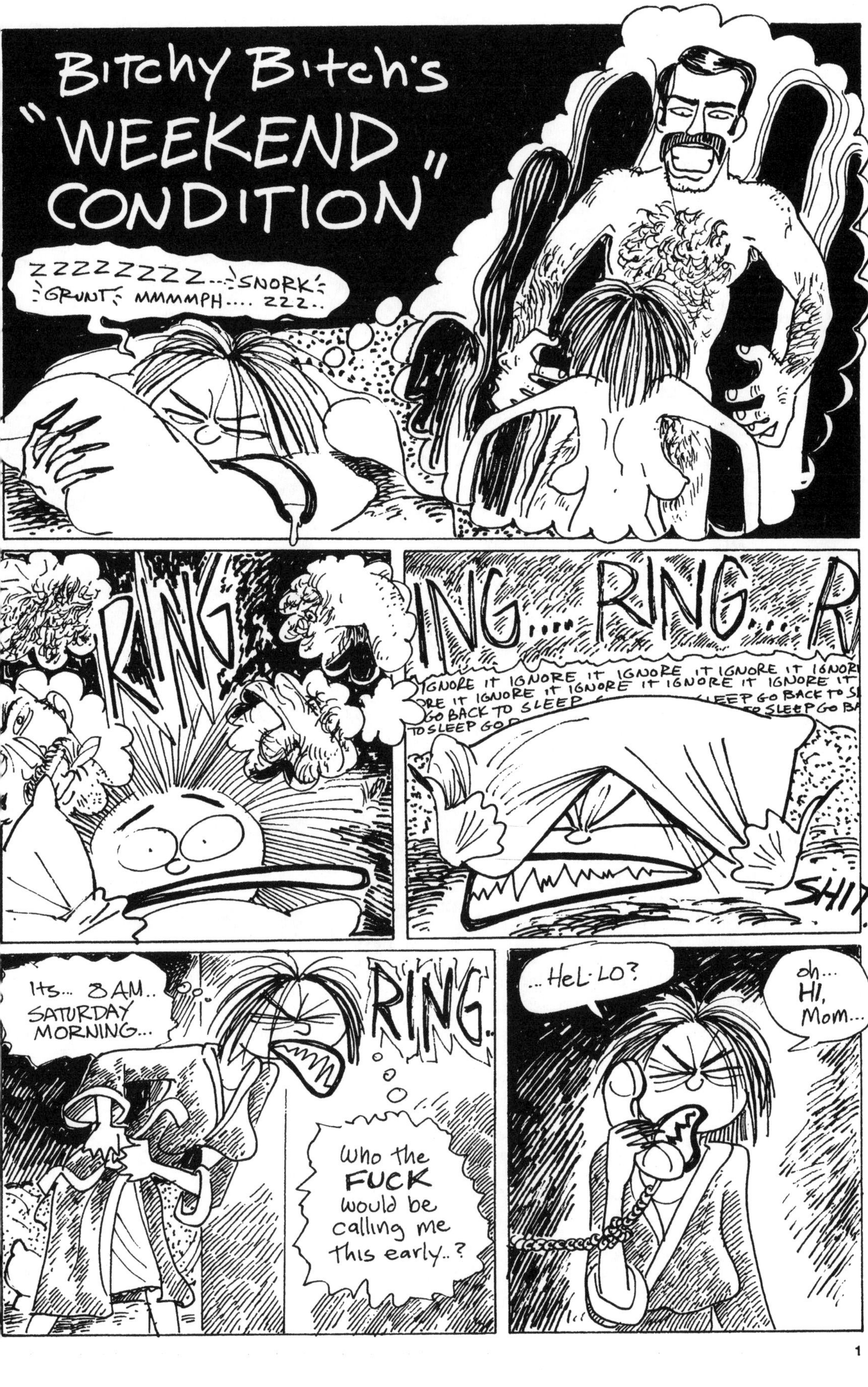
Bitchy Bitch's
"WEEKEND" CONDITION
ZZZZZZZZ... SNORK GRUNT MMMMPH.... ZZZ..
RING
ING.... RING.... R
IGNORE IT IGNORE IT IGNORE IT IGNORE IT IGNORE IT
GO BACK TO SLEEP GO BACK TO SLEEP GO BACK TO SLEEP GO
SHIT!
Its... 8 AM.. SATURDAY MORNING...
RING..
Who the FUCK would be calling me this early..?
...HeL-LO?
oh... HI, Mom...

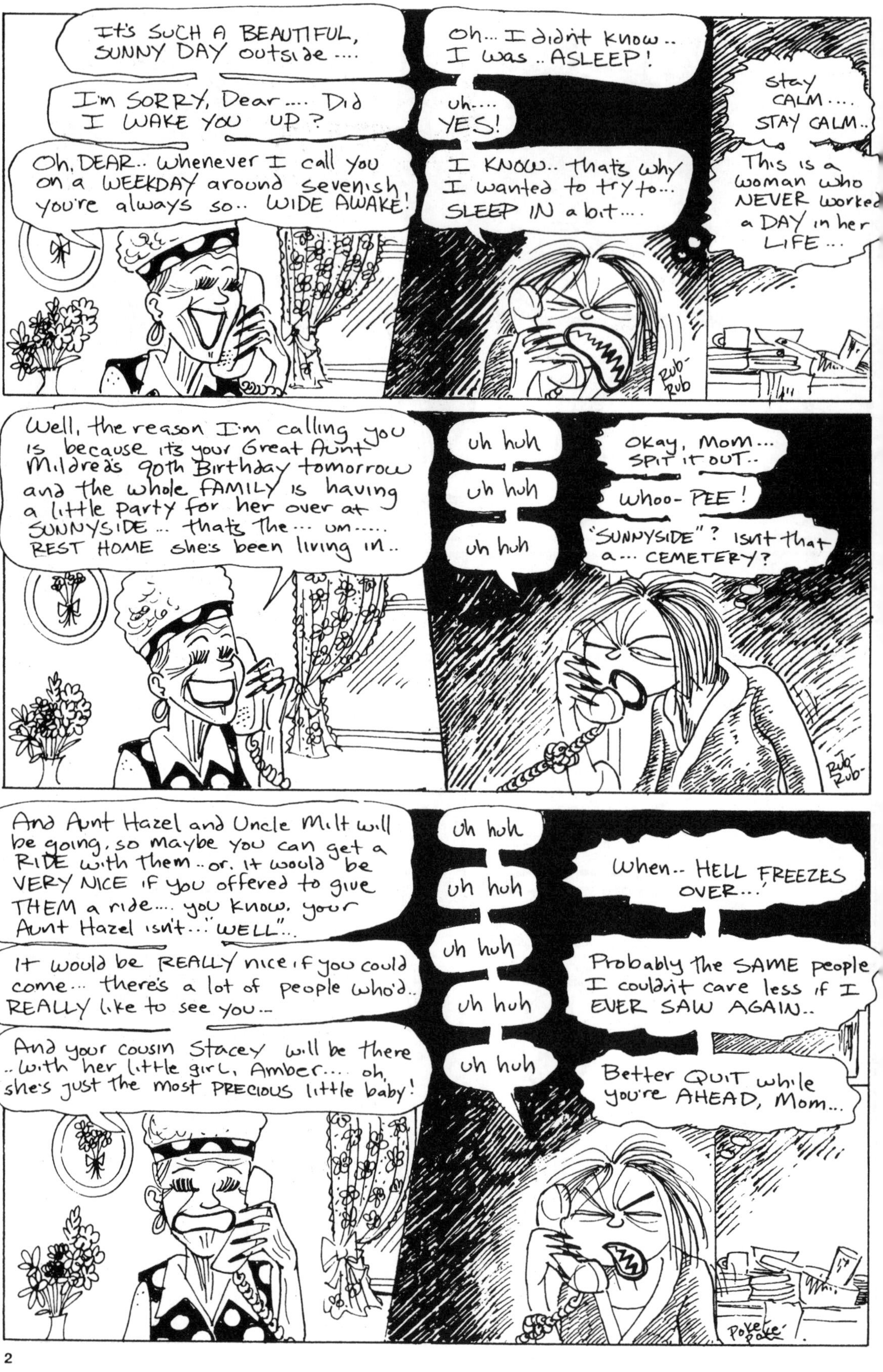
It's SUCH A BEAUTIFUL, SUNNY DAY outside....
I'm SORRY, Dear.... Did I WAKE YOU UP?
Oh, DEAR.. whenever I call you on a WEEKDAY around sevenish you're always so.. WIDE AWAKE!
Oh... I didn't know.. I was.. ASLEEP!
uh.... YES!
I KNOW.. that's why I wanted to try to... SLEEP IN a bit....
Rub-Rub
Stay CALM.... STAY CALM..
This is a woman who NEVER worked a DAY in her LIFE...
Well, the reason I'm calling you is because it's your Great Aunt Mildred's 90th Birthday tomorrow and the whole FAMILY is having a little party for her over at SUNNYSIDE... that's the... um..... REST HOME she's been living in..
uh huh
uh huh
uh huh
Okay, Mom... SPIT IT OUT..
Whoo-PEE!
"SUNNYSIDE"? Isn't that a... CEMETERY?
Rub-Rub-
And Aunt Hazel and Uncle Milt will be going, so maybe you can get a RIDE with them.. or, it would be VERY NICE if you offered to give THEM a ride.... you know, your Aunt Hazel isn't..."WELL"..
It would be REALLY nice if you could come... there's a lot of people who'd.. REALLY like to see you..
And your cousin Stacey will be there ..with her little girl, Amber.... oh, she's just the most PRECIOUS little baby!
uh huh
uh huh
uh huh
uh huh
uh huh
When.. HELL FREEZES OVER...
Probably the SAME people I couldn't care less if I EVER SAW AGAIN..
Better QUIT while you're AHEAD, Mom...
Poke-Poke

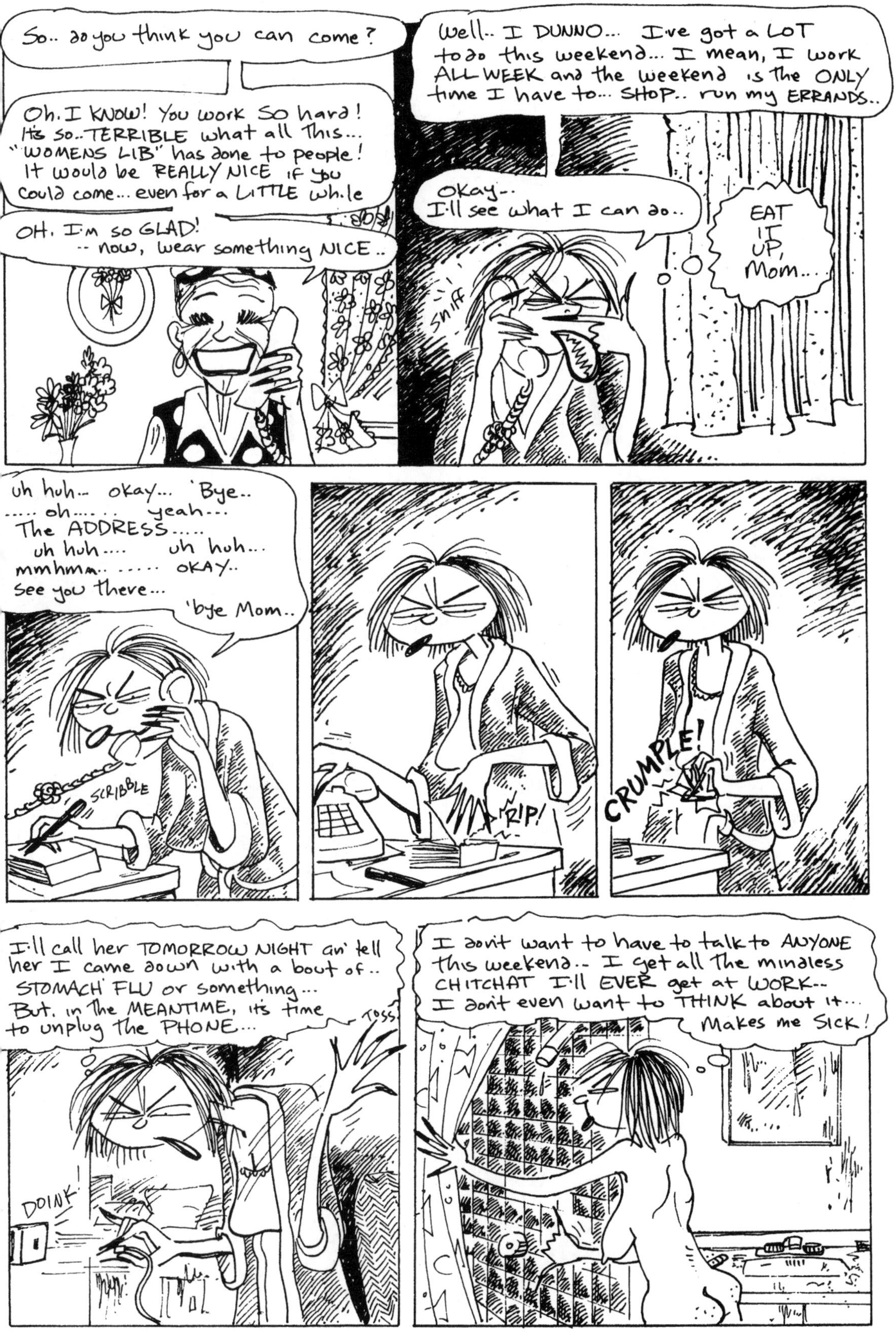
So.. do you think you can come?
Well.. I DUNNO... I've got a LOT to do this weekend... I mean, I work ALL WEEK and the weekend is the ONLY time I have to... SHOP.. run my ERRANDS..
Oh. I KNOW! You work SO hard! It's so.. TERRIBLE what all this... "WOMENS LIB" has done to people! It would be REALLY NICE if you could come... even for a LITTLE while
Okay-.. I'll see what I can do..
EAT IT UP, Mom....
OH. I'M so GLAD! -- now, wear something NICE..
SNIFF
uh huh.. okay... 'Bye.. ..... oh..... yeah... The ADDRESS..... uh huh.... uh huh... mmhmm.. ...... OKAY.. See you there... 'bye Mom..
SCRIBBLE
RIP!
CRUMPLE!
I'll call her TOMORROW NIGHT an' tell her I came down with a bout of.. STOMACH FLU or something... But. in the MEANTIME, it's time to unplug the PHONE...
TOSS
DOINK
I don't want to have to talk to ANYONE this weekend.. I get all the mindless CHITCHAT I'll EVER get at WORK.. I don't even want to THINK about it... Makes me SICK!

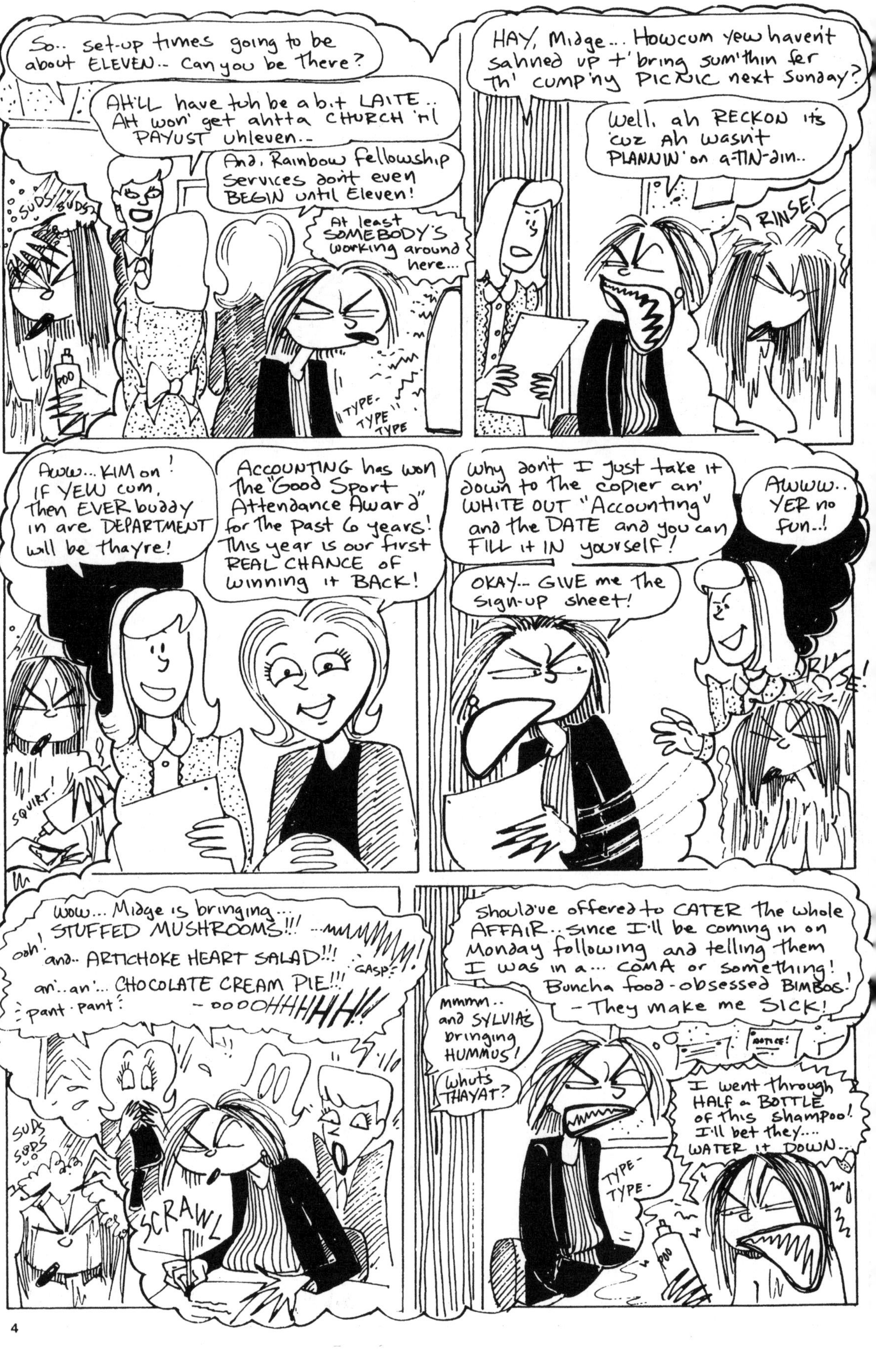
So.. set-up times going to be about ELEVEN.. Can you be there?
AH'LL have tuh be a bit LAITE.. AH won' get ahtta CHURCH 'til PAYUST uhleven..
And, Rainbow fellowship services don't even BEGIN until Eleven!
SUDS SUDS
At least SOMEBODY'S working around here...
POO
TYPE TYPE TYPE
HAY, Midge... Howcum yew haven't sahned up t' bring sum'thin fer th' cump'ny PICNIC next Sunday?
Well, ah RECKON it's 'cuz Ah wasn't PLANNIN' on a-TIN-din..
RINSE!
Aww... KIM on! IF YEW cum, then EVER buddy in are DEPARTMENT will be thayre!
ACCOUNTING has won the "Good Sport Attendance Award" for the past 6 years! This year is our first REAL CHANCE of winning it BACK!
SQUIRT!
Why don't I just take it down to the copier an' WHITE OUT "Accounting" and the DATE and you can FILL it IN yourself!
OKAY.. GIVE me the sign-up sheet!
AWWW.. YER no fun..!
Wow... Midge is bringing... STUFFED MUSHROOMS!!! ...MMMM
ooh! and.. ARTICHOKE HEART SALAD!!!
GASP
an'..an'... CHOCOLATE CREAM PIE!!!
pant · pant
- OOOOHHHHHH!!
SUDS SUDS
SCRAWL
Should've offered to CATER the whole AFFAIR.. since I'll be coming in on Monday following and telling them I was in a... COMA or something! Buncha food-obsessed BIMBOS! - They make me SICK!
mmmm.. and SYLVIA'S bringing HUMMUS!
Whut's THAYAT?
NOTICE!
I went through HALF a BOTTLE of this shampoo! I'll bet they.... WATER it DOWN...
TYPE- TYPE-
POO

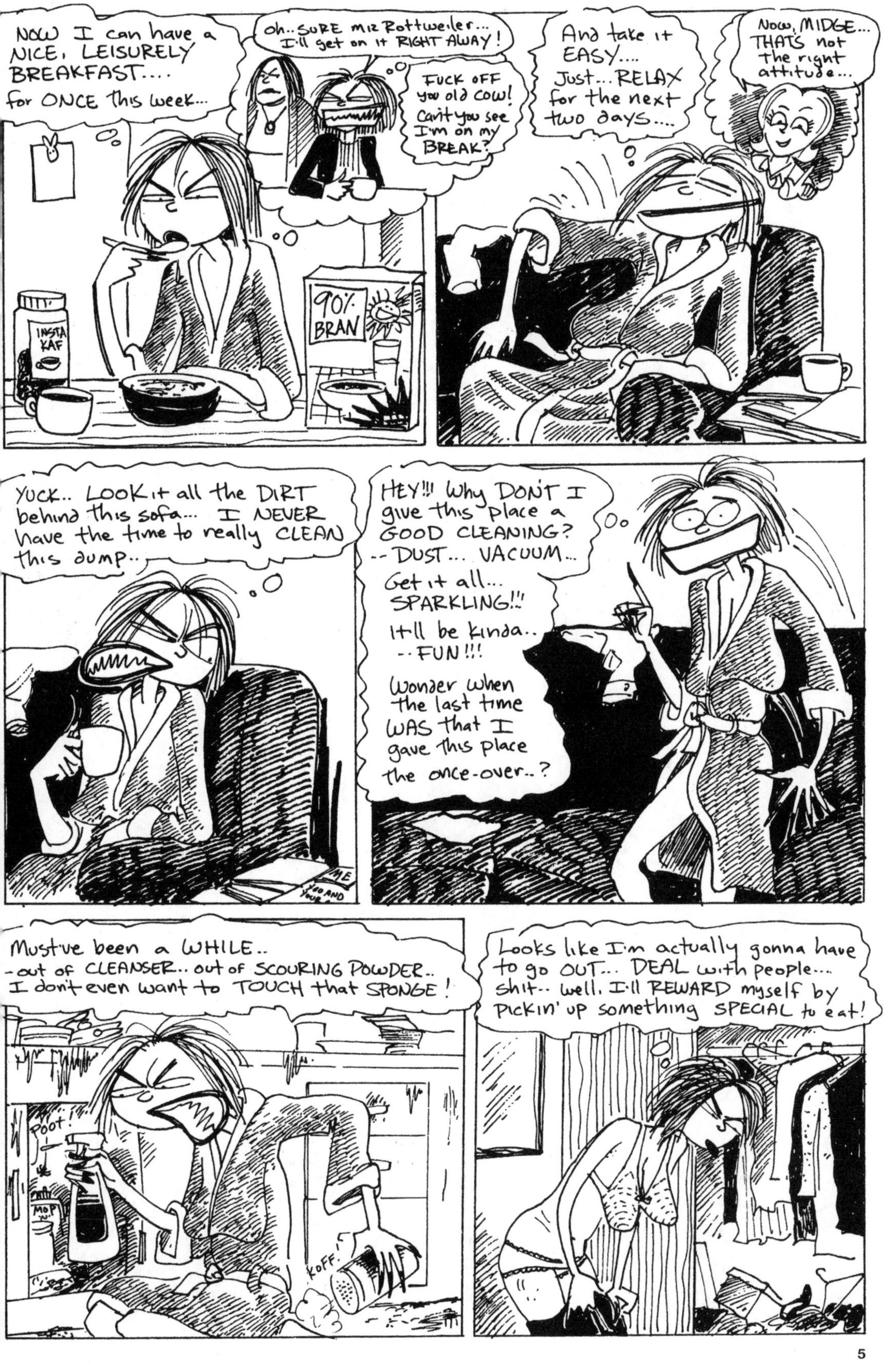
NOW I can have a NICE, LEISURELY BREAKFAST.... for ONCE this week...
oh.. SURE miz Rottweiler... I'll get on it RIGHT AWAY!
FUCK OFF you old cow! Can't you see I'm on my BREAK?
INSTA KAF
90% BRAN
And take it EASY.... Just... RELAX for the next two days....
Now, MIDGE... THAT'S not the right attitude...
YUCK.. LOOK it all the DIRT behind this sofa... I NEVER have the time to really CLEAN this dump..
HEY!!! Why DON'T I give this place a GOOD CLEANING? --DUST... VACUUM... Get it all... SPARKLING!!! It'll be kinda.. --FUN!!! Wonder when the last time WAS that I gave this place the once-over..?
Must've been a WHILE.. -out of CLEANSER.. out of SCOURING POWDER.. I don't even want to TOUCH that SPONGE!
POOT!
MOP
KOFF!
Looks like I'm actually gonna have to go OUT... DEAL with people.... shit.. well, I'll REWARD myself by Pickin' up something SPECIAL to eat!

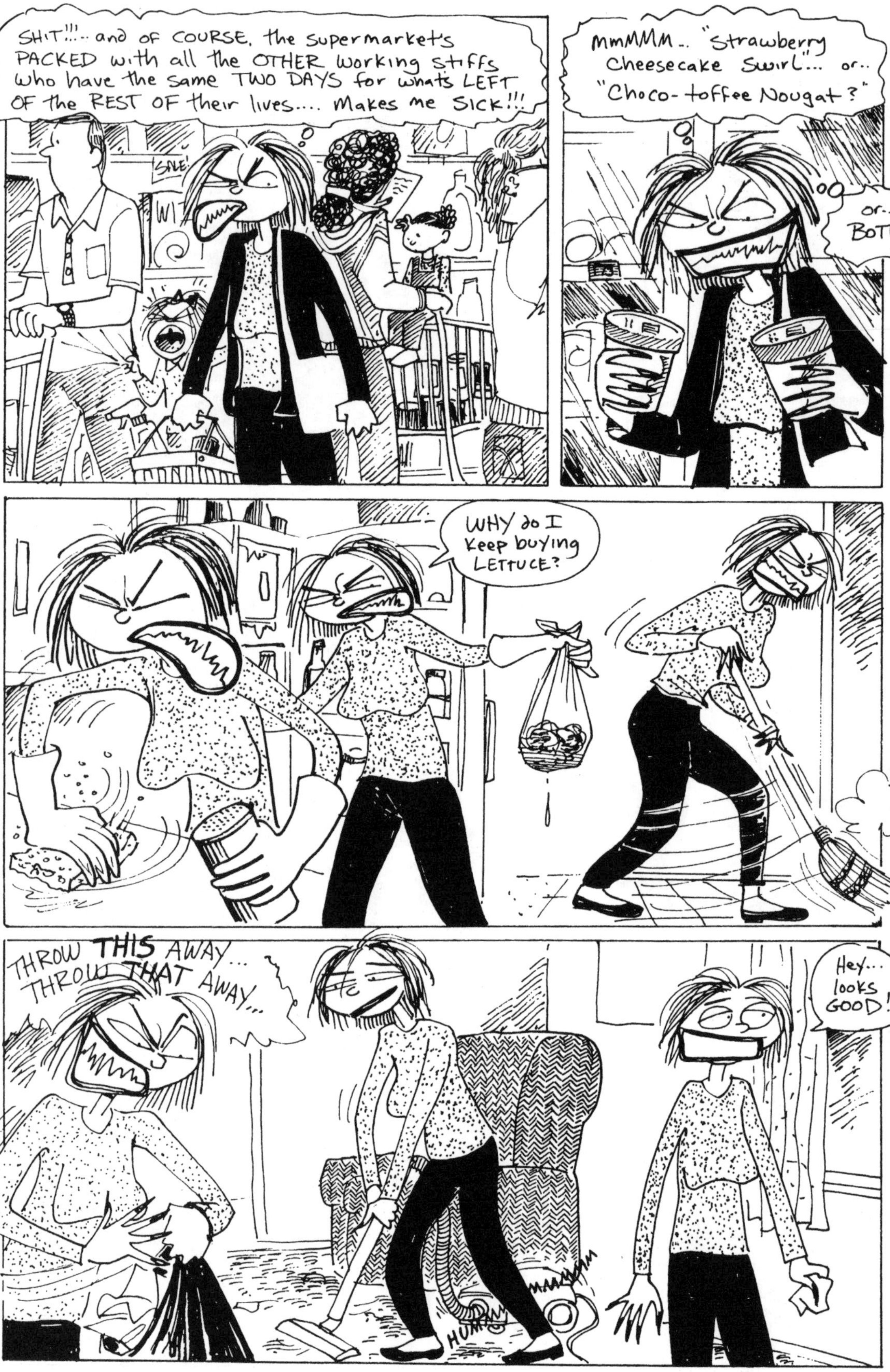

SHIT!!!.. and OF COURSE, the supermarket's PACKED with all the OTHER working stiffs who have the same TWO DAYS for what's LEFT OF the REST OF their lives.... Makes me SICK!!!
SALE!
MmMMM.. "Strawberry Cheesecake Swirl"... or.. "Choco-toffee Nougat?"
WHY do I keep buying LETTUCE?
THROW THIS AWAY... THROW THAT AWAY...
Hey... looks GOOD!

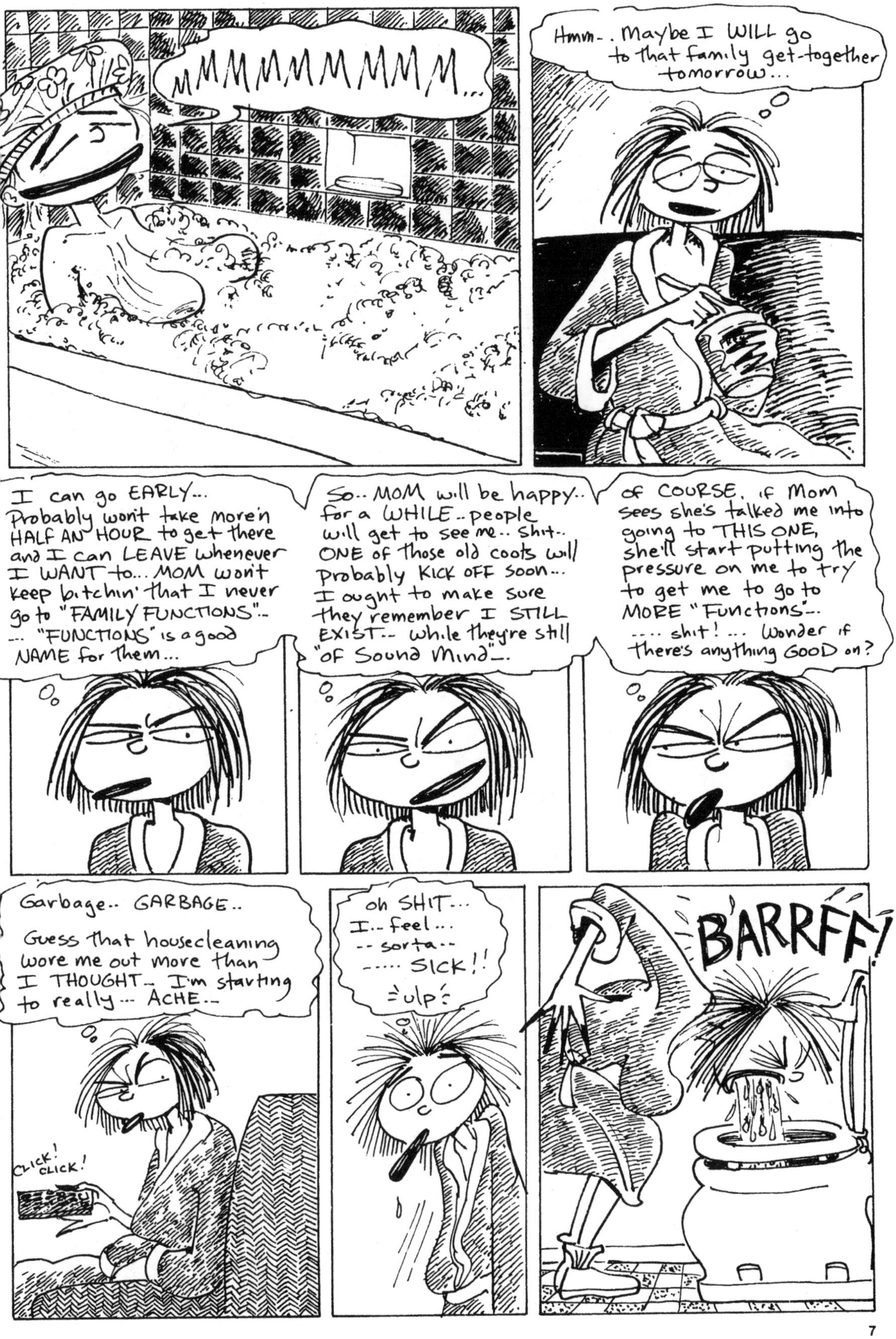

MMMMMMMMMM...
Hmm.. Maybe I WILL go to that family get-together tomorrow...
I can go EARLY... Probably won't take more'n HALF AN HOUR to get there and I can LEAVE whenever I WANT to... MOM won't keep bitchin' that I never go to "FAMILY FUNCTIONS"... "FUNCTIONS" is a good NAME for them...
So.. MOM will be happy.. for a WHILE.. people will get to see me.. shit.. ONE of those old coots will probably KICK OFF soon... I ought to make sure they remember I STILL EXIST.. while they're still "of Sound Mind"...
OF COURSE, if Mom sees she's talked me into going to THIS ONE, she'll start putting the pressure on me to try to get me to go to MORE "Functions"... ....shit! ... Wonder if there's anything GOOD on?
Garbage.. GARBAGE..
Guess that housecleaning wore me out more than I THOUGHT.. I'm starting to really... ACHE..
CLICK! CLICK!
oh SHIT... I.. feel... -- sorta.. ..... SICK!!
ulp
BARRFF!

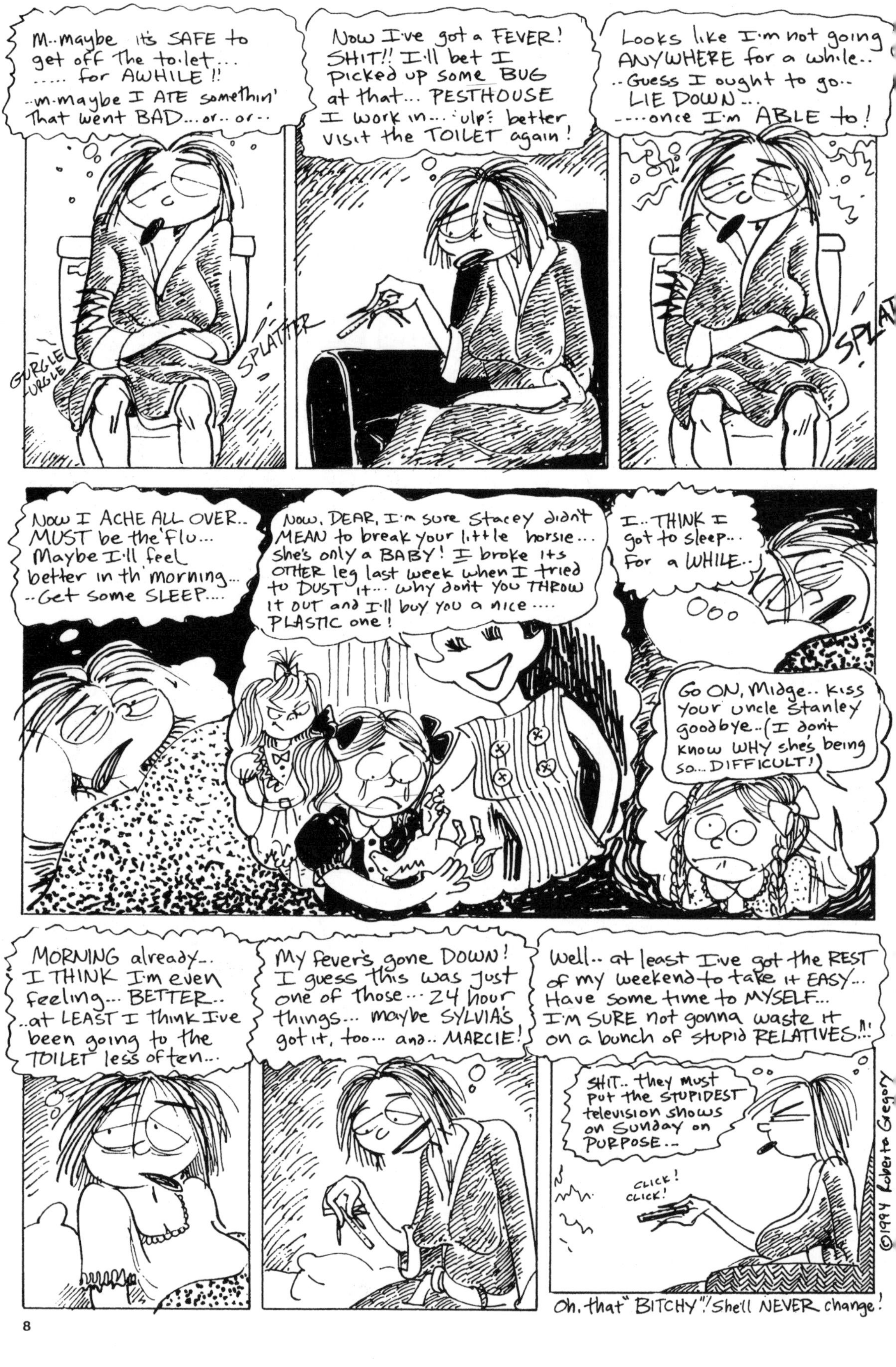

M..maybe it's SAFE to get off the toilet... ..... for AWHILE!! ..m..maybe I ATE somethin' that went BAD....or.. or..
GURGLE GURGLE
SPLATTER
Now I've got a FEVER! SHIT!! I'll bet I picked up some BUG at that... PESTHOUSE I work in... :ulp: better visit the TOILET again!
Looks like I'm not going ANYWHERE for a while.. ..Guess I ought to go.. LIE DOWN... ....once I'm ABLE to!
SPLAT
Now I ACHE ALL OVER.. MUST be the 'Flu... Maybe I'll feel better in th' morning... ..Get some SLEEP....
Now, DEAR, I'm sure Stacey didn't MEAN to break your little horsie... she's only a BABY! I broke its OTHER leg last week when I tried to DUST it... why don't you THROW it out and I'll buy you a nice.... PLASTIC one!
I.. THINK I got to sleep... For a WHILE..
Go ON, Midge.. kiss your uncle Stanley goodbye..(I don't know WHY she's being so... DIFFICULT!)
MORNING already.. I THINK I'm even feeling... BETTER.. ..at LEAST I think I've been going to the TOILET less often..
My fever's gone DOWN! I guess this was just one of those... 24 hour things... maybe SYLVIA'S got it, too... and.. MARCIE!
Well.. at least I've got the REST of my weekend to take it EASY... Have some time to MYSELF... I'M SURE not gonna waste it on a bunch of stupid RELATIVES!!!
SHIT.. they must put the STUPIDEST television shows on Sunday on PURPOSE..
CLICK! CLICK!
©1994 Roberta Gregory
Oh, that "BITCHY"! She'll NEVER change!

Bitsy Bitch goes to School
And then she goes HOME!

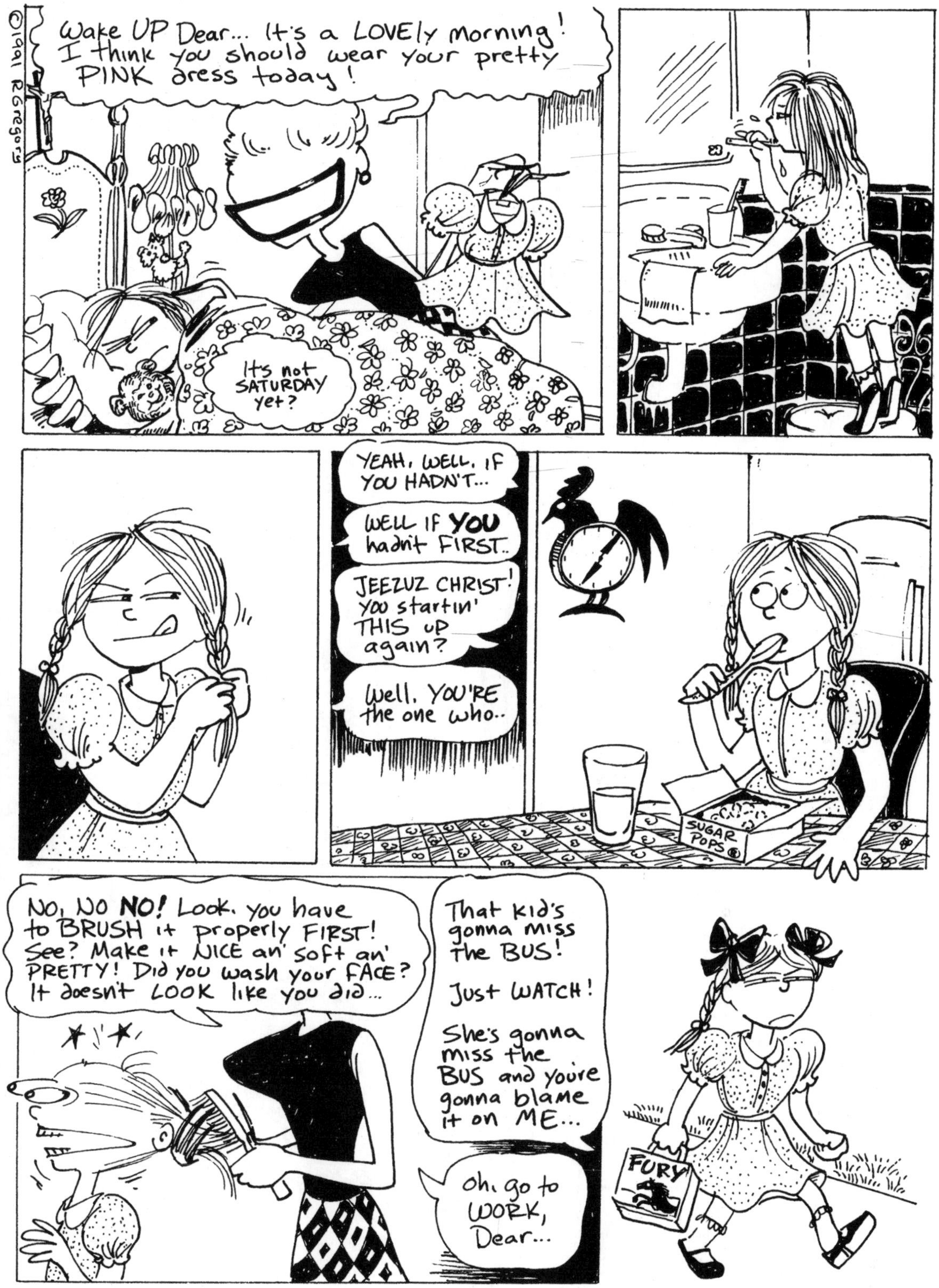
©1991 R.Gregory
Wake UP Dear... It's a LOVEly morning! I think you should wear your pretty PINK dress today!
It's not SATURDAY yet?
YEAH, WELL, IF YOU HADN'T...
WELL IF YOU hadn't FIRST..
JEEZUZ CHRIST! you startin' THIS up again?
Well, YOU'RE the one who..
SUGAR POPS
No, NO NO! Look, you have to BRUSH it properly FIRST! See? Make it NICE an' soft an' PRETTY! Did you wash your FACE? It doesn't LOOK like you did...
That kid's gonna miss the BUS!
Just WATCH!
She's gonna miss the BUS and you're gonna blame it on ME...
Oh, go to WORK, Dear...
FURY

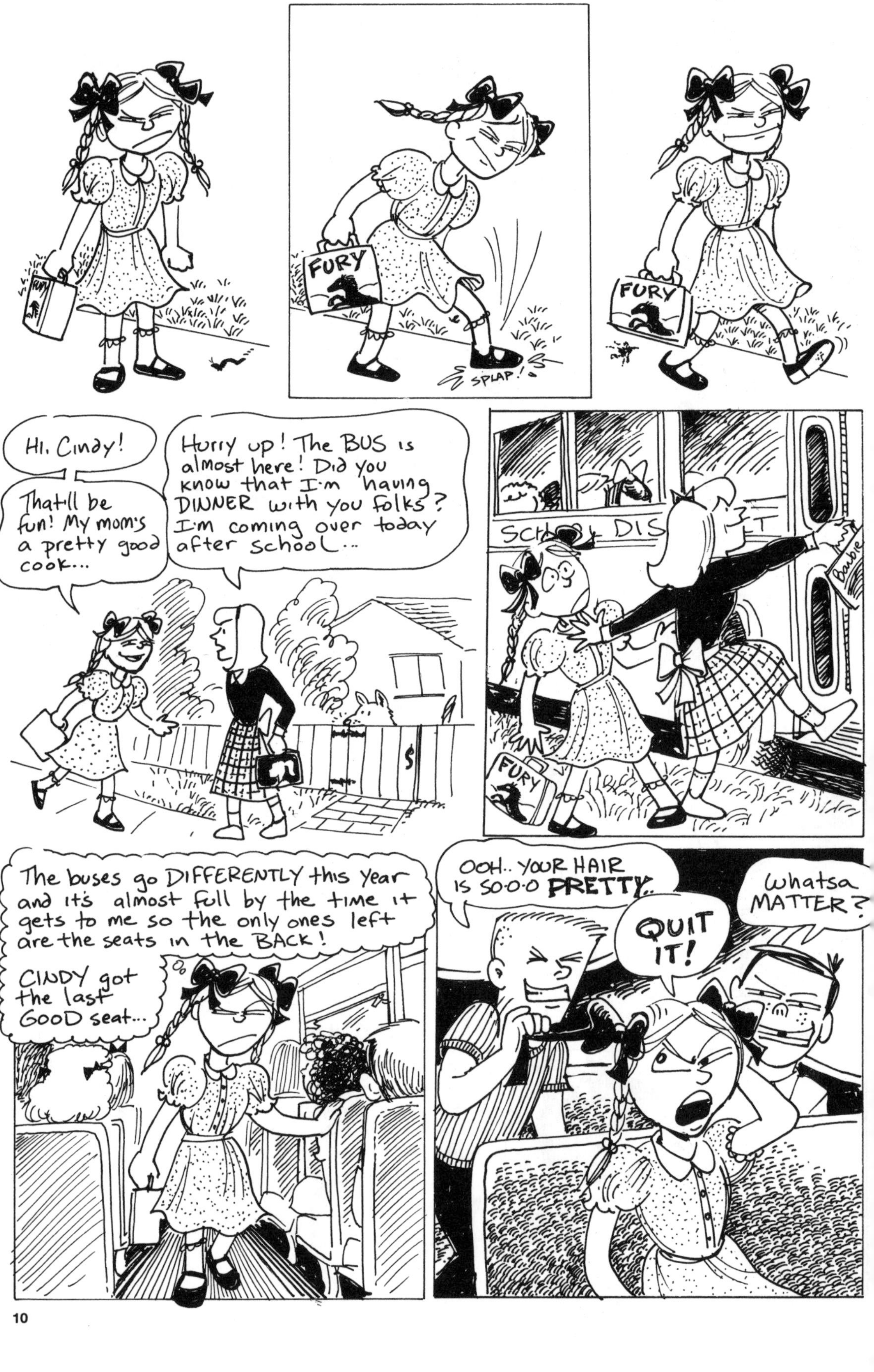
FURY
FURY
SPLAP!
FURY
Hi, Cindy!
Hurry up! The BUS is almost here! Did you know that I'm having DINNER with you folks? I'm coming over today after school...
That'll be fun! My mom's a pretty good cook...
SCHOOL DIS
Barbie
FURY
The buses go DIFFERENTLY this year and it's almost full by the time it gets to me so the only ones left are the seats in the BACK!
CINDY got the last GOOD seat...
OOH.. YOUR HAIR IS SO-O-O PRETTY..
QUIT IT!
Whatsa MATTER?

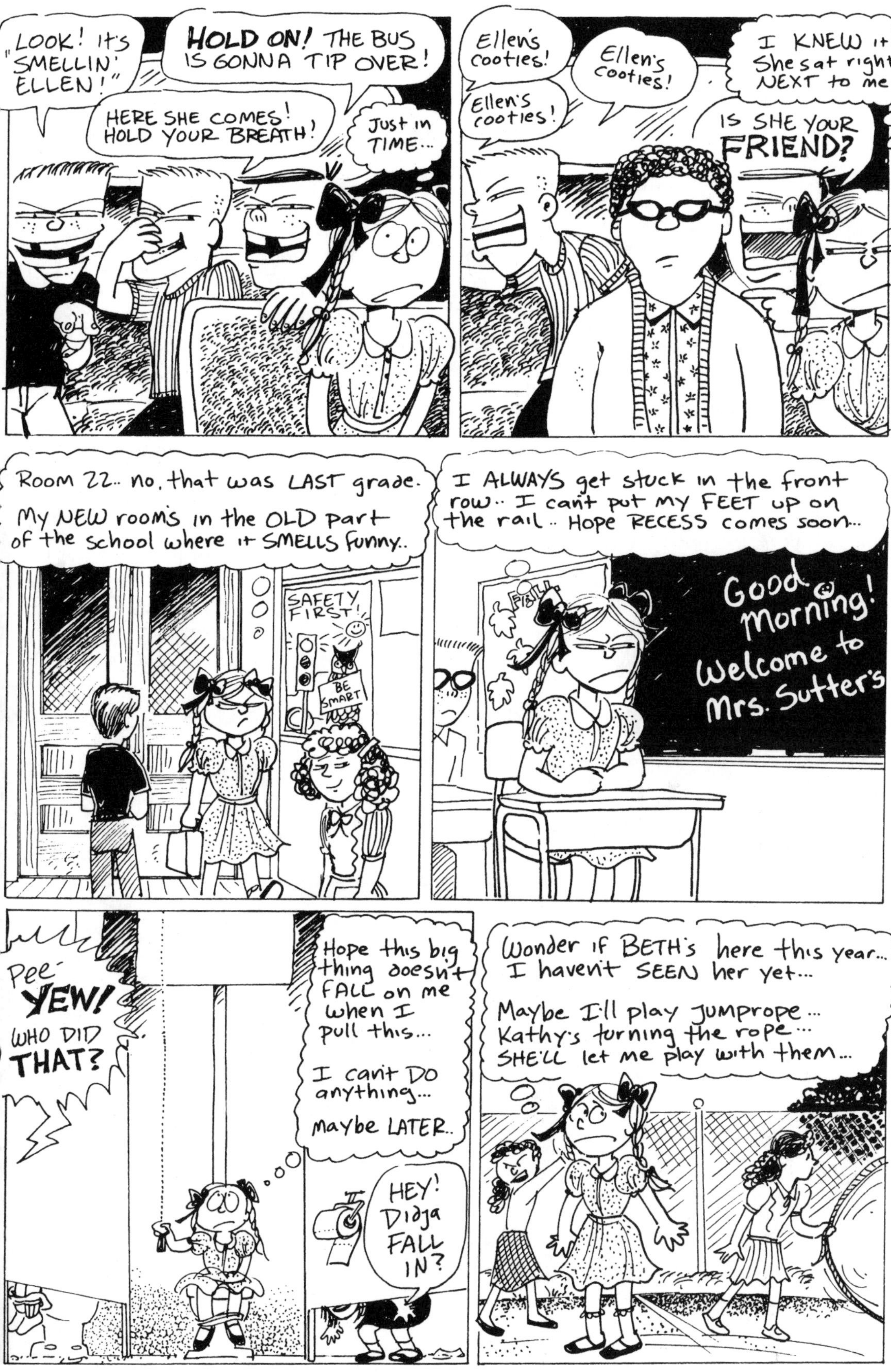
LOOK! It's "SMELLIN' ELLEN!"
HOLD ON! THE BUS IS GONNA TIP OVER!
HERE SHE COMES! HOLD YOUR BREATH!
Just in TIME...
Ellen's cooties!
Ellen's cooties!
Ellen's cooties!
I KNEW it! She sat right NEXT to me!
IS SHE YOUR FRIEND?
Room 22.. no, that was LAST grade.
My NEW room's in the OLD part of the school where it SMELLS funny..
SAFETY FIRST!
BE SMART
I ALWAYS get stuck in the front row.. I can't put my FEET up on the rail.. Hope RECESS comes soon...
Good morning! Welcome to Mrs. Sutter's
Pee-YEW! WHO DID THAT?
Hope this big thing doesn't FALL on me when I pull this...
I can't DO anything...
Maybe LATER..
HEY! Didja FALL IN?
Wonder if BETH's here this year... I haven't SEEN her yet...
Maybe I'll play JUMPROPE... Kathy's turning the rope... SHE'LL let me play with them...

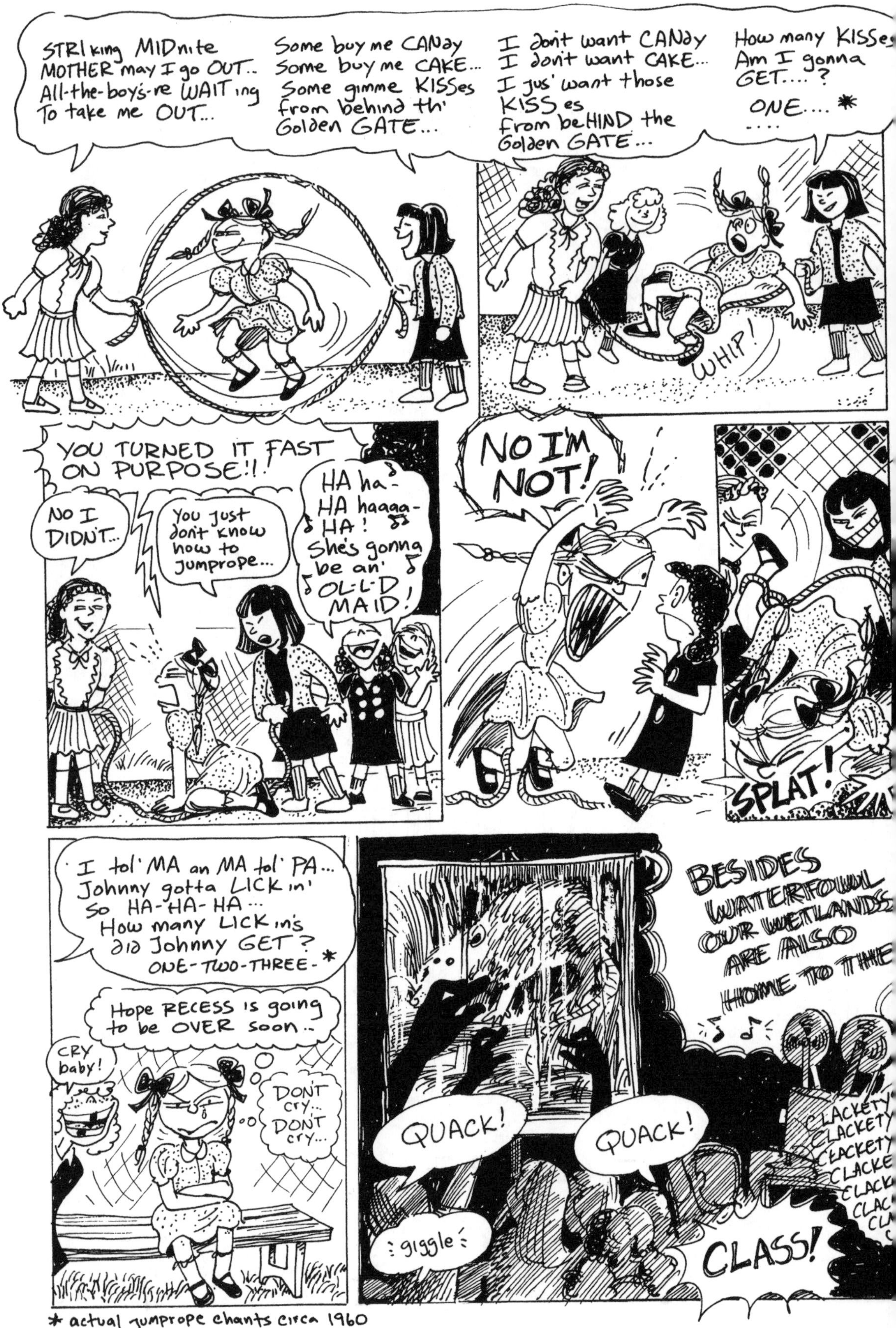
STRIking MIDnite MOTHER may I go OUT.. All-the-boys-re WAITing To take me OUT...
Some buy me CANdy Some buy me CAKE... Some gimme KISSes from behind th' Golden GATE...
I don't want CANdy I don't want CAKE... I jus' want those KISSes from beHIND the Golden GATE...
How many KISSes Am I gonna GET....? ONE....* ....
WHIP!
YOU TURNED IT FAST ON PURPOSE!!
NO I DIDN'T...
You just don't know how to jumprope...
HA ha HA haaaa-HA! She's gonna be an' OL-L-D MAID!
NO I'M NOT!
SPLAT!
I tol' MA an MA tol' PA... Johnny gotta LICKin' so HA-HA-HA... How many LICKin's did Johnny GET? ONE-TWO-THREE-*
Hope RECESS is going to be OVER soon..
CRY baby!
DON'T cry... DON'T cry...
BESIDES WATERFOWL OUR WETLANDS ARE ALSO HOME TO THE
QUACK!
QUACK!
giggle
CLACKETY
CLACKETY
CLACKETY
CLACKE
CLACK
CLACK
CLAC
CLASS!

* actual jumprope chants circa 1960

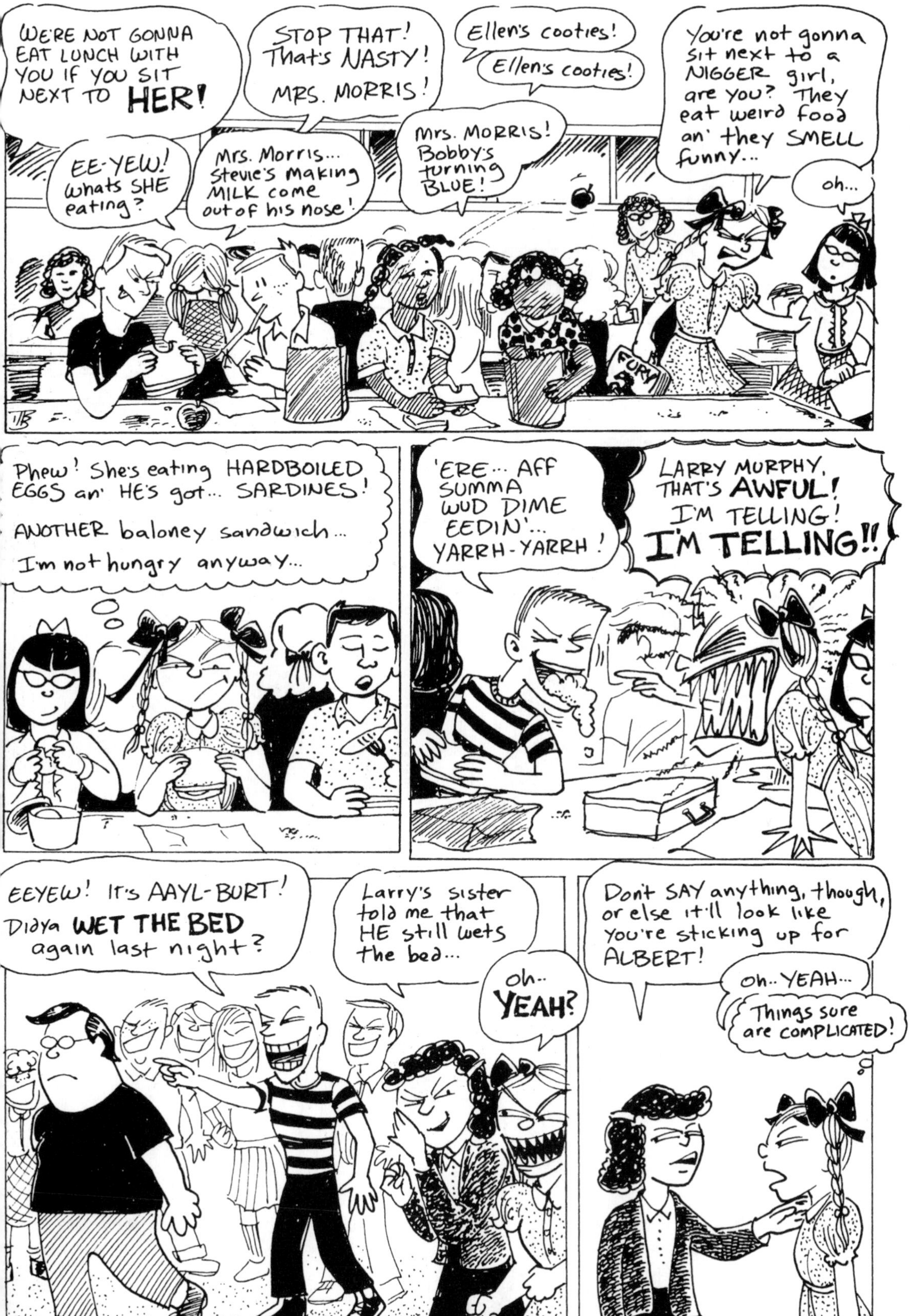

WE'RE NOT GONNA EAT LUNCH WITH YOU IF YOU SIT NEXT TO HER!
STOP THAT! That's NASTY! MRS. MORRIS!
Ellen's cooties!
Ellen's cooties!
You're not gonna sit next to a NIGGER girl, are you? They eat weird food an' they SMELL funny...
EE-YEW! whats SHE eating?
Mrs. Morris... Stevie's making MILK come out of his nose!
Mrs. MORRIS! Bobby's turning BLUE!
oh...
FURY
Phew! She's eating HARDBOILED EGGS an' HE'S got... SARDINES!
ANOTHER baloney sandwich...
I'm not hungry anyway...
'ERE... AFF SUMMA WUD DIME EEDIN'... YARRH-YARRH!
LARRY MURPHY, THAT'S AWFUL! I'M TELLING! I'M TELLING!!
EEYEW! It's AAYL-BURT! Didya WET THE BED again last night?
Larry's sister told me that HE still wets the bed...
oh.. YEAH?
Don't SAY anything, though, or else it'll look like you're sticking up for ALBERT!
oh.. YEAH...
Things sure are COMPLICATED!

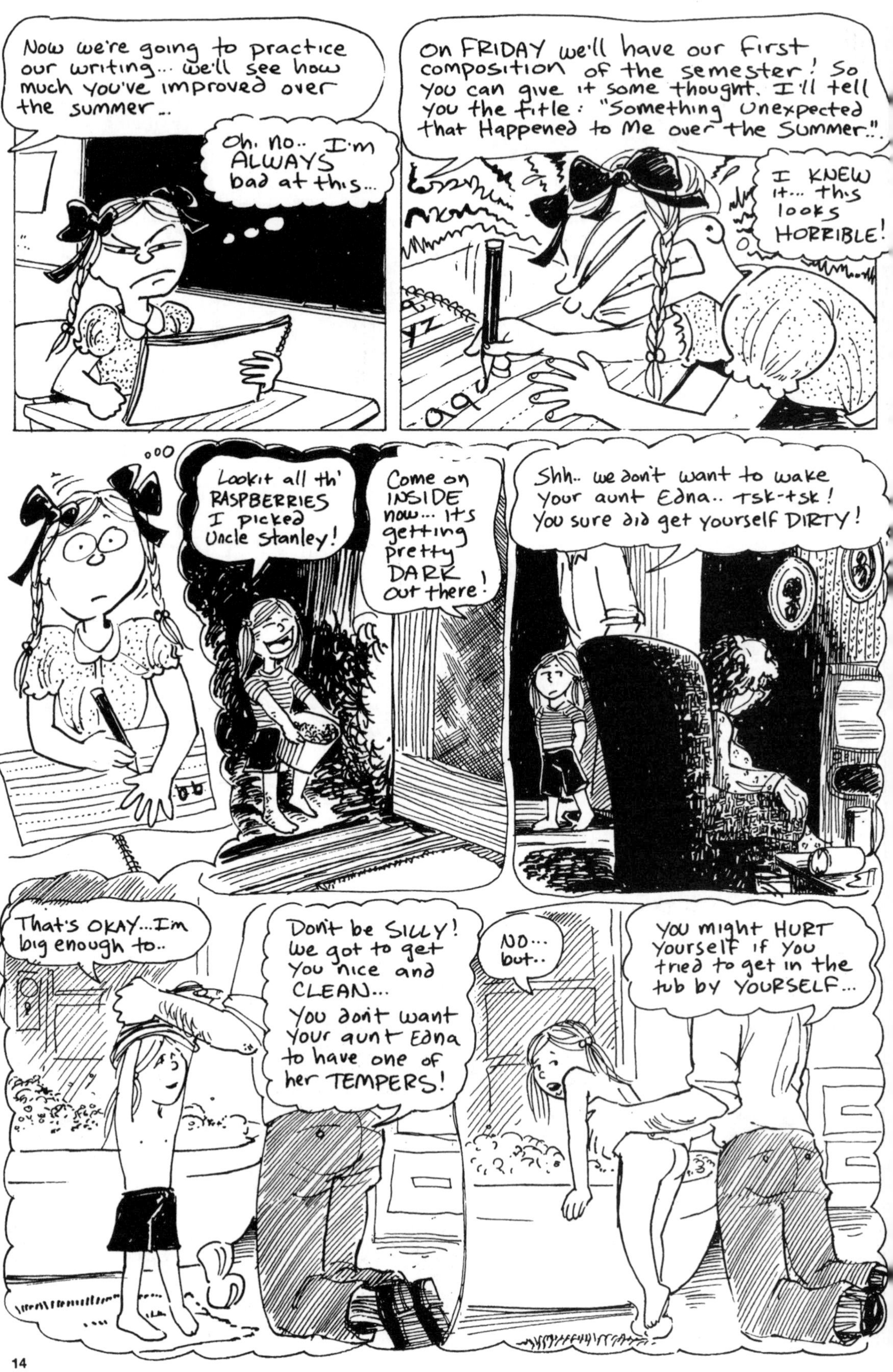
Now we're going to practice our writing... we'll see how much you've improved over the summer..
Oh, no.. I'm ALWAYS bad at this...
On FRIDAY we'll have our first composition of the semester! So you can give it some thought. I'll tell you the title: "Something Unexpected that Happened to Me over the Summer."
I KNEW it... this looks HORRIBLE!
Lookit all th' RASPBERRIES I picked Uncle Stanley!
Come on INSIDE now... It's getting pretty DARK out there!
Shh.. we don't want to wake your aunt Edna.. tsk-tsk! You sure did get yourself DIRTY!
That's OKAY...I'm big enough to..
Don't be SILLY! We got to get you nice and CLEAN... You don't want your aunt Edna to have one of her TEMPERS!
NO... but..
You might HURT yourself if you tried to get in the tub by YOURSELF...

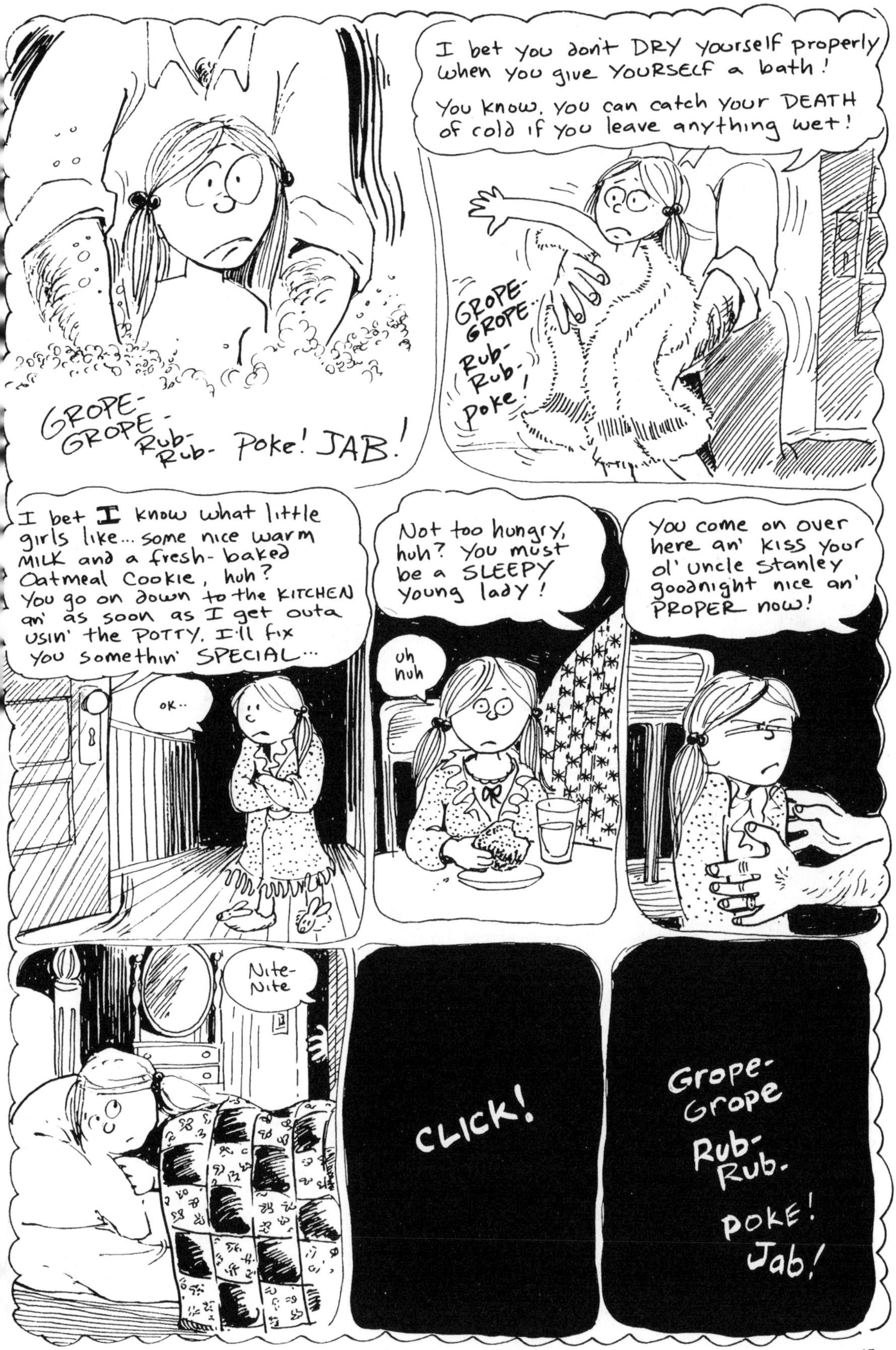

GROPE- GROPE- Rub- Rub- Poke! JAB!
I bet you don't DRY yourself properly when you give YOURSELF a bath!
You know, you can catch your DEATH of cold if you leave anything wet!
GROPE- GROPE- Rub- Rub- Poke!
I bet I know what little girls like... some nice warm MILK and a fresh-baked Oatmeal Cookie, huh? You go on down to the KITCHEN an' as soon as I get outa usin' the POTTY, I'll fix you somethin' SPECIAL...
ok..
Not too hungry, huh? You must be a SLEEPY young lady!
uh huh
You come on over here an' kiss your ol' uncle Stanley goodnight nice an' PROPER now!
Nite-Nite
CLICK!
Grope-Grope Rub-Rub. POKE! Jab!

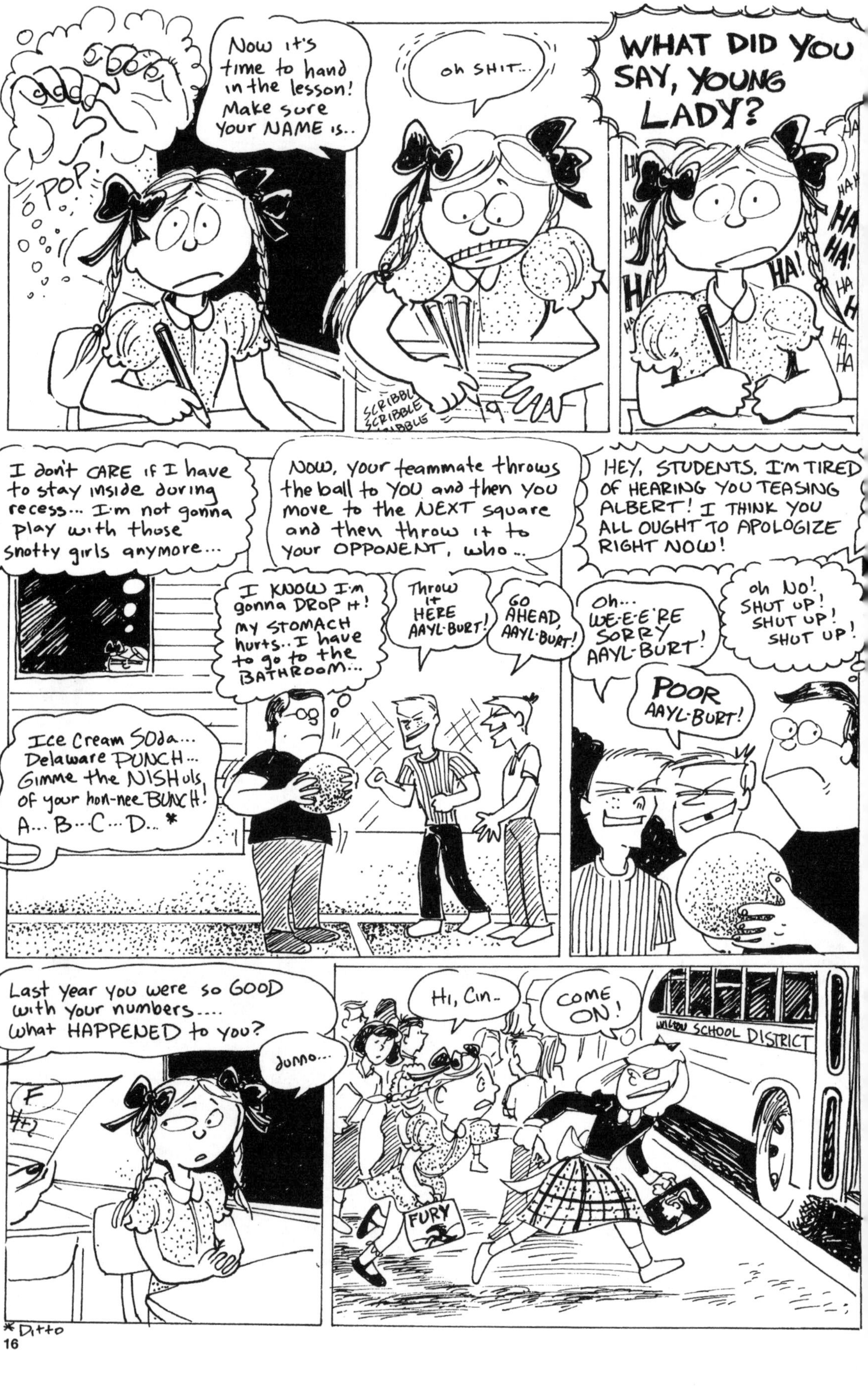
POP!
Now it's time to hand in the lesson! Make sure your NAME is..
oh SHIT...
SCRIBBLE SCRIBBLE
WHAT DID YOU SAY, YOUNG LADY?
HA HA HA HA HA! HA! HA HA HA! HA HA
I don't CARE if I have to stay inside during recess... I'm not gonna play with those snotty girls anymore...
Ice Cream SOda... Delaware PUNCH... Gimme the NISHuls of your hon-nee BUNCH! A... B...C...D...*
NOW, your teammate throws the ball to YOU and then you move to the NEXT square and then throw it to your OPPONENT, who...
I KNOW I'm gonna DROP it! My STOMACH hurts.. I have to go to the BATHROOM...
Throw it HERE AAYL-BURT!
GO AHEAD, AAYL-BURT!
HEY, STUDENTS. I'M TIRED OF HEARING YOU TEASING ALBERT! I THINK YOU ALL OUGHT TO APOLOGIZE RIGHT NOW!
Oh... WE-E-E'RE SORRY AAYL-BURT!
oh NO! SHUT UP! SHUT UP! SHUT UP!
POOR AAYL-BURT!
Last year you were so GOOD with your numbers.... What HAPPENED to you?
F
dunno...
Hi, Cin..
COME ON!
SCHOOL DISTRICT
FURY

*Ditto

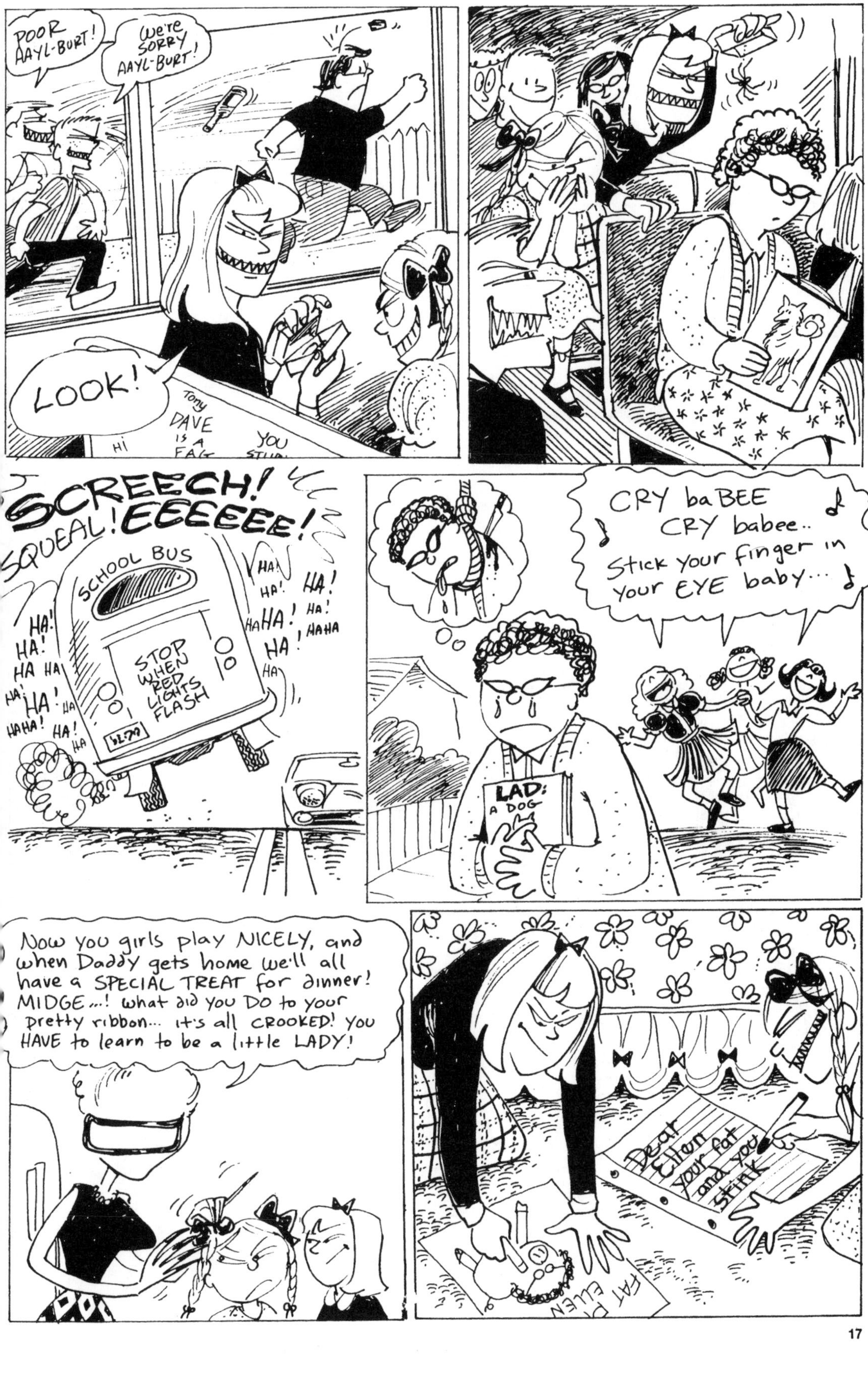
POOR AAYL-BURT!
We're SORRY AAYL-BURT!
LOOK!
Tony
DAVE IS A
HI
SCREECH!
SQUEAL! EEEEEEE!
SCHOOL BUS
STOP WHEN RED LIGHTS FLASH
HA! HA! HA HA HA! HA! HAHA! HA! HA
HA! HA! HA! HA! HAHA! HA! HAHA
CRY baBEE CRY babee.. Stick your finger in your EYE baby...
LAD: A DOG
Now you girls play NICELY, and when Daddy gets home we'll all have a SPECIAL TREAT for dinner! MIDGE...! what did you DO to your pretty ribbon... it's all CROOKED! You HAVE to learn to be a little LADY!
Dear Ellen your fat and you stink
FAT ELLEN

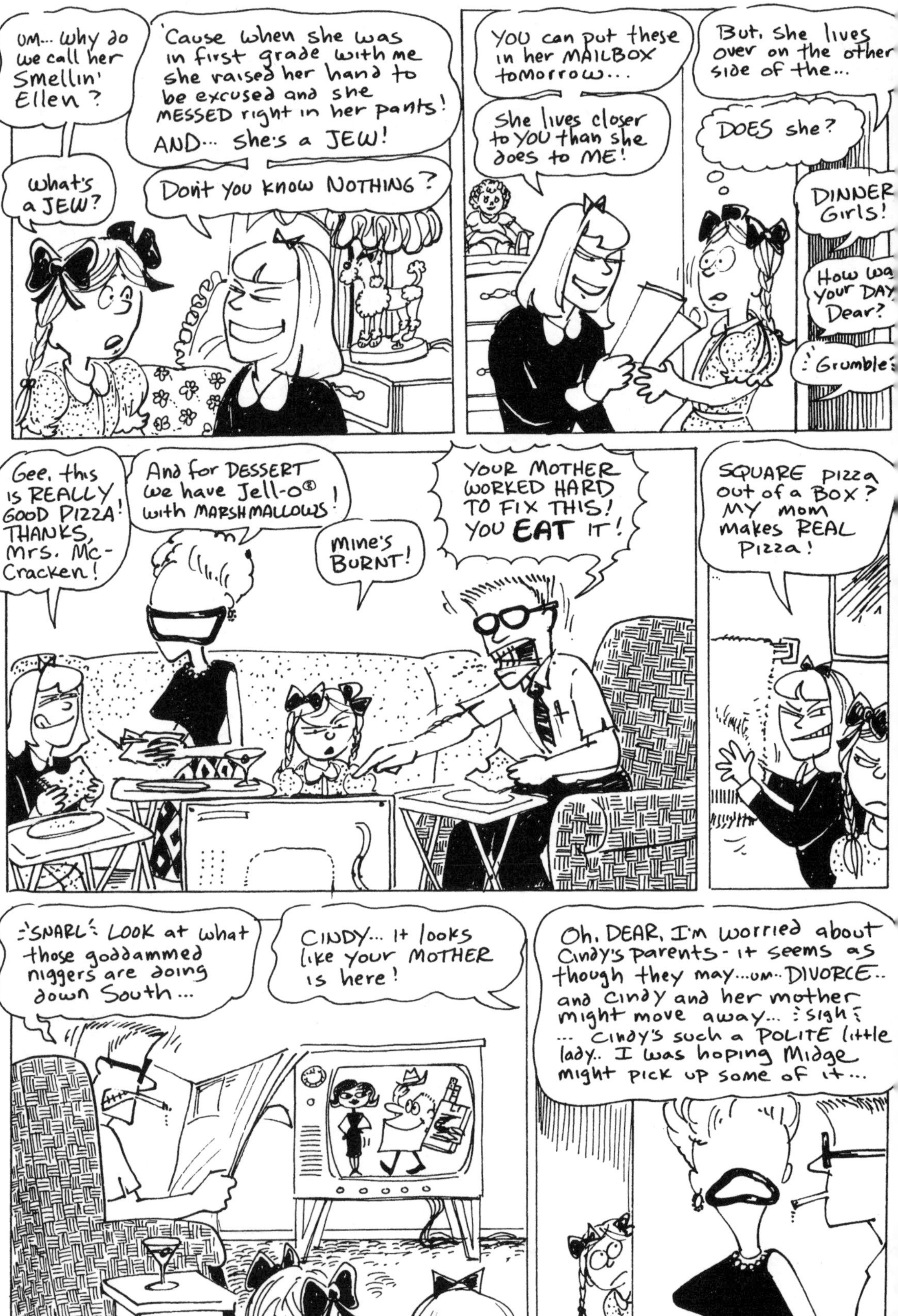
UM... why do we call her Smellin' Ellen?
'Cause when she was in first grade with me she raised her hand to be excused and she MESSED right in her pants! AND... she's a JEW!
What's a JEW?
Don't you know NOTHING?
YOU can put these in her MAILBOX tomorrow...
But, she lives over on the other side of the...
She lives closer to YOU than she does to ME!
DOES she?
DINNER Girls!
How wa your DAY Dear?
:Grumble:
Gee, this is REALLY GOOD PIZZA! THANKS, Mrs. Mc-Cracken!
And for DESSERT we have Jell-O® with MARSHMALLOWS!
Mine's BURNT!
YOUR MOTHER WORKED HARD TO FIX THIS! YOU EAT IT!
SQUARE pizza out of a BOX? MY mom makes REAL Pizza!
:SNARL: LOOK at what those goddammed niggers are doing down South...
CINDY... it looks like your MOTHER is here!
Oh, DEAR, I'm worried about Cindy's parents - it seems as though they may...um.. DIVORCE... and Cindy and her mother might move away... :sigh: ... Cindy's such a POLITE little lady.. I was hoping Midge might pick up some of it...

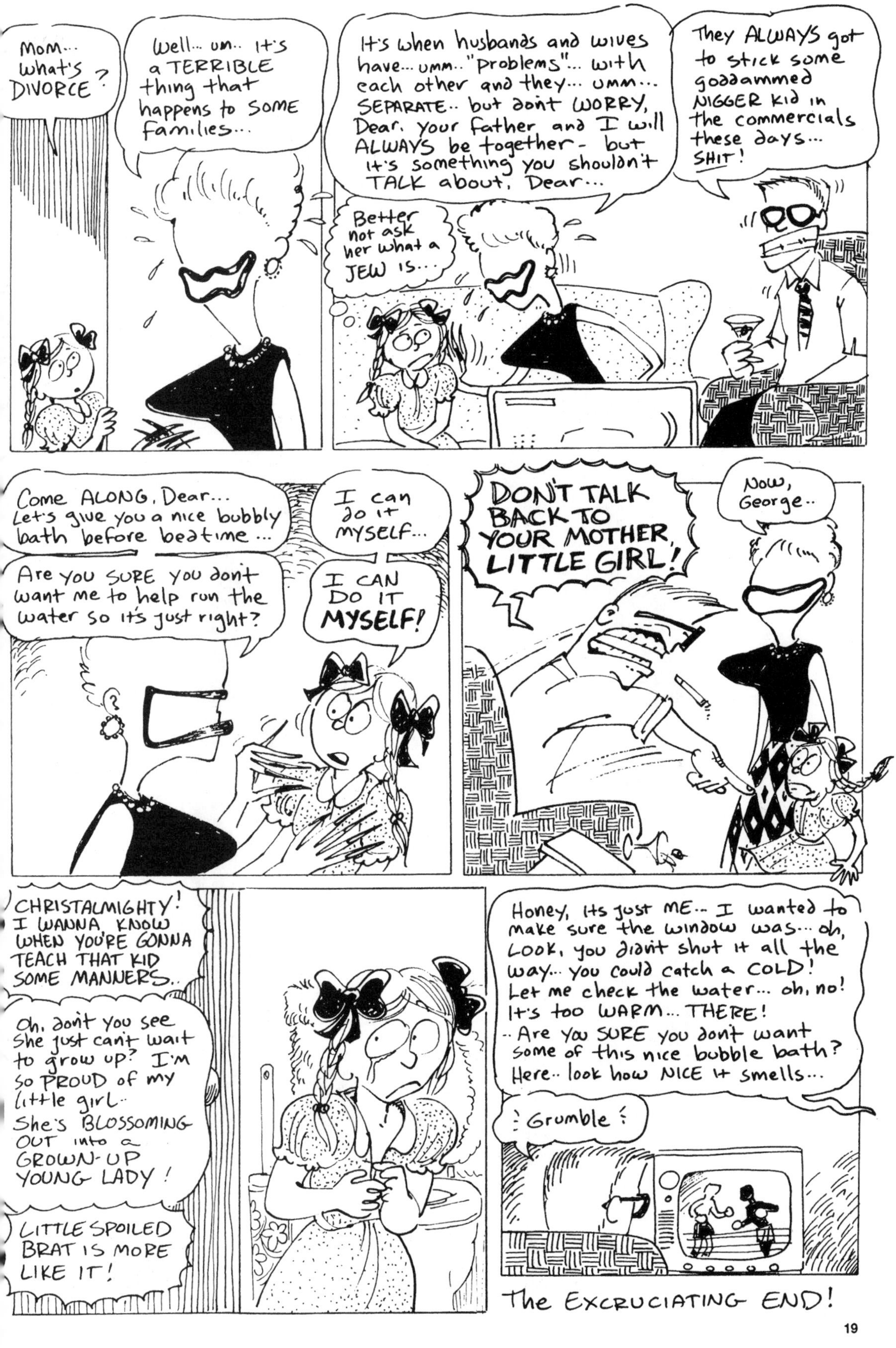

Mom... what's DIVORCE?
Well... um.. it's a TERRIBLE thing that happens to SOME families...
It's when husbands and wives have... umm.. "problems"... with each other and they... umm... SEPARATE.. but don't WORRY, Dear. your father and I will ALWAYS be together - but it's something you shouldn't TALK about, Dear...
Better not ask her what a JEW is...
They ALWAYS got to stick some goddammed NIGGER kid in the commercials these days... SHIT!
Come ALONG, Dear... Let's give you a nice bubbly bath before bedtime...
I can do it MYSELF...
Are you SURE you don't want me to help run the water so it's just right?
I CAN DO IT MYSELF!
DON'T TALK BACK TO YOUR MOTHER, LITTLE GIRL!
Now, George..
CHRISTALMIGHTY! I WANNA KNOW WHEN YOU'RE GONNA TEACH THAT KID SOME MANNERS..
Oh, don't you see She just can't wait to grow up? I'm so PROUD of my little girl.. She's BLOSSOMING OUT into a GROWN-UP YOUNG LADY!
LITTLE SPOILED BRAT IS MORE LIKE IT!
Honey, its just ME.. I wanted to make sure the window was... oh, LOOK, you didn't shut it all the way.. you could catch a COLD! Let me check the water... oh, no! It's too WARM... THERE! ..Are you SURE you don't want some of this nice bubble bath? Here.. look how NICE it smells...
Grumble
The EXCRUCIATING END!

UNHAPPY HOLIDAYS PART ONE

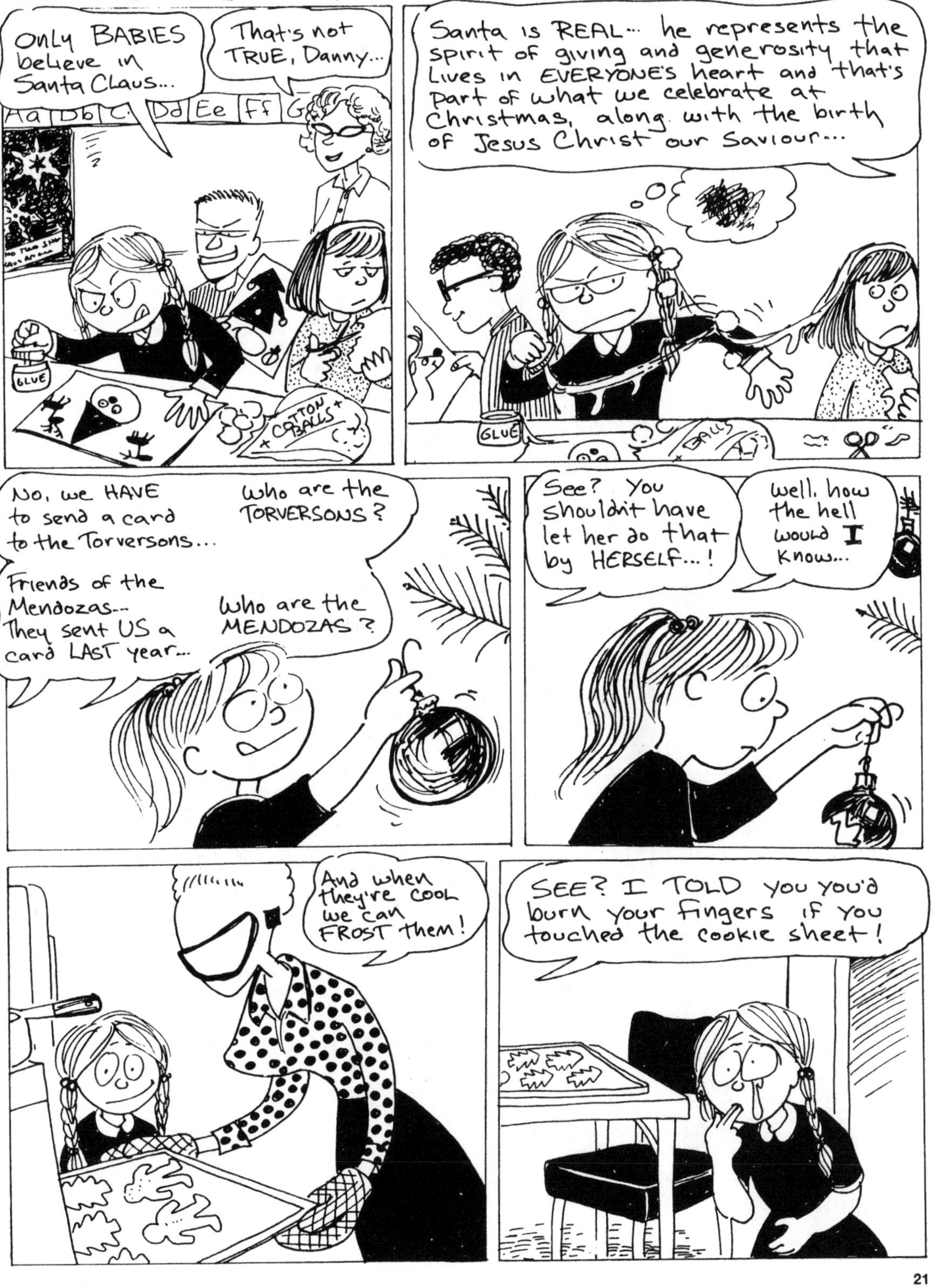
Only BABIES believe in Santa Claus...
That's not TRUE, Danny...
Aa Bb Cc Dd Ee Ff G
GLUE
COTTON BALLS
Santa is REAL... he represents the spirit of giving and generosity that lives in EVERYONE'S heart and that's part of what we celebrate at Christmas, along with the birth of Jesus Christ our Saviour...
GLUE
No, we HAVE to send a card to the Torversons...
Who are the TORVERSONS?
Friends of the Mendozas... They sent US a card LAST year...
Who are the MENDOZAS?
See? You shouldn't have let her do that by HERSELF...!
Well, how the hell would I know...
And when they're COOL we can FROST them!
SEE? I TOLD you you'd burn your fingers if you touched the cookie sheet!

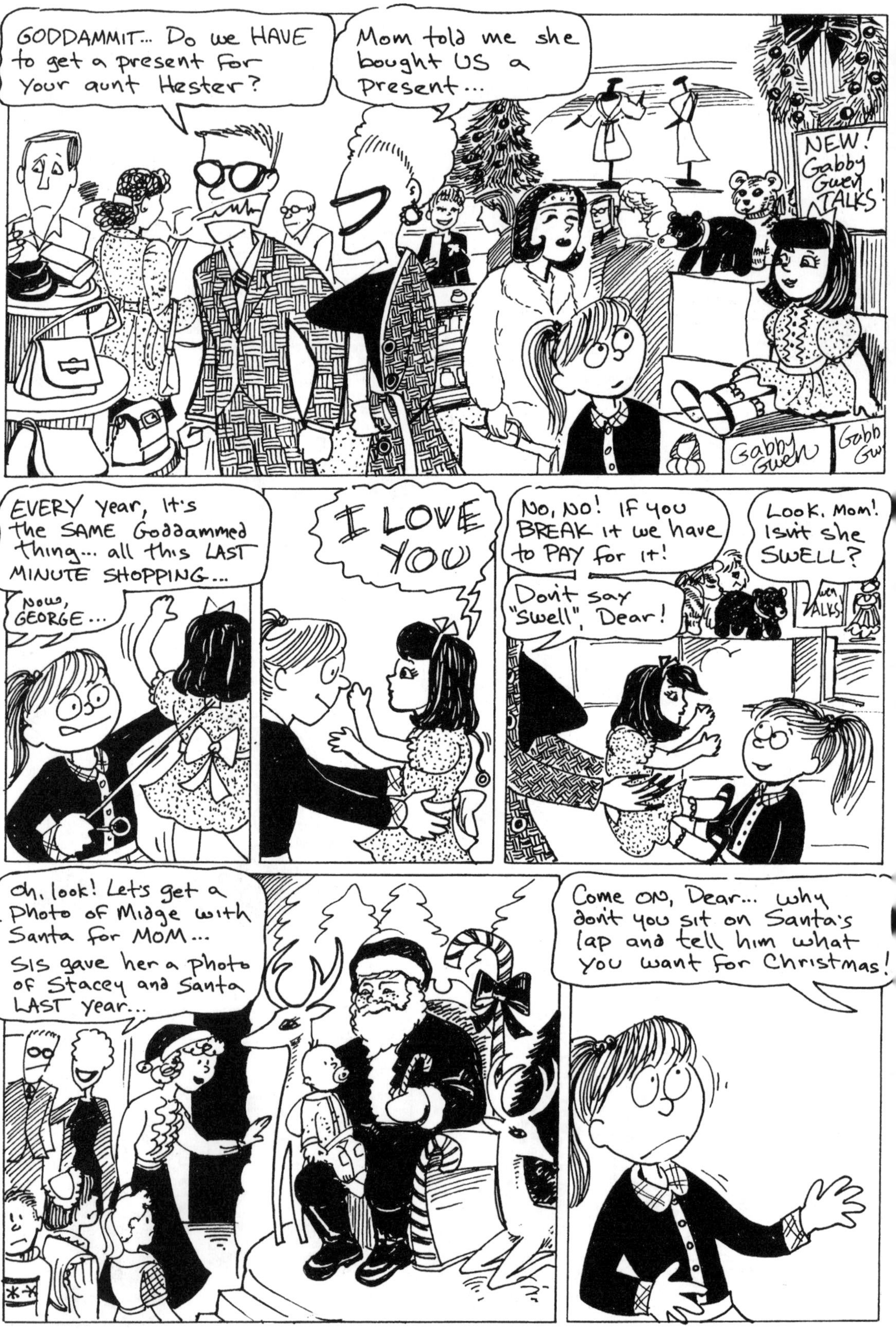
GODDAMMIT... Do we HAVE to get a present for your aunt Hester?
Mom told me she bought US a present...
NEW! Gabby Gwen TALKS!
Gabby Gwen
EVERY year, it's the SAME Goddammed thing... all this LAST MINUTE SHOPPING...
Now, GEORGE...
I LOVE YOU
No, NO! If you BREAK it we have to PAY for it!
Look, Mom! Isn't she SWELL?
Don't say "Swell", Dear!
Oh, look! Let's get a photo of Midge with Santa for MOM...
Sis gave her a photo of Stacey and Santa LAST year...
Come ON, Dear... why don't you sit on Santa's lap and tell him what you want for Christmas!

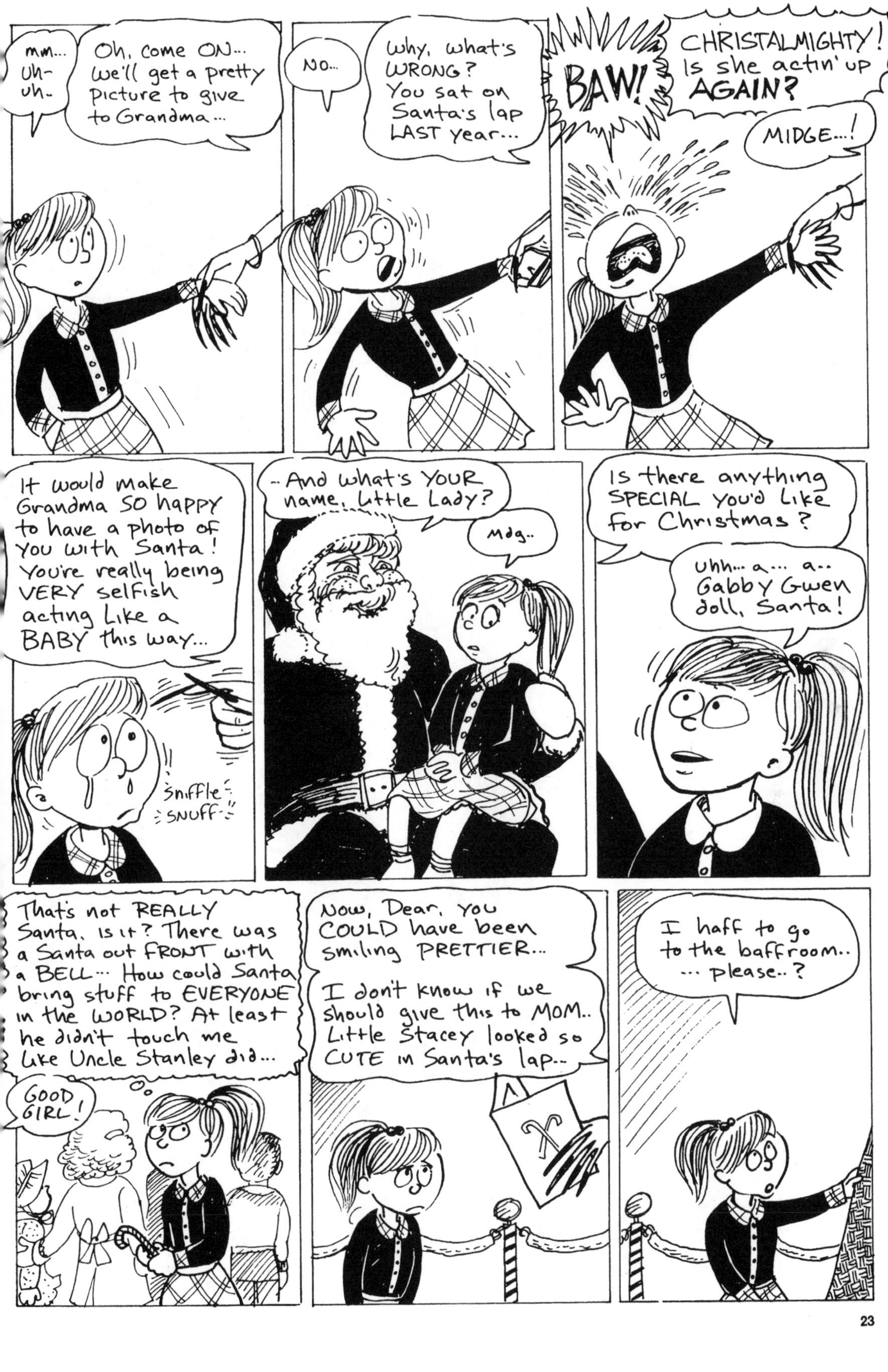
mm... uh-uh..
Oh, come ON... We'll get a pretty picture to give to Grandma...
NO...
Why, what's WRONG? You sat on Santa's lap LAST year...
BAW!
CHRISTALMIGHTY! Is she actin' up AGAIN?
MIDGE...!
It would make Grandma SO happy to have a photo of you with Santa! You're really being VERY selfish acting like a BABY this way...
sniffle
SNUFF
..And what's YOUR name, little Lady?
Mdg..
Is there anything SPECIAL you'd like for Christmas?
Uhh... a... a.. Gabby Gwen doll, Santa!
That's not REALLY Santa, is it? There was a Santa out FRONT with a BELL... How could Santa bring stuff to EVERYONE in the WORLD? At least he didn't touch me like Uncle Stanley did...
GOOD GIRL!
Now, Dear, you COULD have been smiling PRETTIER...
I don't know if we should give this to MOM.. Little Stacey looked so CUTE in Santa's lap..
I haff to go to the baffroom.. ... please..?

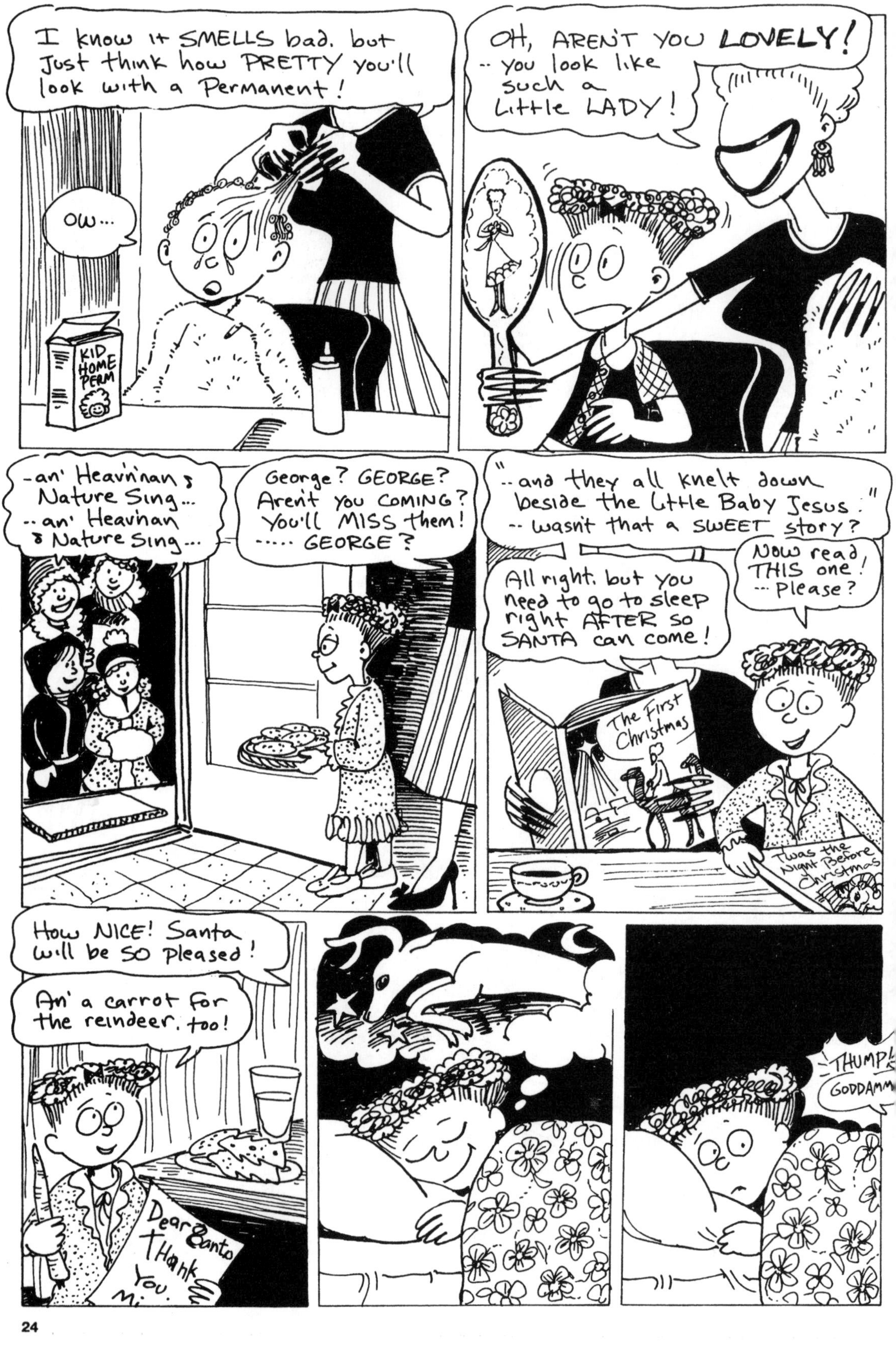

I know it SMELLS bad. but Just think how PRETTY you'll look with a Permanent!
OW...
KID HOME PERM
OH, AREN'T YOU LOVELY!
-- you look like such a Little LADY!
-an' Heav'nan & Nature Sing... -- an' Heav'nan & Nature Sing...
George? GEORGE? Aren't you COMING? You'll MISS them! ..... GEORGE?
".. and they all knelt down beside the Little Baby Jesus." -- wasn't that a SWEET story?
Now read THIS one! -- Please?
All right. but you need to go to sleep right AFTER so SANTA can come!
The First Christmas
Twas the Night Before Christmas
How NICE! Santa will be SO pleased!
An' a carrot for the reindeer, too!
Dear Santa THank You.
THUMP!
GODDAMM

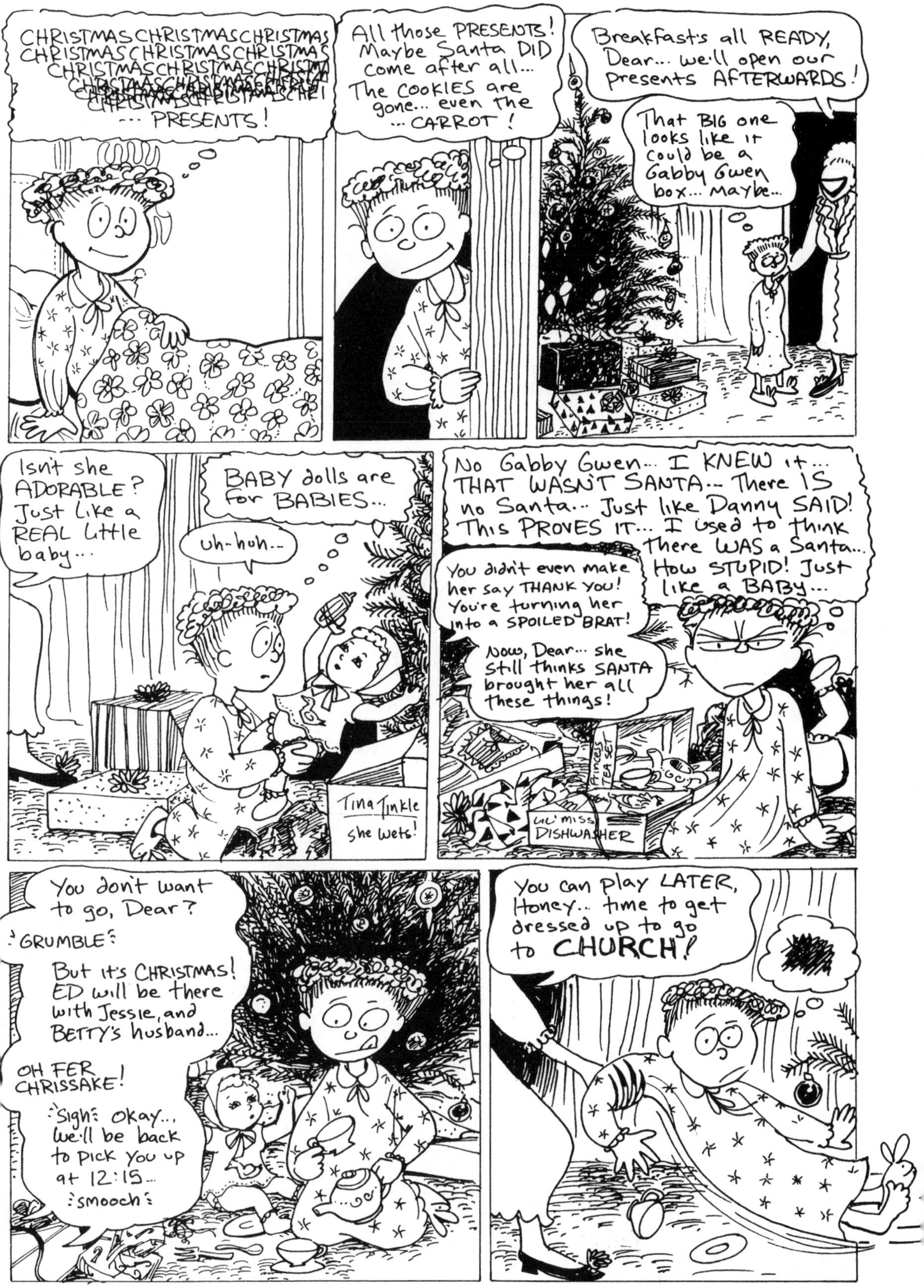
CHRISTMAS CHRISTMAS CHRISTMAS CHRISTMAS CHRISTMAS CHRISTMAS CHRISTMAS CHRISTMAS CHRISTMAS
... PRESENTS!
All those PRESENTS! Maybe Santa DID come after all... The COOKIES are gone... even the ... CARROT!
Breakfast's all READY, Dear... we'll open our presents AFTERWARDS!
That BIG one looks like it could be a Gabby Gwen box... maybe...
Isn't she ADORABLE? Just like a REAL little baby...
BABY dolls are for BABIES...
uh-huh...
Tina Tinkle
she wets!
No Gabby Gwen... I KNEW it... THAT WASN'T SANTA... There IS no Santa... Just like Danny SAID! This PROVES IT... I used to think there WAS a Santa... How STUPID! Just like a BABY...
You didn't even make her say THANK YOU! You're turning her into a SPOILED BRAT!
Now, Dear... she still thinks SANTA brought her all these things!
Princess TEA SET
Lil' miss DISHWASHER
You don't want to go, Dear?
:GRUMBLE:
But it's CHRISTMAS! ED will be there with Jessie, and BETTY's husband...
OH FER CHRISSAKE!
:Sigh: Okay... We'll be back to pick you up at 12:15...
:smooch:
You can play LATER, Honey... time to get dressed up to go to CHURCH!

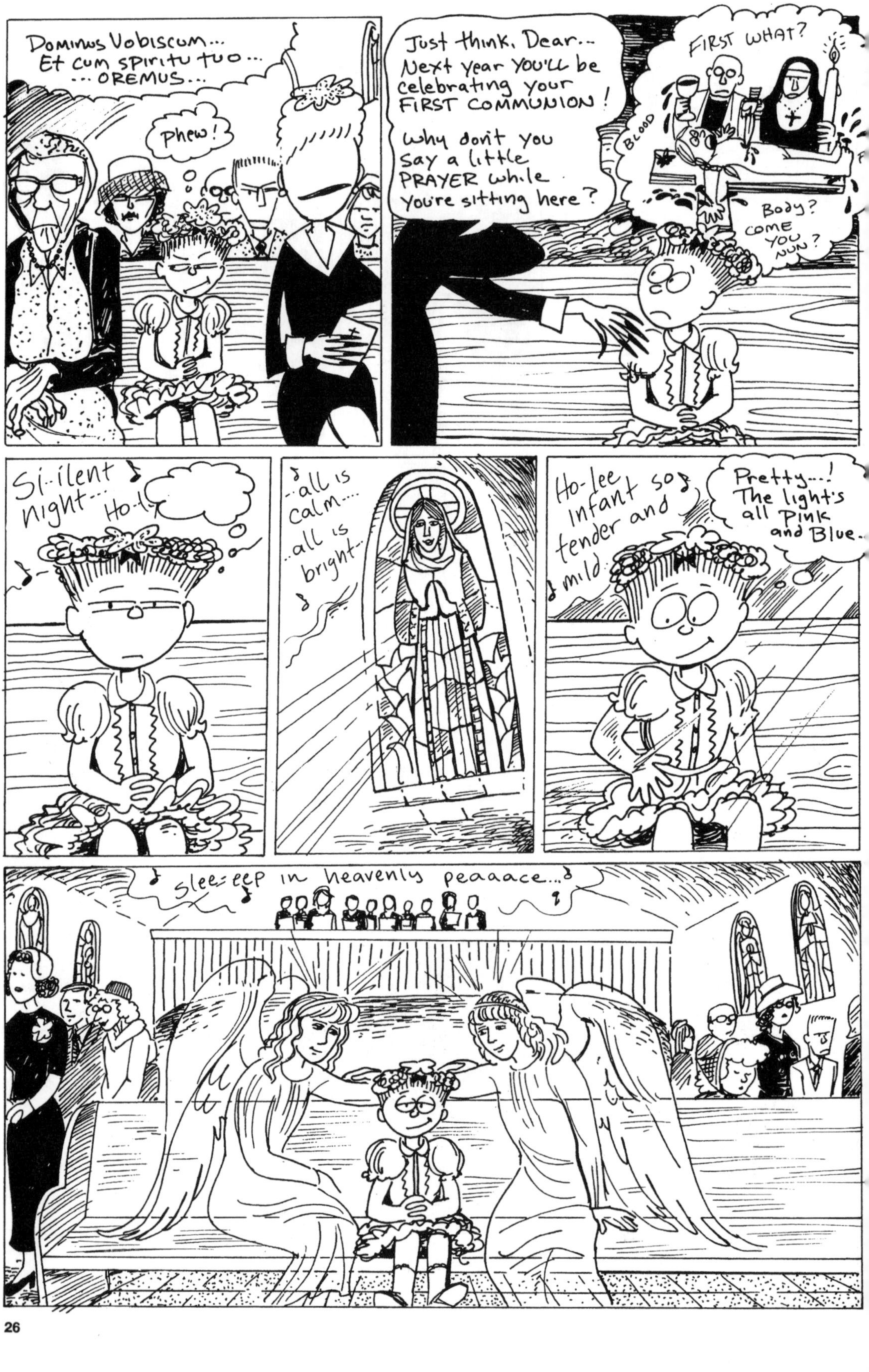
Dominus Vobiscum...
Et cum spiritu tuo...
...OREMUS...
Phew!
Just think, Dear... Next year YOU'LL be celebrating your FIRST COMMUNION!
Why don't you say a little PRAYER while you're sitting here?
FIRST WHAT?
BLOOD
Body? COME YOU NUN?
Si-ilent night... Ho-ly
...all is calm... ...all is bright...
Ho-lee Infant so tender and mild
Pretty...! The light's all Pink and Blue...
slee-eep in heavenly peaaace...

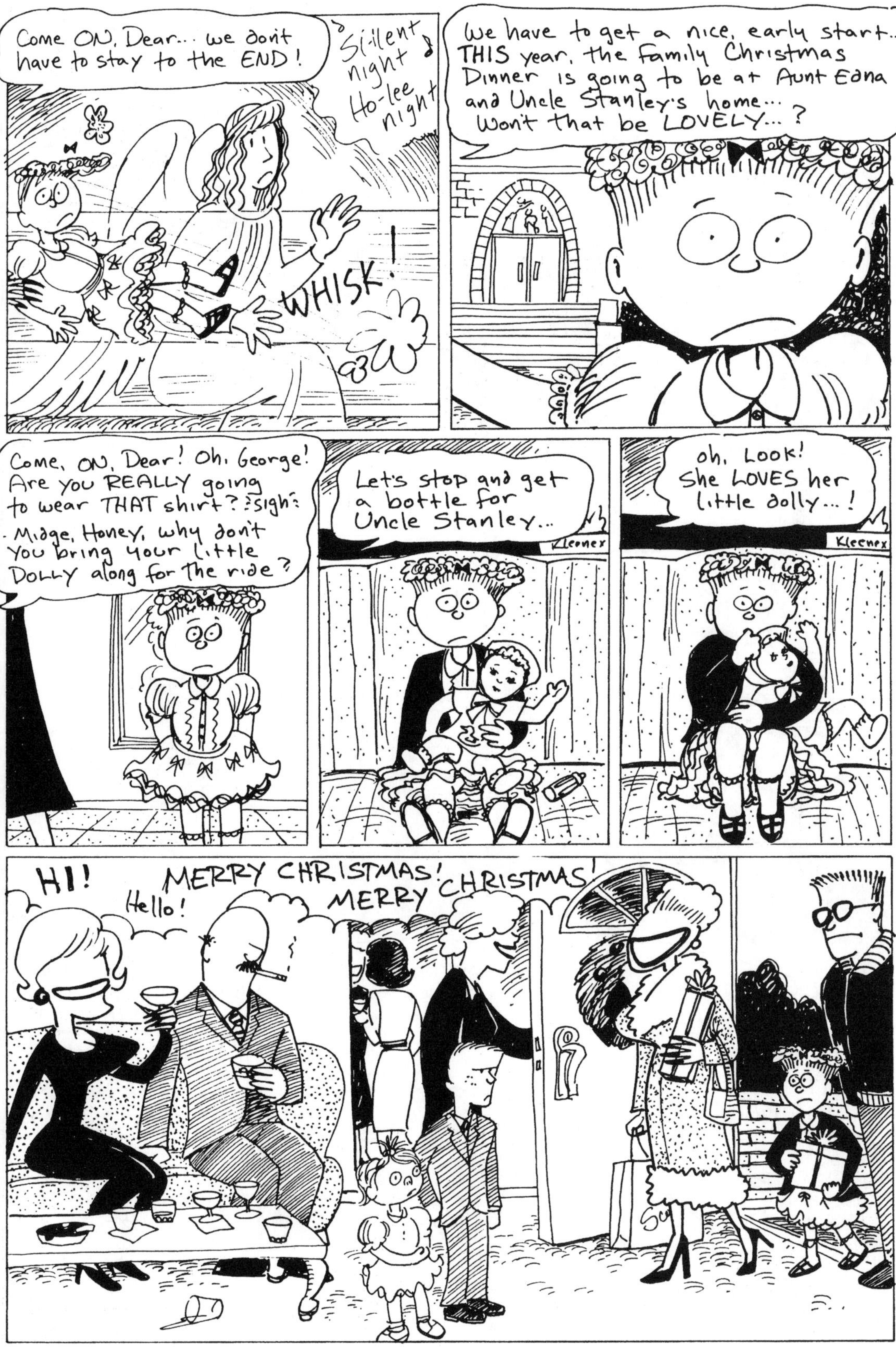

Come ON, Dear... we don't have to stay to the END!
Si-ilent night Ho-lee night
WHISK!
We have to get a nice, early start... THIS year, the family Christmas Dinner is going to be at Aunt Edna and Uncle Stanley's home... Won't that be LOVELY...?
Come, ON, Dear! Oh, George! Are you REALLY going to wear THAT shirt? :sigh:
Midge, Honey, why don't you bring your little DOLLY along for the ride?
Let's stop and get a bottle for Uncle Stanley...
Kleenex
oh, Look! She LOVES her little dolly...!
Kleenex
HI!
Hello!
MERRY CHRISTMAS!
MERRY CHRISTMAS!

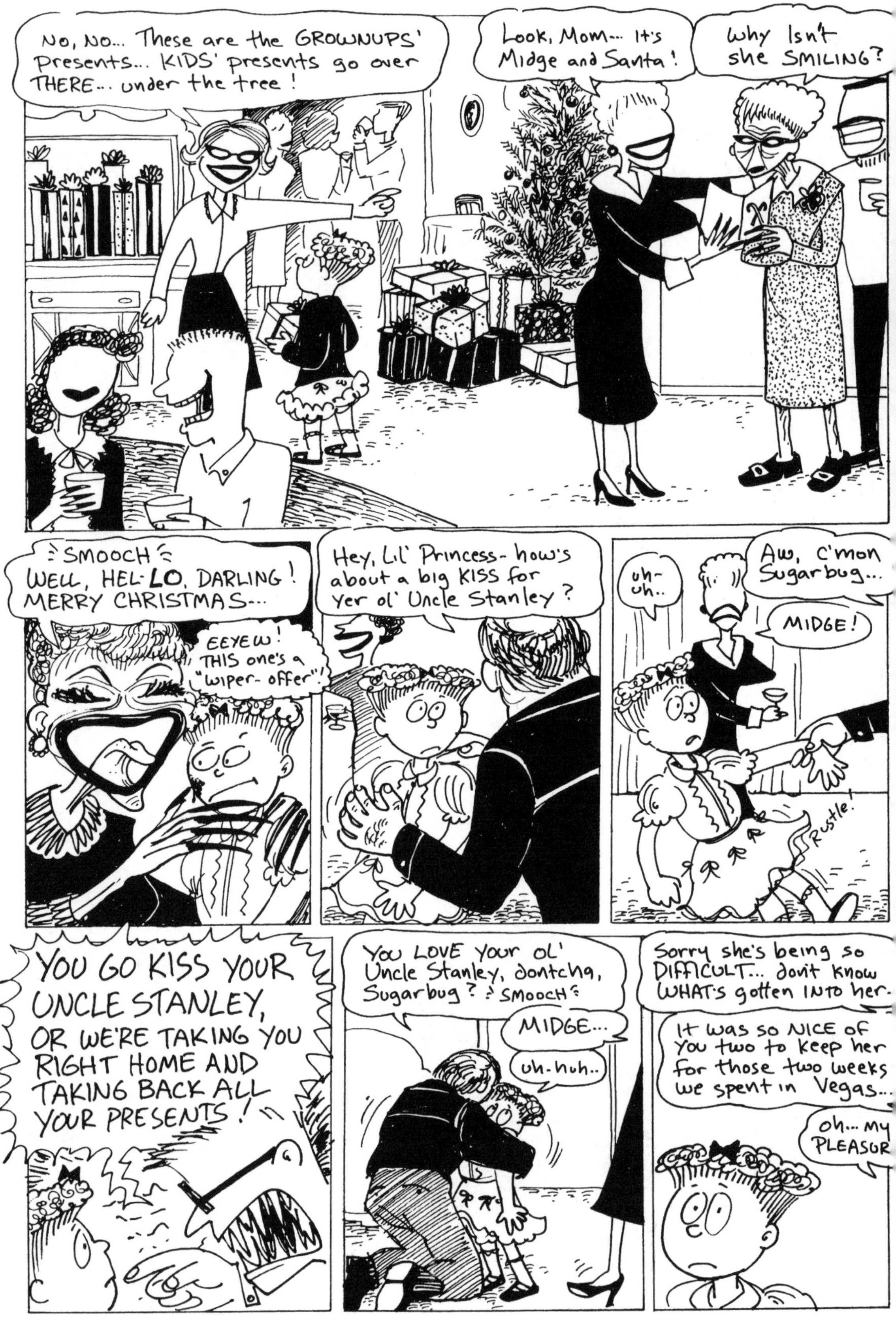
No, No... These are the GROWNUPS' presents... KIDS' presents go over THERE... under the tree!
Look, Mom... It's Midge and Santa!
Why Isn't she SMILING?
SMOOCH
WELL, HEL-LO, DARLING! MERRY CHRISTMAS...
EEYEW! THIS one's a "wiper-offer"!
Hey, Lil' Princess- how's about a big KISS for Yer ol' Uncle Stanley?
oh-uh..
Aw, c'mon Sugarbug...
MIDGE!
Rustle!
YOU GO KISS YOUR UNCLE STANLEY, OR WE'RE TAKING YOU RIGHT HOME AND TAKING BACK ALL YOUR PRESENTS!
You LOVE your ol' Uncle Stanley, dontcha, Sugarbug? SMOOCH
MIDGE...
uh-huh..
Sorry she's being so DIFFICULT... don't know WHAT's gotten INTO her.
It was so NICE of You two to keep her for those two weeks we spent in Vegas...
oh... MY PLEASUR

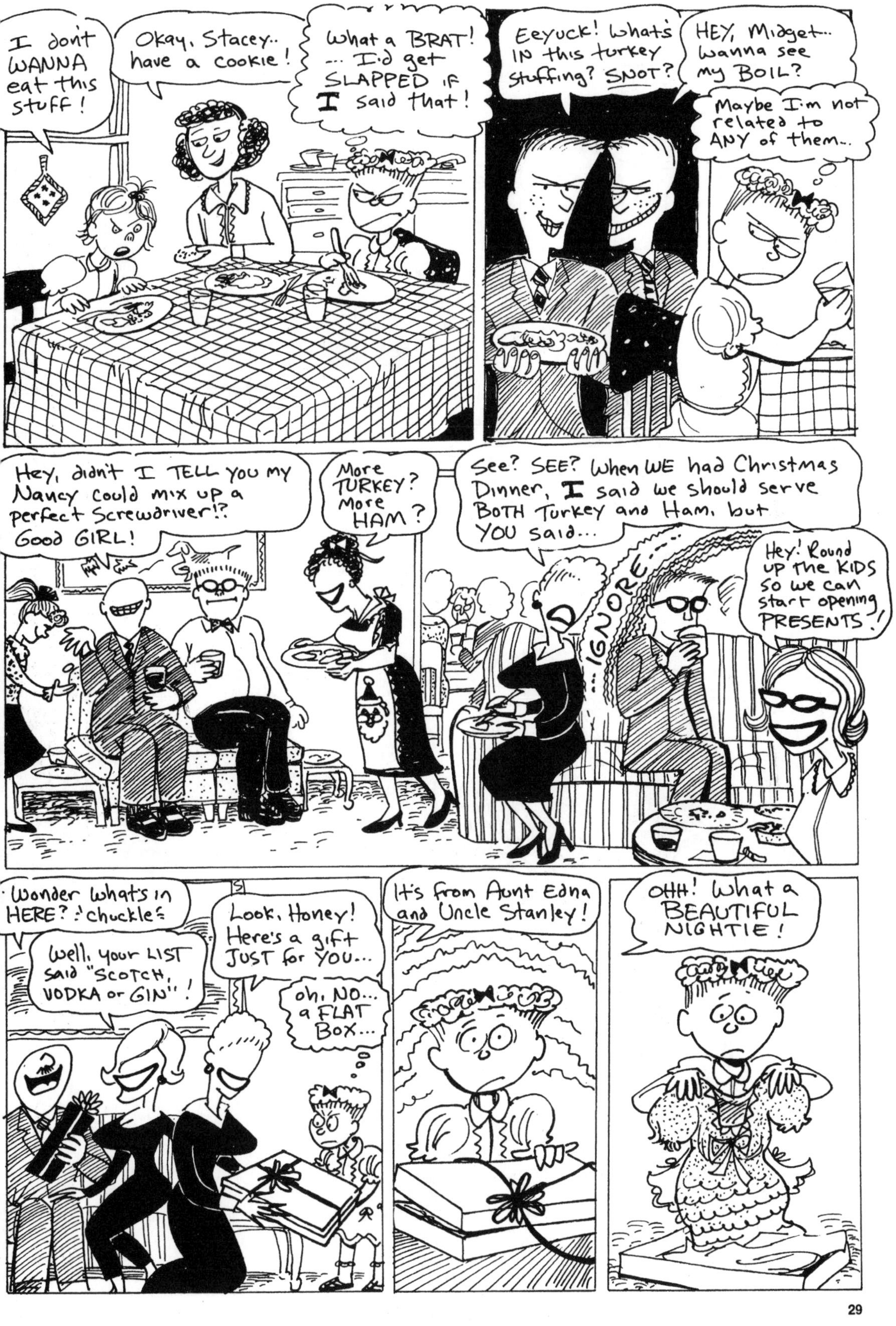

I don't WANNA eat this stuff!
Okay, Stacey.. have a cookie!
What a BRAT! ... I'd get SLAPPED if I said that!
Eeyuck! What's in this turkey stuffing? SNOT?
HEY, Midget.. wanna see my BOIL?
Maybe I'm not related to ANY of them..
Hey, didn't I TELL you my Nancy could mix up a perfect Screwdriver!? Good GIRL!
More TURKEY? More HAM?
See? SEE? When WE had Christmas Dinner, I said we should serve BOTH Turkey and Ham, but YOU said...
...IGNORE...
Hey! Round up the KIDS so we can start opening PRESENTS!
Wonder what's in HERE? chuckle
Well, your LIST said "SCOTCH, VODKA or GIN"!
Look, Honey! Here's a gift JUST for YOU...
oh, NO... a FLAT Box...
It's from Aunt Edna and Uncle Stanley!
OHH! What a BEAUTIFUL NIGHTIE!

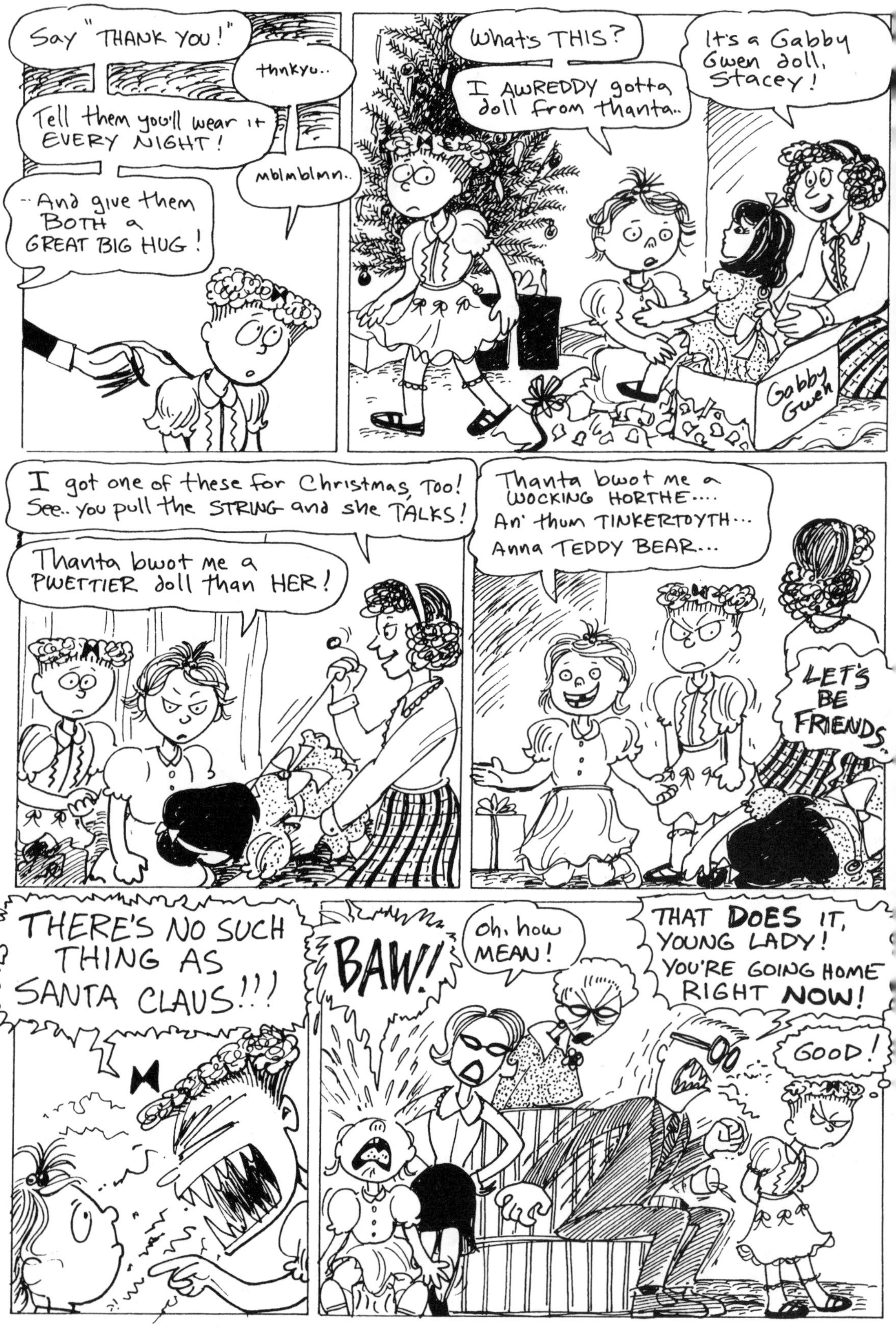
Say "THANK YOU!"
thnkyu..
Tell them you'll wear it EVERY NIGHT!
mblmblmn..
..And give them BOTH a GREAT BIG HUG!
What's THIS?
I AWREDDY gotta doll from thanta..
It's a Gabby Gwen doll, Stacey!
Gabby Gwen
I got one of these for Christmas, Too! See.. you pull the STRING and she TALKS!
Thanta bwot me a PWETTIER doll than HER!
Thanta bwot me a WOCKING HORTHE.... An' thum TINKERTOYTH... Anna TEDDY BEAR...
LET'S BE FRIENDS.
THERE'S NO SUCH THING AS SANTA CLAUS!!!
BAW!
Oh, how MEAN!
THAT DOES IT, YOUNG LADY! YOU'RE GOING HOME RIGHT NOW!
GOOD!

UNHAPPY HOLIDAYS PART TWO

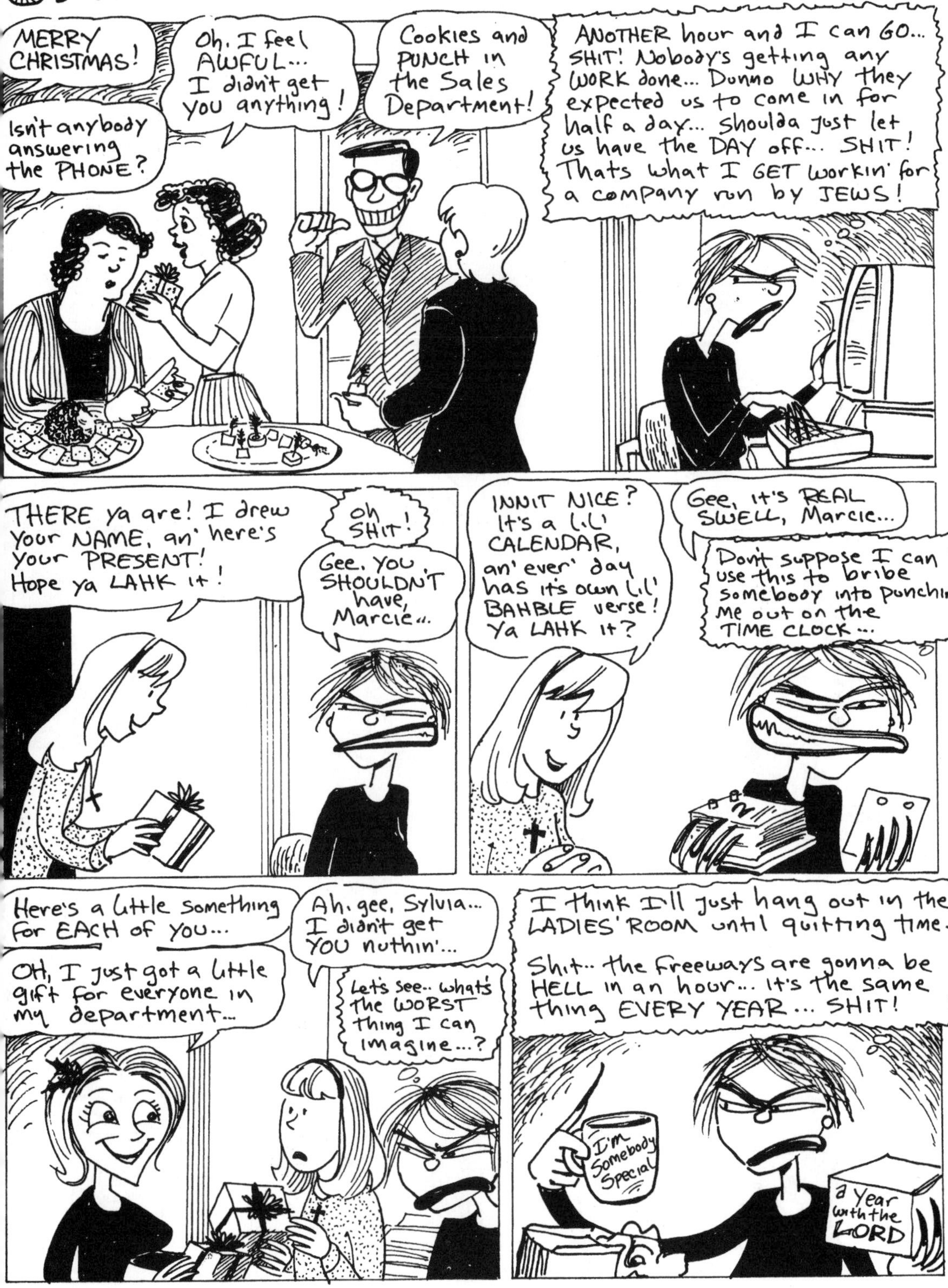
MERRY CHRISTMAS!
Isn't anybody answering the PHONE?
Oh, I feel AWFUL... I didn't get you anything!
Cookies and PUNCH in the Sales Department!
ANOTHER hour and I can GO... SHIT! Nobody's getting any WORK done... Dunno WHY they expected us to come in for half a day... shoulda just let us have the DAY off... SHIT! Thats what I GET workin' for a company run by JEWS!
THERE ya are! I drew your NAME, an' here's your PRESENT! Hope ya LAHK it!
oh SHIT!
Gee, YOU SHOULDN'T have, Marcie...
INNIT NICE? It's a LiL' CALENDAR, an' ever' day has its own LiL' BAHBLE verse! Ya LAHK it?
Gee, it's REAL SWELL, Marcie...
Don't suppose I can use this to bribe somebody into punchin' me out on the TIME CLOCK...
Here's a little something for EACH of you...
OH, I just got a little gift for everyone in my department...
Ah, gee, Sylvia... I didn't get YOU nothin'...
Let's see... what's the WORST thing I can imagine...?
I think I'll just hang out in the LADIES' ROOM until quitting time...
Shit... the freeways are gonna be HELL in an hour... It's the same thing EVERY YEAR... SHIT!
I'm Somebody Special
a Year with the LORD

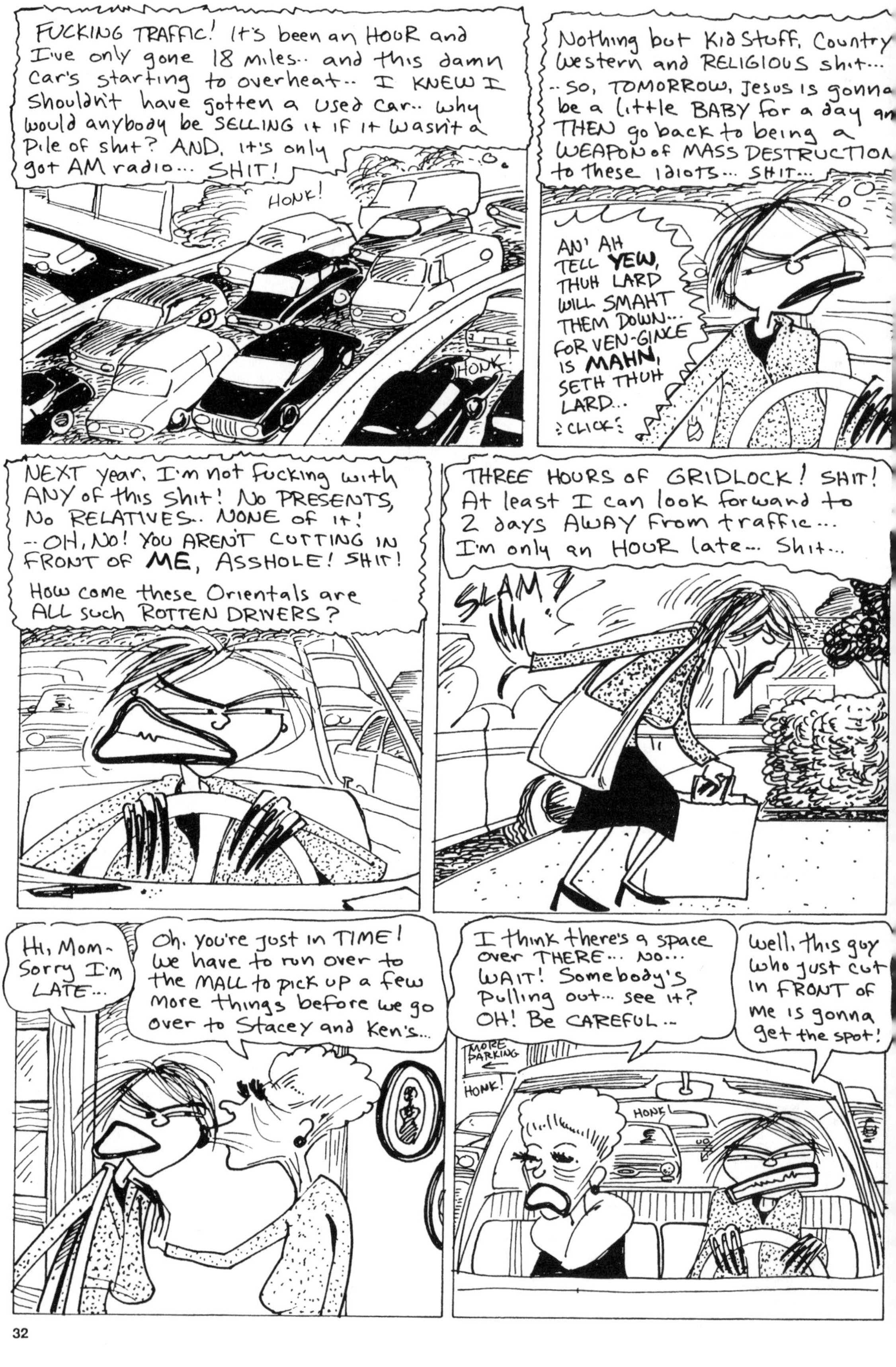
FUCKING TRAFFIC! It's been an HOUR and I've only gone 18 miles.. and this damn car's starting to overheat.. I KNEW I shouldn't have gotten a used car.. why would anybody be SELLING it if it wasn't a pile of shit? AND, it's only got AM radio... SHIT!
HONK!
HONK!
Nothing but kid stuff, Country Western and RELIGIOUS shit... ..so, TOMORROW, Jesus is gonna be a little BABY for a day an THEN go back to being a WEAPON of MASS DESTRUCTION to these idiots... SHIT...
AN' AH TELL YEW, THUH LARD WILL SMAHT THEM DOWN... FOR VEN-GINCE IS MAHN, SETH THUH LARD...
CLICK
NEXT year, I'm not fucking with ANY of this shit! No PRESENTS, No RELATIVES.. NONE of it! ..OH, NO! YOU AREN'T CUTTING IN FRONT OF ME, ASSHOLE! SHIT!
How come these Orientals are ALL such ROTTEN DRIVERS?
THREE HOURS of GRIDLOCK! SHIT! At least I can look forward to 2 days AWAY from traffic... I'm only an HOUR late... Shit...
SLAM!
Hi, Mom- Sorry I'm LATE...
Oh, you're just in TIME! We have to run over to the MALL to pick up a few more things before we go over to Stacey and Ken's...
I think there's a space over THERE... No... WAIT! Somebody's pulling out... see it? OH! Be CAREFUL..
Well, this guy who just cut in FRONT of me is gonna get the spot!
MORE PARKING
HONK!
HONK!

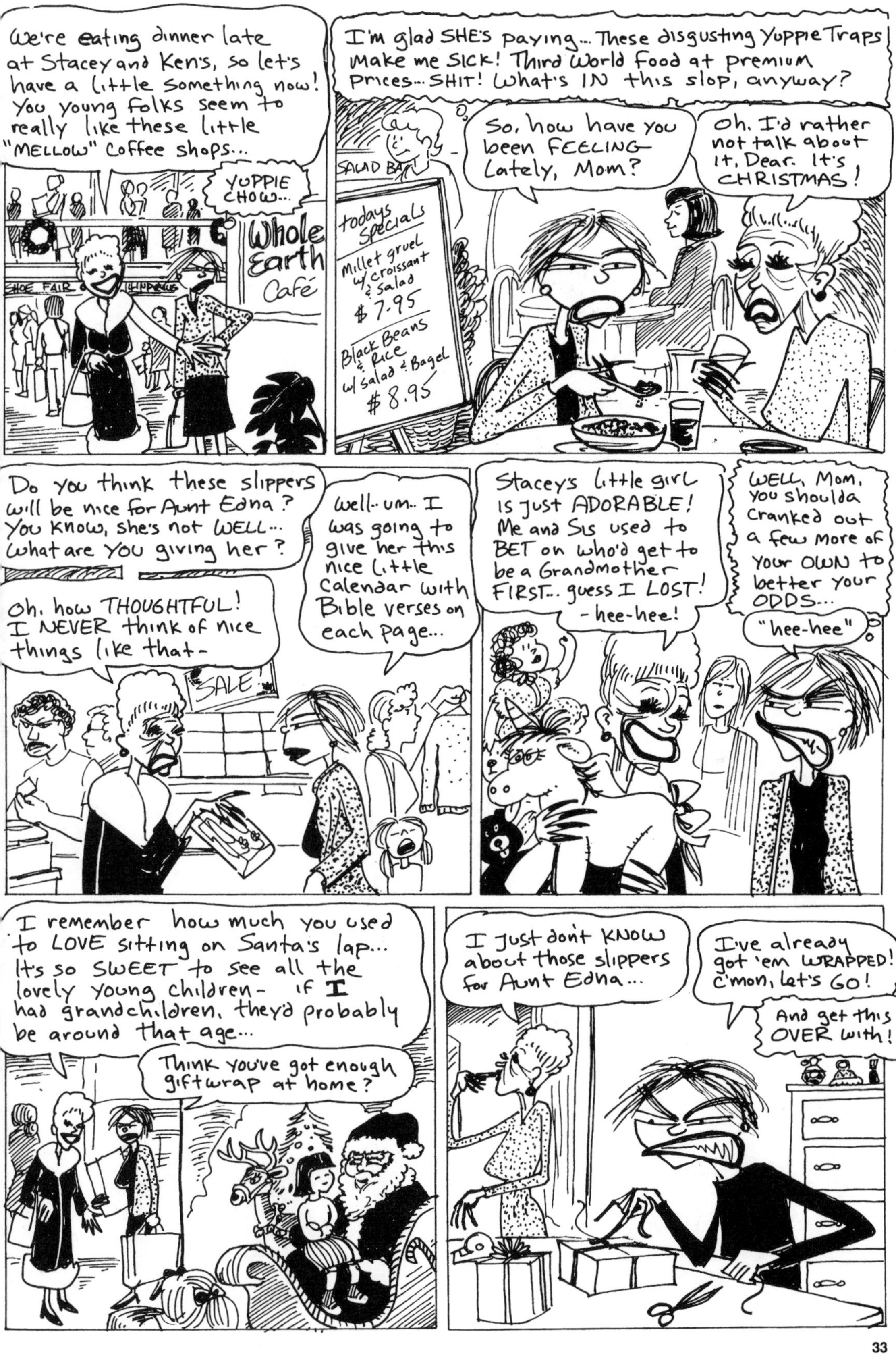
We're eating dinner late at Stacey and Ken's, so let's have a little something now! You young folks seem to really like these little "MELLOW" Coffee shops...
YUPPIE CHOW...
Whole Earth Café
SHOE FAIR
I'm glad SHE'S paying... These disgusting Yuppie Traps make me SICK! Third World food at premium prices... SHIT! What's IN this slop, anyway?
SALAD BAR
todays specials
Millet gruel w/ croissant & salad $7.95
Black Beans & Rice w/ salad & Bagel $8.95
So, how have you been FEELING lately, Mom?
Oh. I'd rather not talk about it, Dear. It's CHRISTMAS!
Do you think these slippers will be nice for Aunt Edna? You know, she's not WELL... What are YOU giving her?
Well.. um.. I was going to give her this nice little calendar with Bible verses on each page...
Oh, how THOUGHTFUL! I NEVER think of nice things like that-
SALE!
Stacey's little girl is just ADORABLE! Me and Sis used to BET on who'd get to be a Grandmother FIRST... guess I LOST!
- hee-hee!
WELL, Mom, you shoulda cranked out a few more of your OWN to better your ODDS...
"hee-hee"
I remember how much you used to LOVE sitting on Santa's lap... It's so SWEET to see all the lovely young children- if I had grandchildren, they'd probably be around that age...
Think you've got enough giftwrap at home?
I just don't KNOW about those slippers for Aunt Edna...
I've already got 'em WRAPPED! C'mon, let's GO!
And get this OVER with!

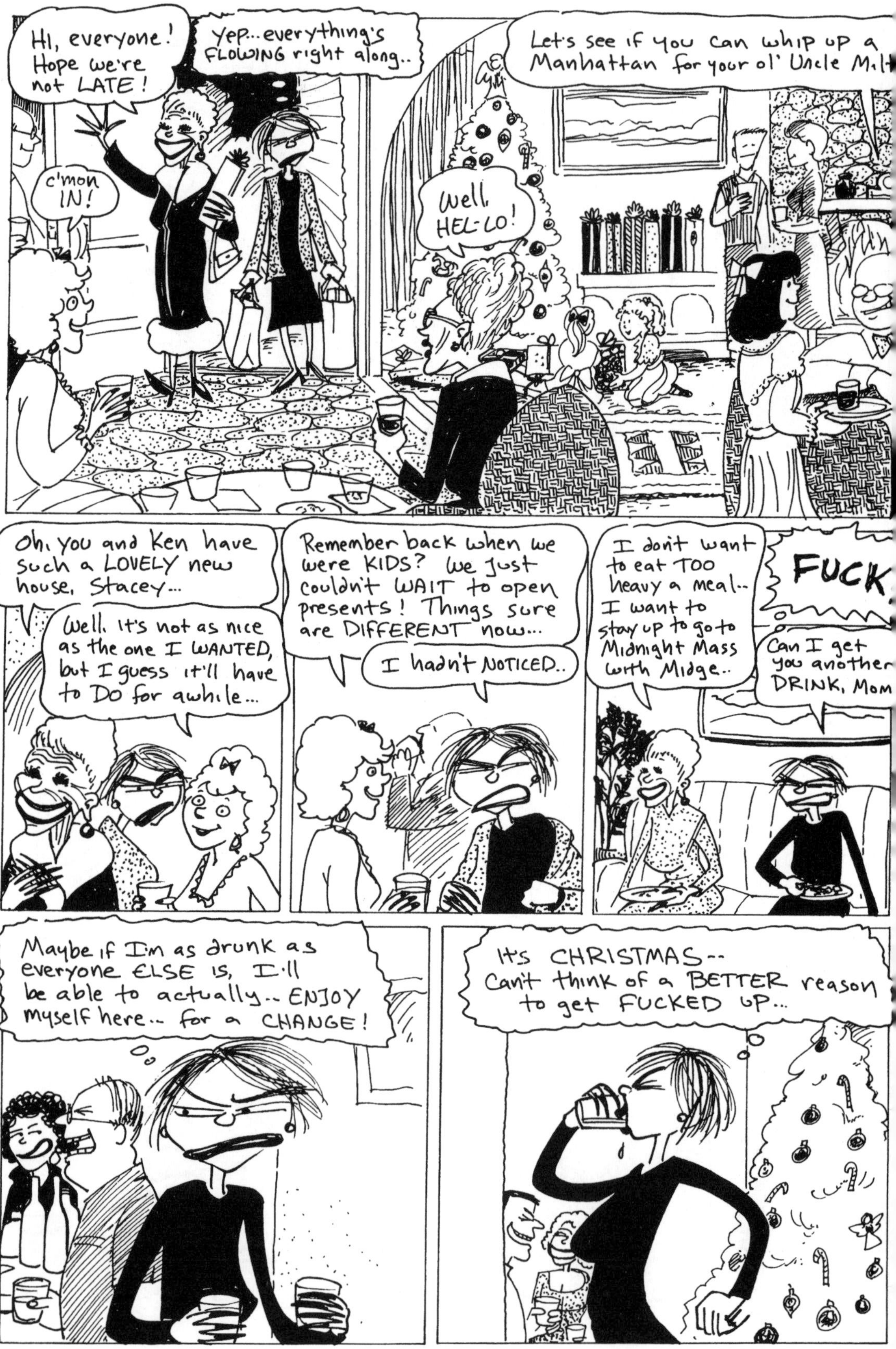
Hi, everyone! Hope we're not LATE!
c'mon IN!
Yep... everything's FLOWING right along..
Let's see if you can whip up a Manhattan for your ol' Uncle Milt
Well, HEL-LO!
Oh, you and Ken have such a LOVELY new house, Stacey...
Well, it's not as nice as the one I WANTED, but I guess it'll have to DO for awhile...
Remember back when we were KIDS? We just couldn't WAIT to open presents! Things sure are DIFFERENT now...
I hadn't NOTICED..
I don't want to eat TOO heavy a meal.. I want to stay up to go to Midnight Mass with Midge..
FUCK
Can I get you another DRINK, Mom
Maybe if I'm as drunk as everyone ELSE is, I'll be able to actually.. ENJOY myself here.. for a CHANGE!
It's CHRISTMAS-- Can't think of a BETTER reason to get FUCKED UP...

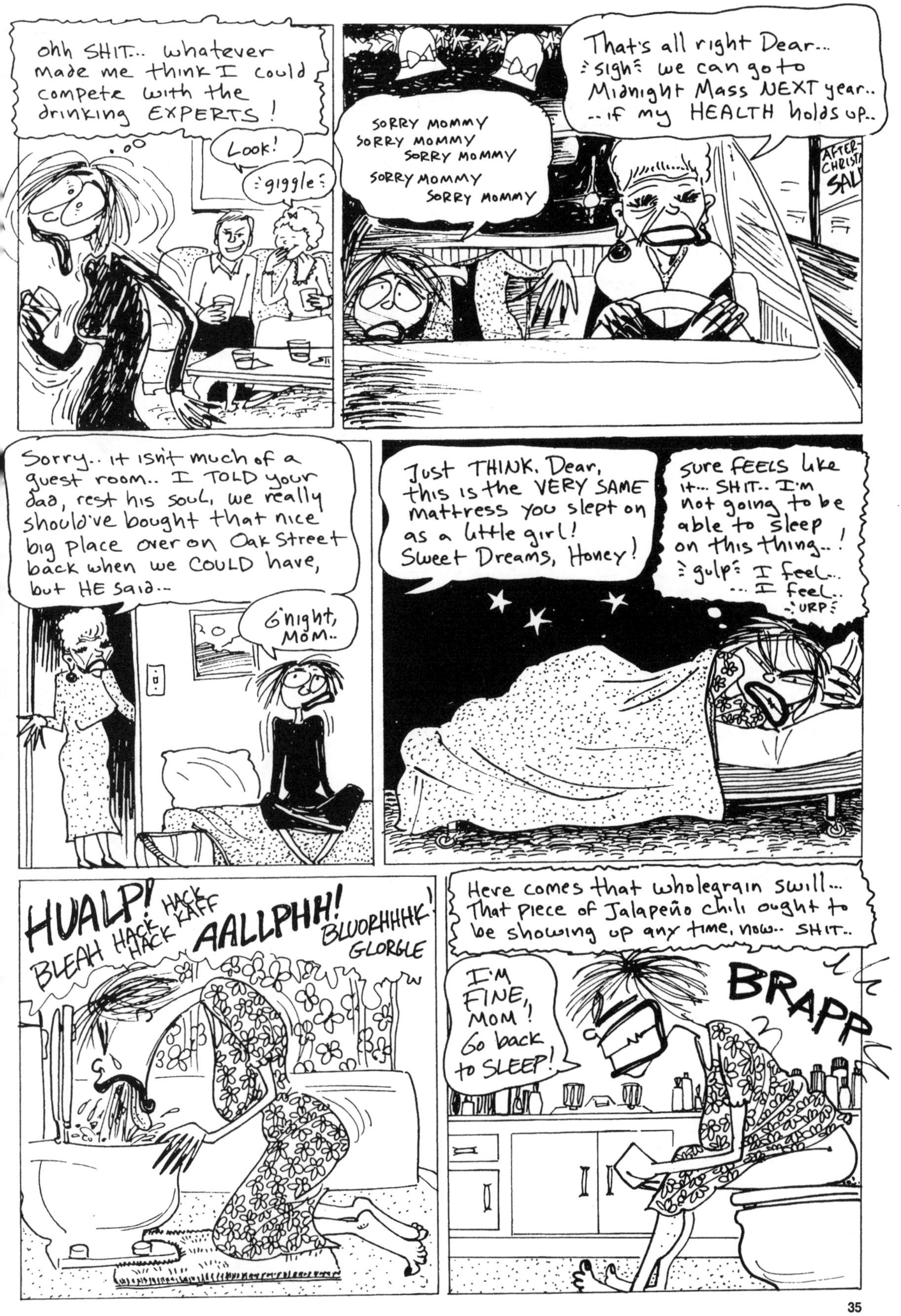
ohh SHIT... whatever made me think I could compete with the drinking EXPERTS!
Look!
giggle
SORRY MOMMY SORRY MOMMY SORRY MOMMY SORRY MOMMY SORRY MOMMY
That's all right Dear... sigh we can go to Midnight Mass NEXT year.. ..if my HEALTH holds up..
Sorry.. it isn't much of a guest room.. I TOLD your dad, rest his soul, we really should've bought that nice big place over on Oak Street back when we COULD have, but HE said..
G'night, MOM..
Just THINK, Dear, this is the VERY SAME mattress you slept on as a little girl! Sweet Dreams, Honey!
sure FEELS like it... SHIT.. I'm not going to be able to sleep on this thing..! gulp I feel.. ...I feel.. URP
HUALP! HACK KAFF BLEAH HACK HACK AALLPHH! BLUORHHHK! GLORGLE
Here comes that wholegrain swill... That piece of Jalapeño chili ought to be showing up any time, now.. SHIT..
I'M FINE, MOM! Go back to SLEEP!
BRAPP

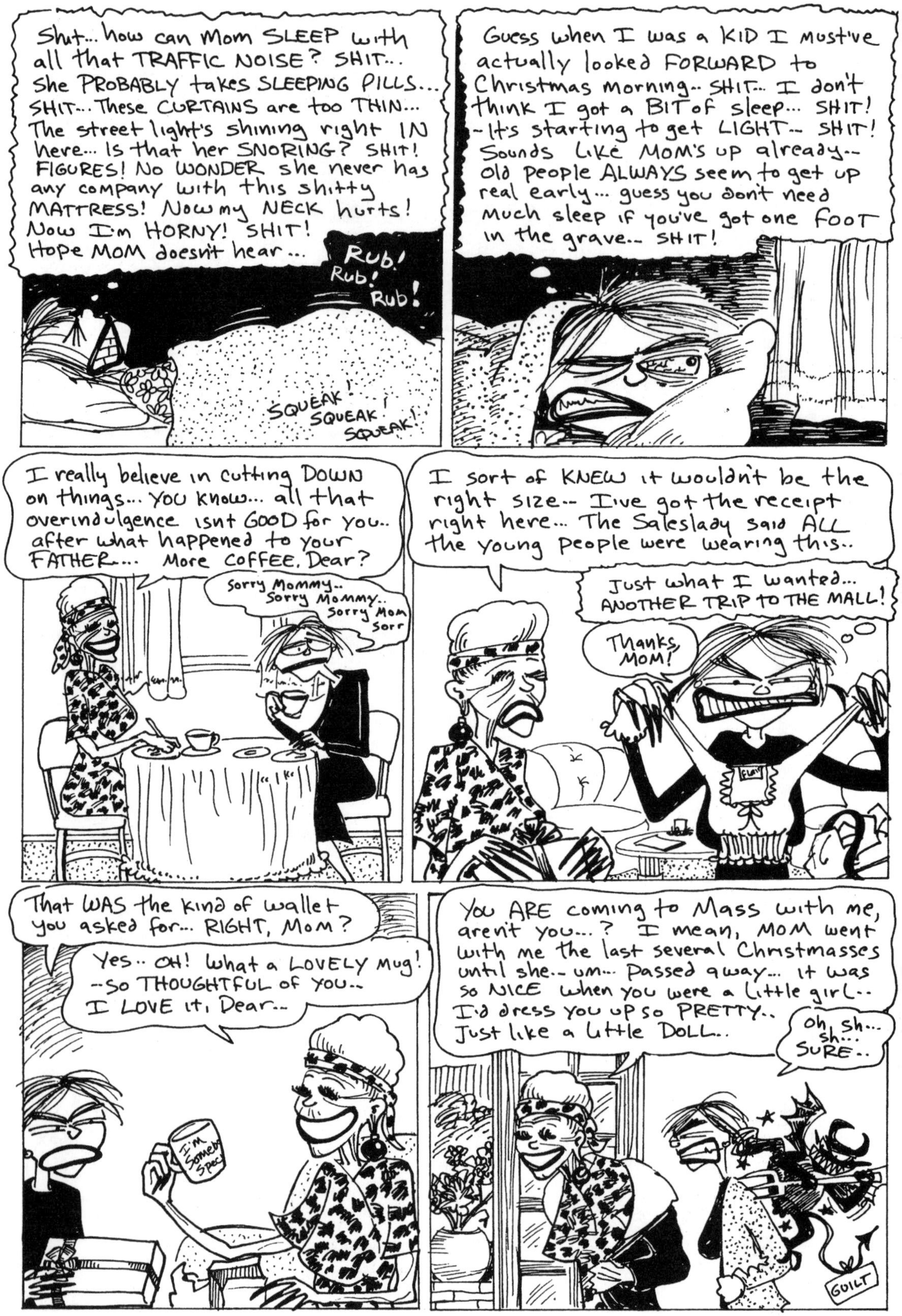
Shit... how can Mom SLEEP with all that TRAFFIC NOISE? SHIT... She PROBABLY takes SLEEPING PILLS... SHIT... These CURTAINS are too THIN... The street light's shining right IN here... Is that her SNORING? SHIT! FIGURES! No WONDER she never has any company with this shitty MATTRESS! Now my NECK hurts! Now I'm HORNY! SHIT! Hope MOM doesn't hear...
Rub! Rub! Rub!
SQUEAK! SQUEAK! SQUEAK!
Guess when I was a KID I must've actually looked FORWARD to Christmas morning.. SHIT.. I don't think I got a BIT of sleep... SHIT! -It's starting to get LIGHT-- SHIT! Sounds like MOM'S up already-- old people ALWAYS seem to get up real early... guess you don't need much sleep if you've got one FOOT in the grave.. SHIT!
I really believe in cutting DOWN on things... you know... all that overindulgence isnt GOOD for you.. after what happened to your FATHER.... More COFFEE, Dear?
Sorry Mommy.. Sorry Mommy.. Sorry Mom Sorr
I sort of KNEW it wouldn't be the right size-- I've got the receipt right here... The Saleslady said ALL the young people were wearing this..
Just what I wanted... ANOTHER TRIP TO THE MALL!
Thanks, MOM!
That WAS the kind of wallet you asked for... RIGHT, Mom?
Yes.. OH! What a LOVELY Mug! --So THOUGHTFUL of you.. I LOVE it, Dear..
You ARE coming to Mass with me, aren't you...? I mean, MOM went with me the last several Christmasses until she.. um.. passed away... it was so NICE when you were a little girl.. I'd dress you up so PRETTY.. Just like a little DOLL..
Oh sh... sh... SURE..
GUILT

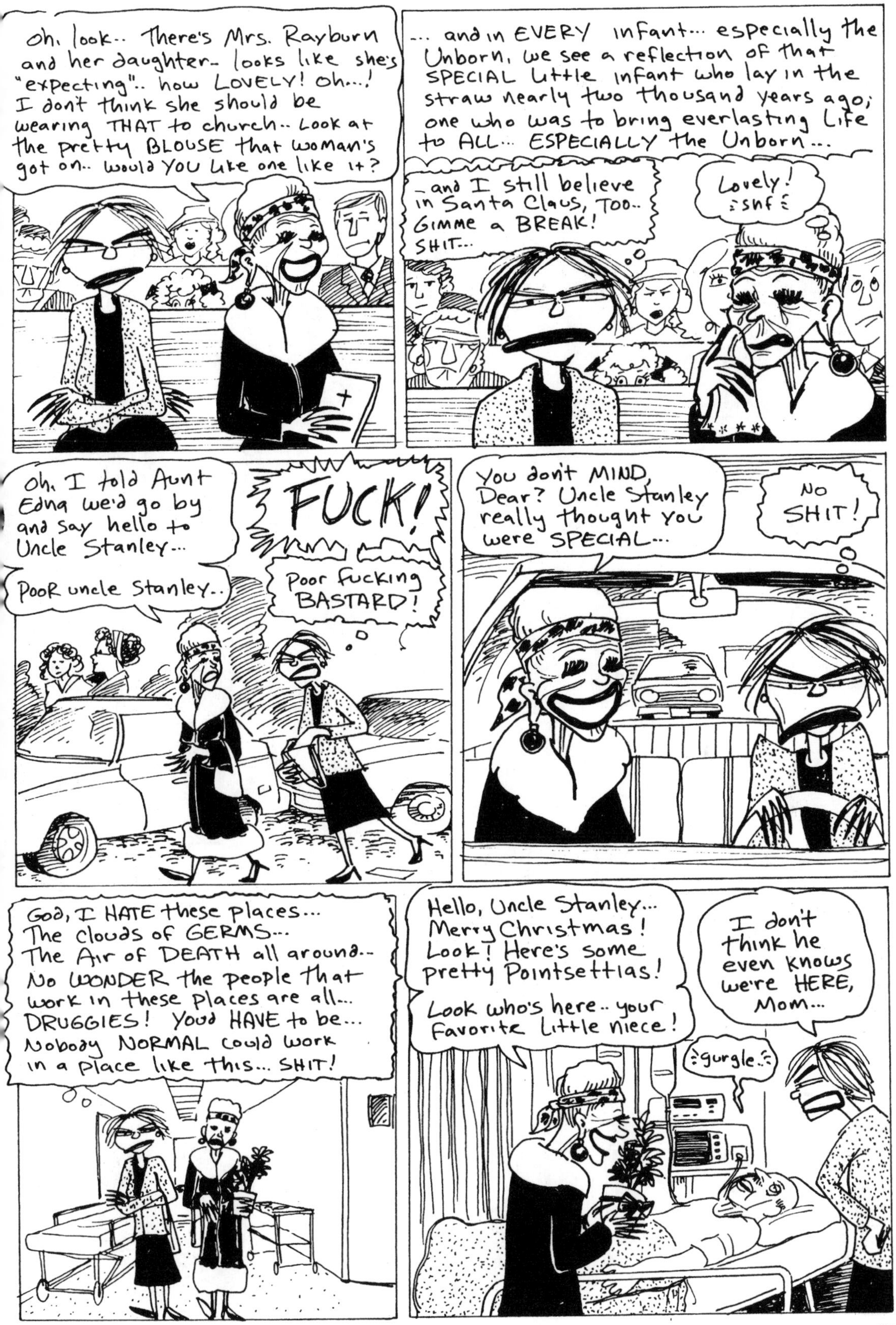
Oh, look.. There's Mrs. Rayburn and her daughter.. looks like she's "expecting".. how LOVELY! Oh...! I don't think she should be wearing THAT to church.. Look at the pretty BLOUSE that woman's got on.. would YOU like one like it?
... and in EVERY infant... especially the Unborn, we see a reflection of that SPECIAL little infant who lay in the straw nearly two thousand years ago; one who was to bring everlasting Life to ALL... ESPECIALLY the Unborn...
..and I still believe in Santa Claus, TOO.. GIMME a BREAK! SHIT...
Lovely! snf
Oh, I told Aunt Edna we'd go by and say hello to Uncle Stanley...
Poor uncle Stanley..
FUCK!
Poor fucking BASTARD!
You don't MIND, Dear? Uncle Stanley really thought you were SPECIAL...
No SHIT!
God, I HATE these places... The clouds of GERMS... The Air of DEATH all around.. No WONDER the people that work in these places are all... DRUGGIES! You'd HAVE to be... Nobody NORMAL could work in a place like this... SHIT!
Hello, Uncle Stanley... Merry Christmas! Look! Here's some pretty Pointsettias!
Look who's here.. your favorite little niece!
I don't think he even knows we're HERE, Mom...
gurgle.

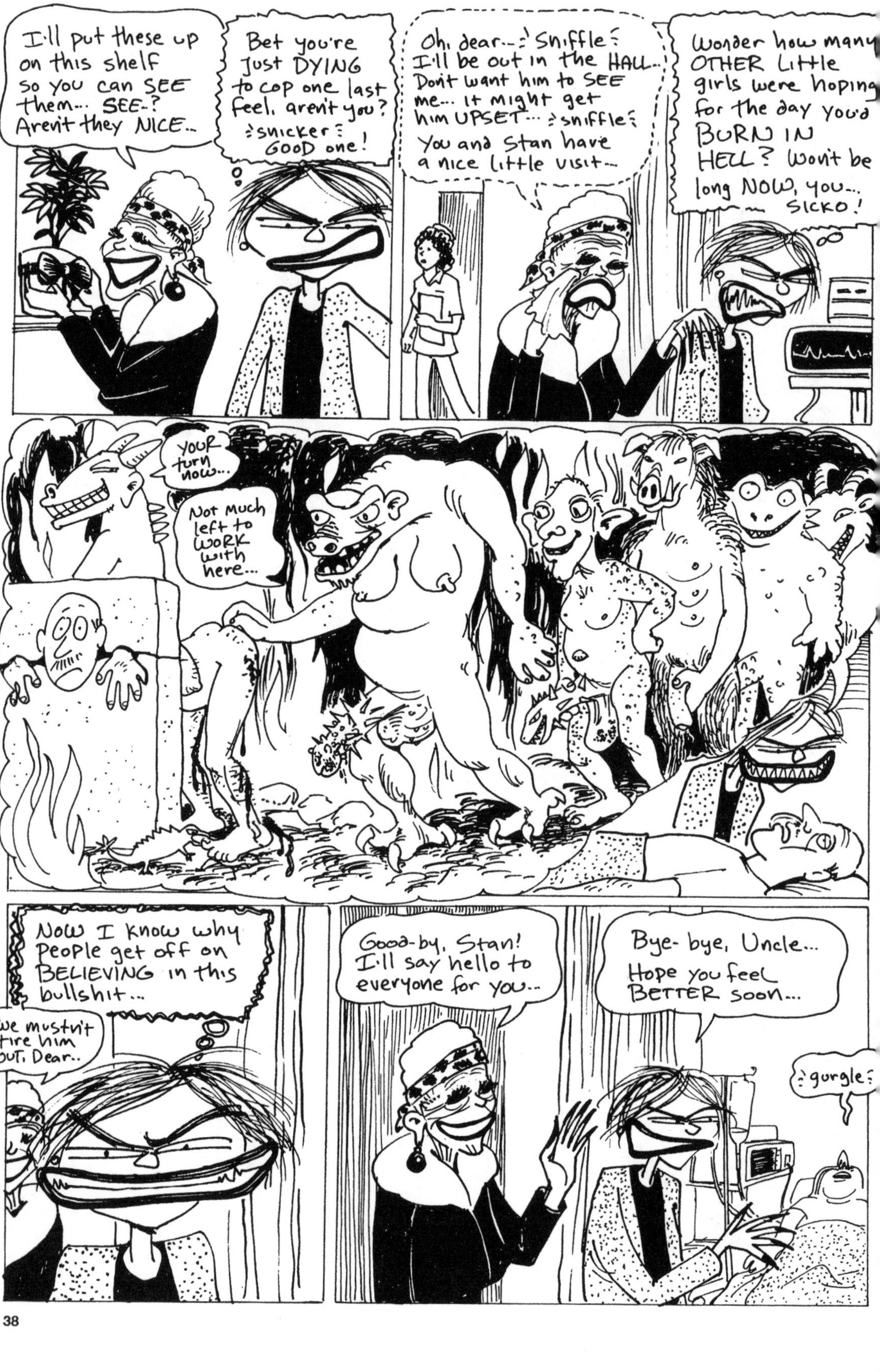
I'll put these up on this shelf so you can SEE them... SEE-? Aren't they NICE..
Bet you're JUST DYING to cop one last feel, aren't you? :snicker: GOOD one!
Oh, dear... :sniffle: I'll be out in the HALL... Don't want him to SEE me... it might get him UPSET... :sniffle: You and Stan have a nice little visit...
Wonder how many OTHER Little girls were hoping for the day you'd BURN IN HELL? Won't be long NOW, you... SICKO!
YOUR turn now...
Not much left to WORK with here...
NOW I know why People get off on BELIEVING in this bullshit...
We mustn't tire him out, Dear..
Good-by, Stan! I'll say hello to everyone for you...
Bye-bye, Uncle... Hope you feel BETTER soon...
:gurgle:

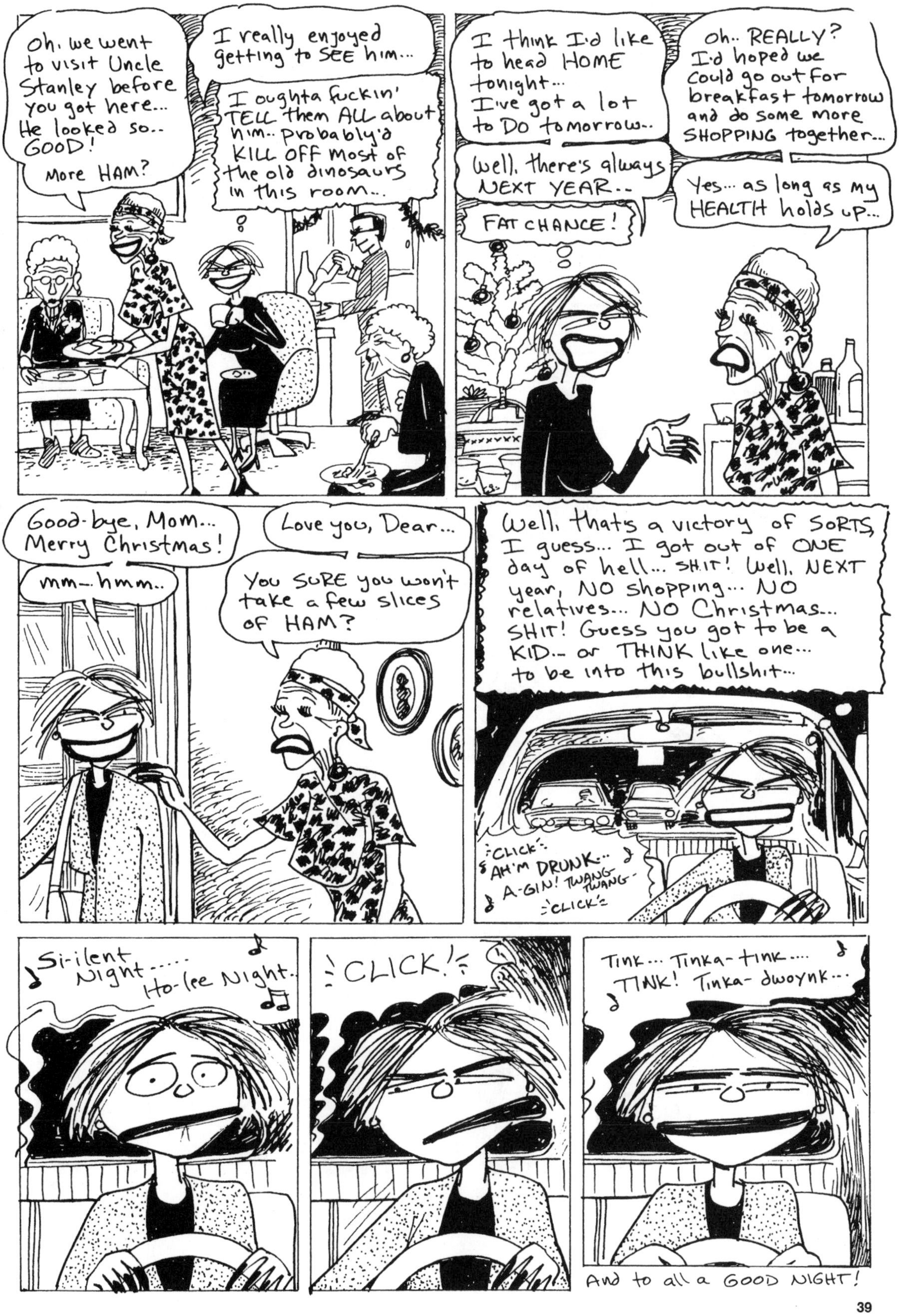
Oh, we went to visit Uncle Stanley before you got here... He looked so.. GOOD!
More HAM?
I really enjoyed getting to SEE him...
I oughta fuckin' TELL them ALL about him.. probably'd KILL OFF most of the old dinosaurs in this room...
I think I'd like to head HOME tonight... I've got a lot to DO tomorrow..
Oh.. REALLY? I'd hoped we could go out for breakfast tomorrow and do some more SHOPPING together...
Well, there's always NEXT YEAR..
FAT CHANCE!
Yes... as long as my HEALTH holds up...
Good-bye, Mom... Merry Christmas!
Love you, Dear...
mm-hmm..
You SURE you won't take a few slices of HAM?
Well, that's a victory of SORTS, I guess... I got out of ONE day of hell... SHIT! Well, NEXT year, NO shopping... NO relatives... NO Christmas... SHIT! Guess you got to be a KID.. or THINK like one... to be into this bullshit...
CLICK
AH'M DRUNK... A-GIN! TWANG TWANG
CLICK
Si-ilent Night..... Ho-lee Night..
CLICK!
Tink... Tinka-tink.... TINK! Tinka-dwoynk...
And to all a GOOD NIGHT!

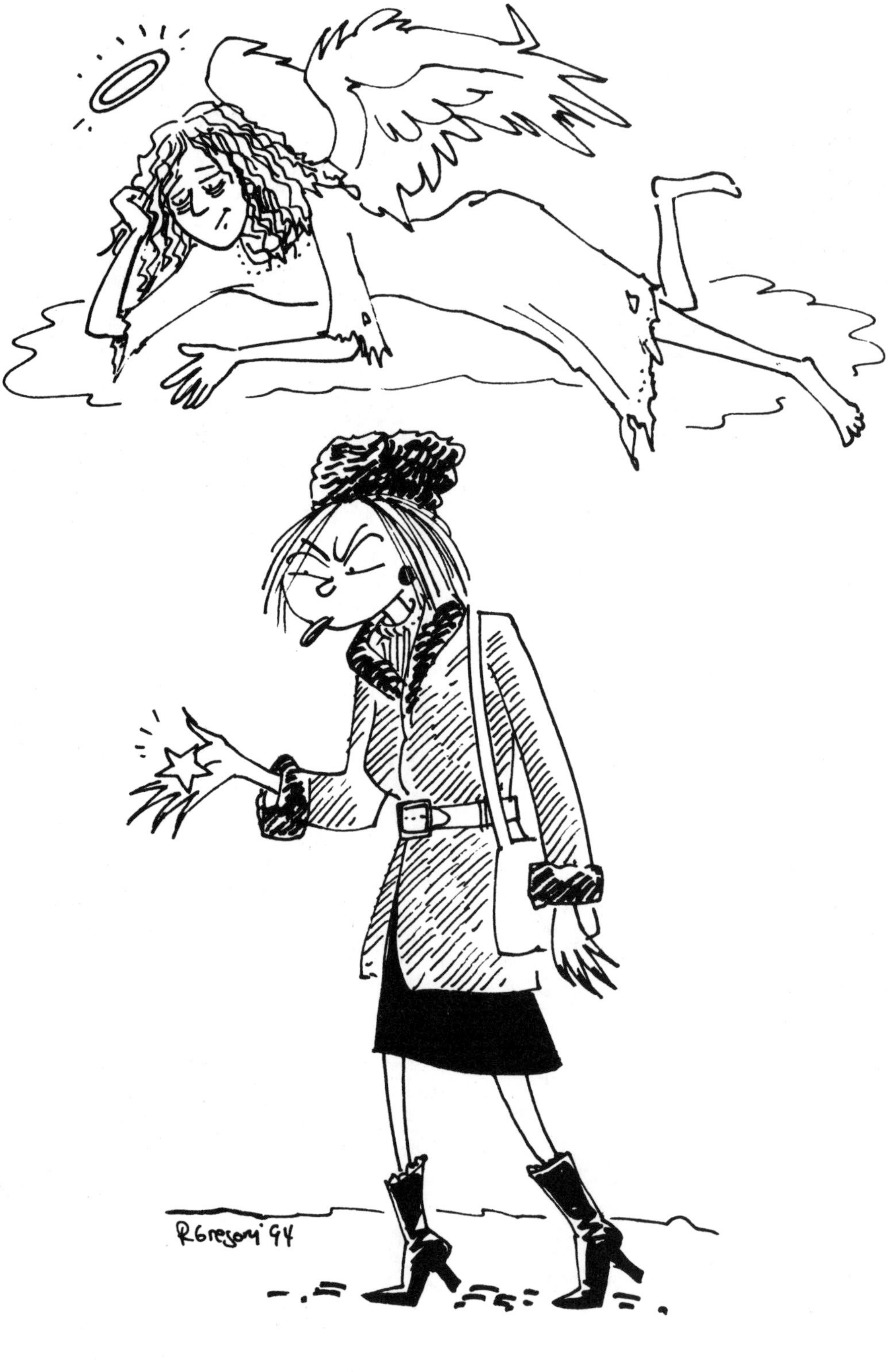
RGregory '94

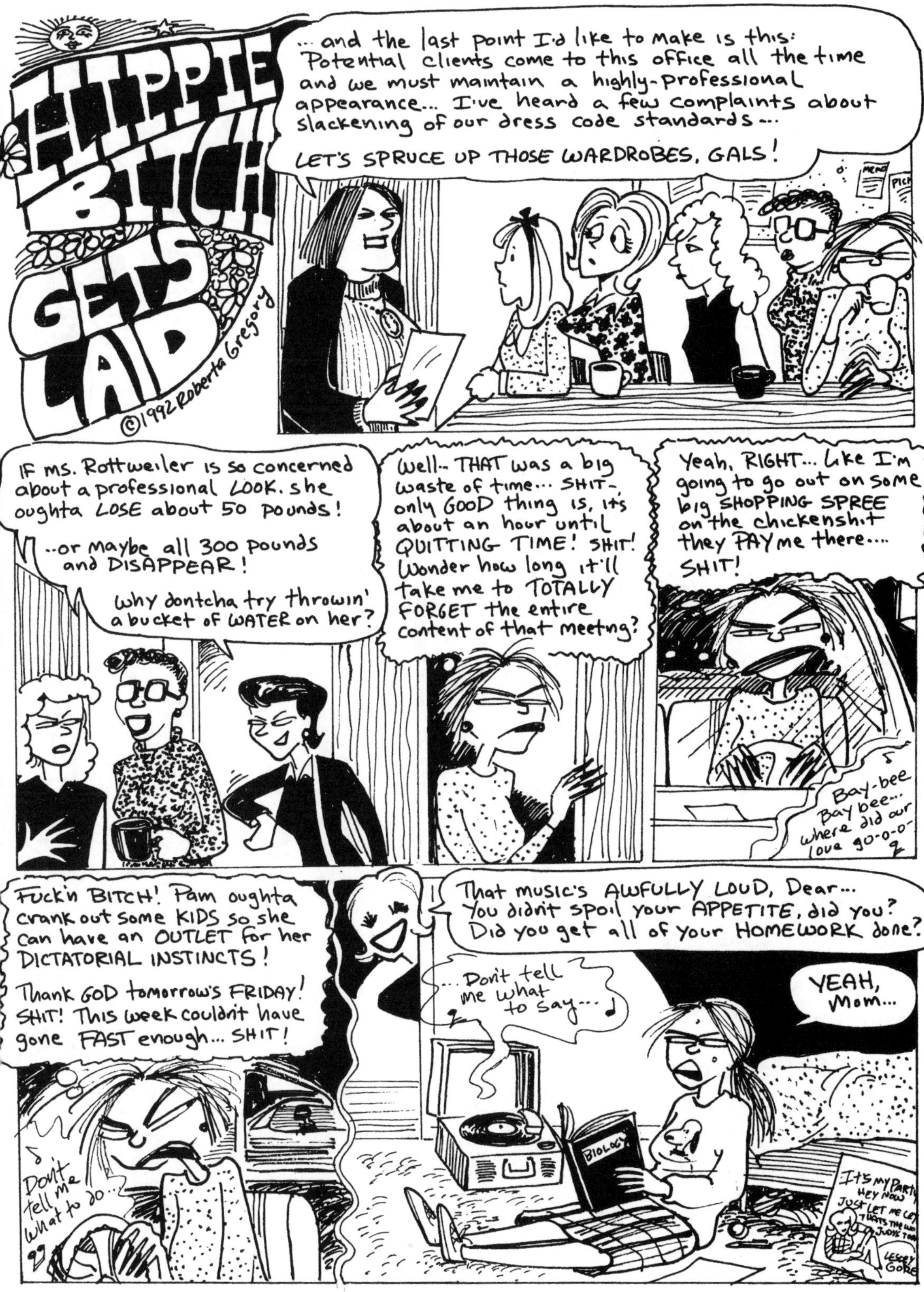
HIPPIE BITCH GETS LAID
©1992 Roberta Gregory
...and the last point I'd like to make is this: Potential clients come to this office all the time and we must maintain a highly-professional appearance... I've heard a few complaints about slackening of our dress code standards...
LET'S SPRUCE UP THOSE WARDROBES, GALS!
MEMO
IF ms. Rottweiler is so concerned about a professional LOOK, she oughta LOSE about 50 pounds!
...or maybe all 300 pounds and DISAPPEAR!
Why dontcha try throwin' a bucket of WATER on her?
Well... THAT was a big waste of time... SHIT... only GOOD thing is, it's about an hour until QUITTING TIME! SHIT! Wonder how long it'll take me to TOTALLY FORGET the entire content of that meeting?
Yeah, RIGHT... Like I'm going to go out on some big SHOPPING SPREE on the chickenshit they PAY me there.... SHIT!
Bay-bee Bay bee... where did our love go-o-o-?
Fuck'n BITCH! Pam oughta crank out some KIDS so she can have an OUTLET for her DICTATORIAL INSTINCTS!
Thank GOD tomorrow's FRIDAY! SHIT! This week couldn't have gone FAST enough... SHIT!
Don't tell me what to do...
That music's AWFULLY LOUD, Dear... You didn't spoil your APPETITE, did you? Did you get all of your HOMEWORK done?
...Don't tell me what to say...
YEAH, Mom...
BIOLOGY
IT'S MY PARTY
LESLEY GORE

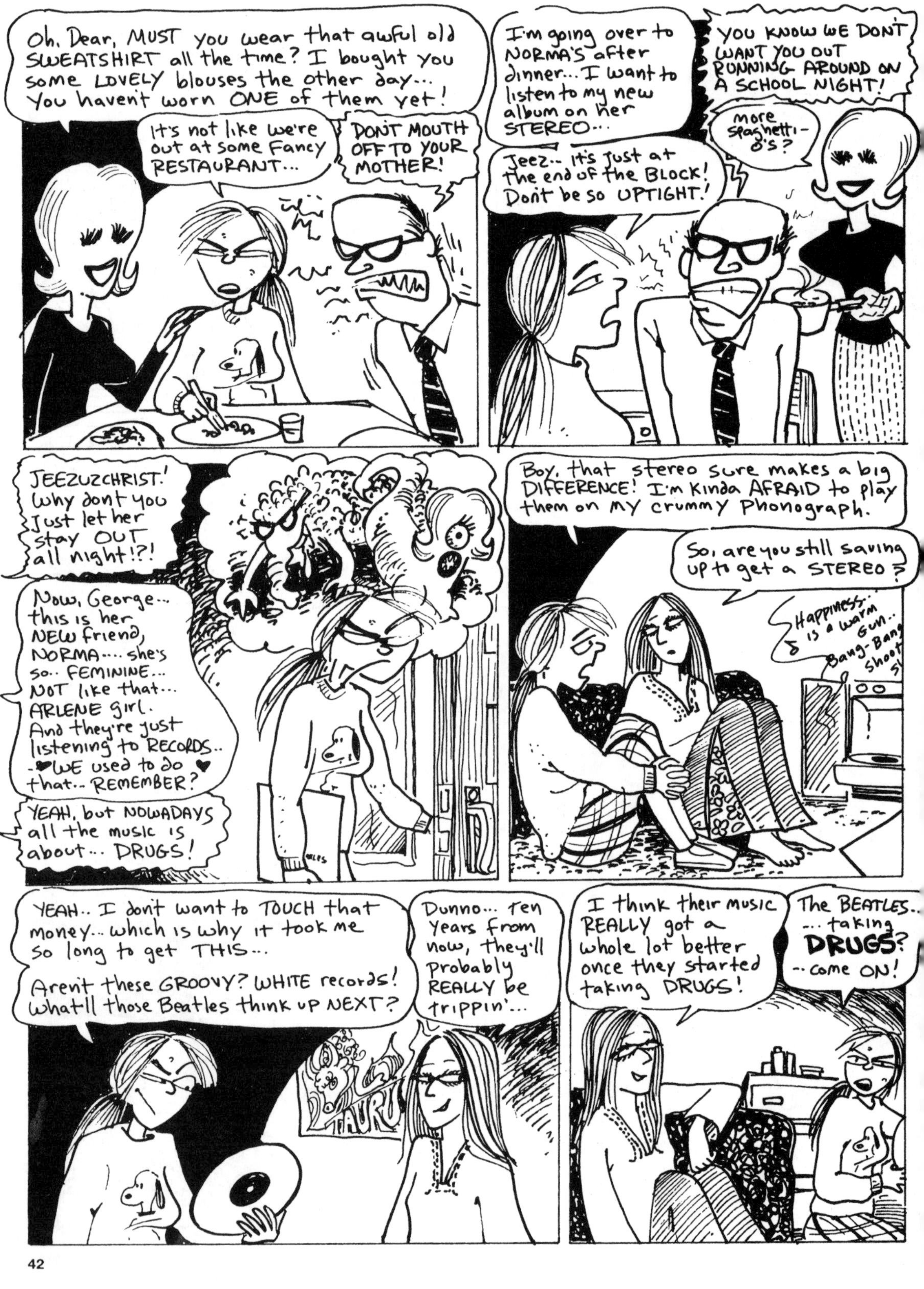
Oh, Dear, MUST you wear that awful old SWEATSHIRT all the time? I bought you some LOVELY blouses the other day... You haven't worn ONE of them yet!
It's not like we're out at some Fancy RESTAURANT...
DON'T MOUTH OFF TO YOUR MOTHER!
I'm going over to NORMA'S after dinner... I want to listen to my new album on her STEREO...
YOU KNOW WE DON'T WANT YOU OUT RUNNING AROUND ON A SCHOOL NIGHT!
more spaghetti-o's?
Jeez.. it's just at the end of the BLOCK! Don't be so UPTIGHT!
JEEZUZCHRIST! Why don't you just let her stay OUT all night!?!
Now, George... this is her NEW friend, NORMA.... she's so.. FEMININE... NOT like that... ARLENE girl. And they're just listening to RECORDS.. -WE used to do that.. REMEMBER?
YEAH, but NOWADAYS all the music is about... DRUGS!
Boy, that stereo sure makes a big DIFFERENCE! I'm kinda AFRAID to play them on my crummy Phonograph.
So, are you still saving up to get a STEREO?
Happiness.. is a warm Gun.. Bang-Bang Shoot
YEAH.. I don't want to TOUCH that money... which is why it took me so long to get THIS...
Aren't these GROOVY? WHITE records! What'll those Beatles think up NEXT?
Dunno... ten years from now, they'll probably REALLY be trippin'...
I think their music REALLY got a whole lot better once they started taking DRUGS!
The BEATLES.. ...taking DRUGS? ..come ON!

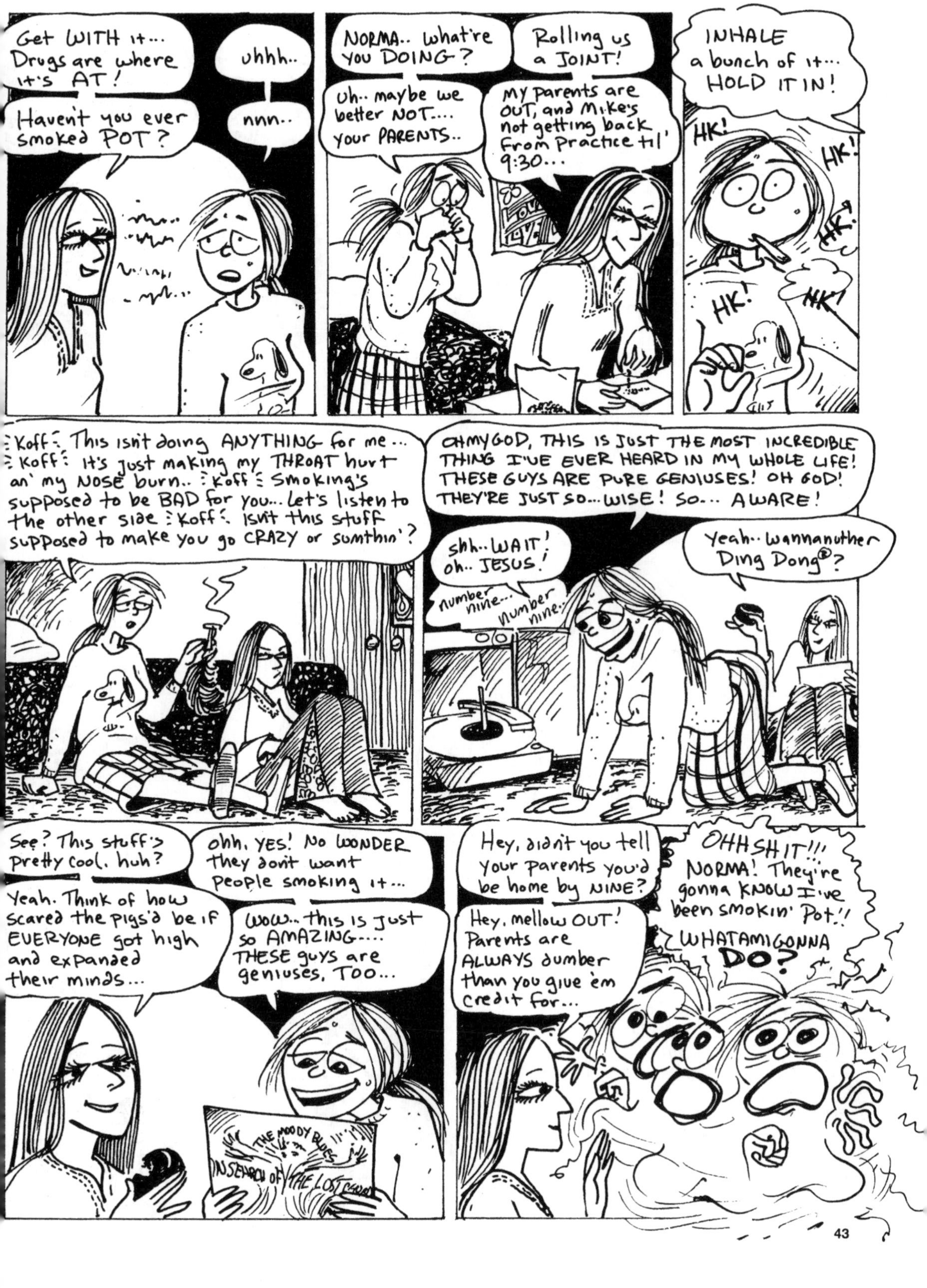

Get WITH it... Drugs are where it's AT!
uhhh..
Haven't you ever smoked POT?
nnn..
NORMA.. what're you DOING?
Rolling us a JOINT!
Uh.. maybe we better NOT.... your PARENTS..
My parents are OUT, and Mike's not getting back from practice til' 9:30...
INHALE a bunch of it... HOLD IT IN!
HK!
HK!
HK!
HK!
HK!
:Koff: This isn't doing ANYTHING for me... :Koff: It's just making my THROAT hurt an' my NOSE burn.. :Koff: Smoking's supposed to be BAD for you... Let's listen to the other side :Koff: Isn't this stuff supposed to make you go CRAZY or sumthin'?
OHMYGOD, THIS IS JUST THE MOST INCREDIBLE THING I'VE EVER HEARD IN MY WHOLE LIFE! THESE GUYS ARE PURE GENIUSES! OH GOD! THEY'RE JUST SO... WISE! SO... AWARE!
shh.. WAIT! oh.. JESUS!
number nine... number nine..
Yeah.. wannanuther Ding Dong®?
See? This stuff's pretty cool, huh?
ohh, YES! No WONDER they don't want people smoking it...
Yeah. Think of how scared the pigs'd be if EVERYONE got high and expanded their minds...
Wow.. this is just so AMAZING.... THESE guys are geniuses, TOO...
THE MOODY BLUES
IN SEARCH OF THE LOST
Hey, didn't you tell your parents you'd be home by NINE?
OHH SHIT!!! NORMA! They're gonna KNOW I've been smokin' pot!!
WHATAMIGONNA DO?
Hey, mellow OUT! Parents are ALWAYS dumber than you give 'em credit for...

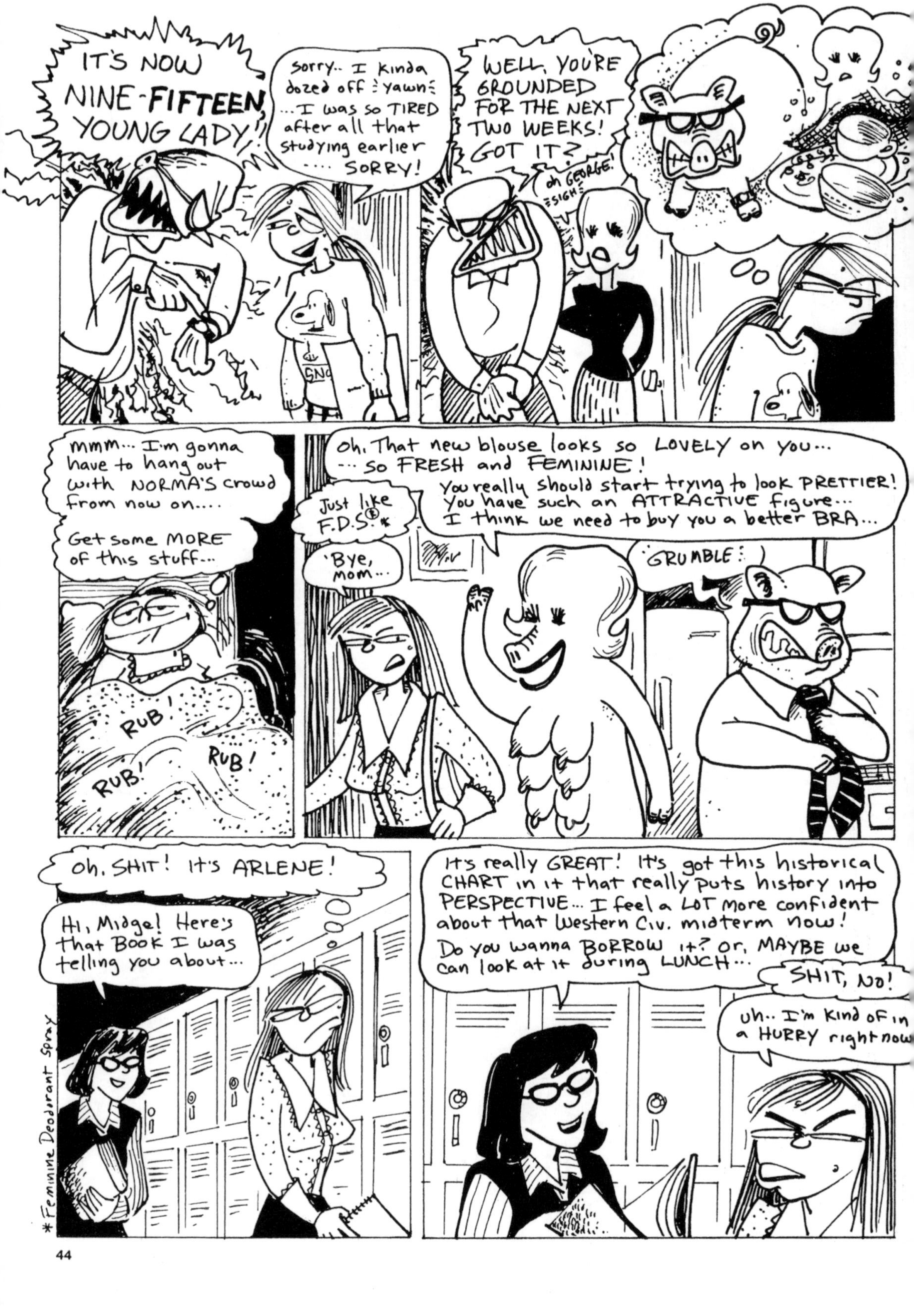

IT'S NOW NINE-FIFTEEN, YOUNG LADY!
Sorry.. I kinda dozed off :yawn: ...I was so TIRED after all that studying earlier .... SORRY!
WELL, YOU'RE GROUNDED FOR THE NEXT TWO WEEKS! GOT IT?
oh GEORGE! :SIGH:
mmm... I'm gonna have to hang out with NORMA'S crowd from now on....
Get some MORE of this stuff...
RUB! RUB! RUB!
Oh, That new blouse looks so LOVELY on you... ...so FRESH and FEMININE!
You really should start trying to look PRETTIER! You have such an ATTRACTIVE figure... I think we need to buy you a better BRA...
Just like F.D.S.® *
'Bye, mom...
GRUMBLE:
Oh, SHIT! It's ARLENE!
Hi, Midge! Here's that BOOK I was telling you about...
It's really GREAT! It's got this historical CHART in it that really puts history into PERSPECTIVE... I feel a LOT more confident about that Western Civ. midterm now! Do you wanna BORROW it? Or, MAYBE we can look at it during LUNCH...
SHIT, NO!
uh.. I'm kind of in a HURRY right now
* Feminine Deodorant Spray

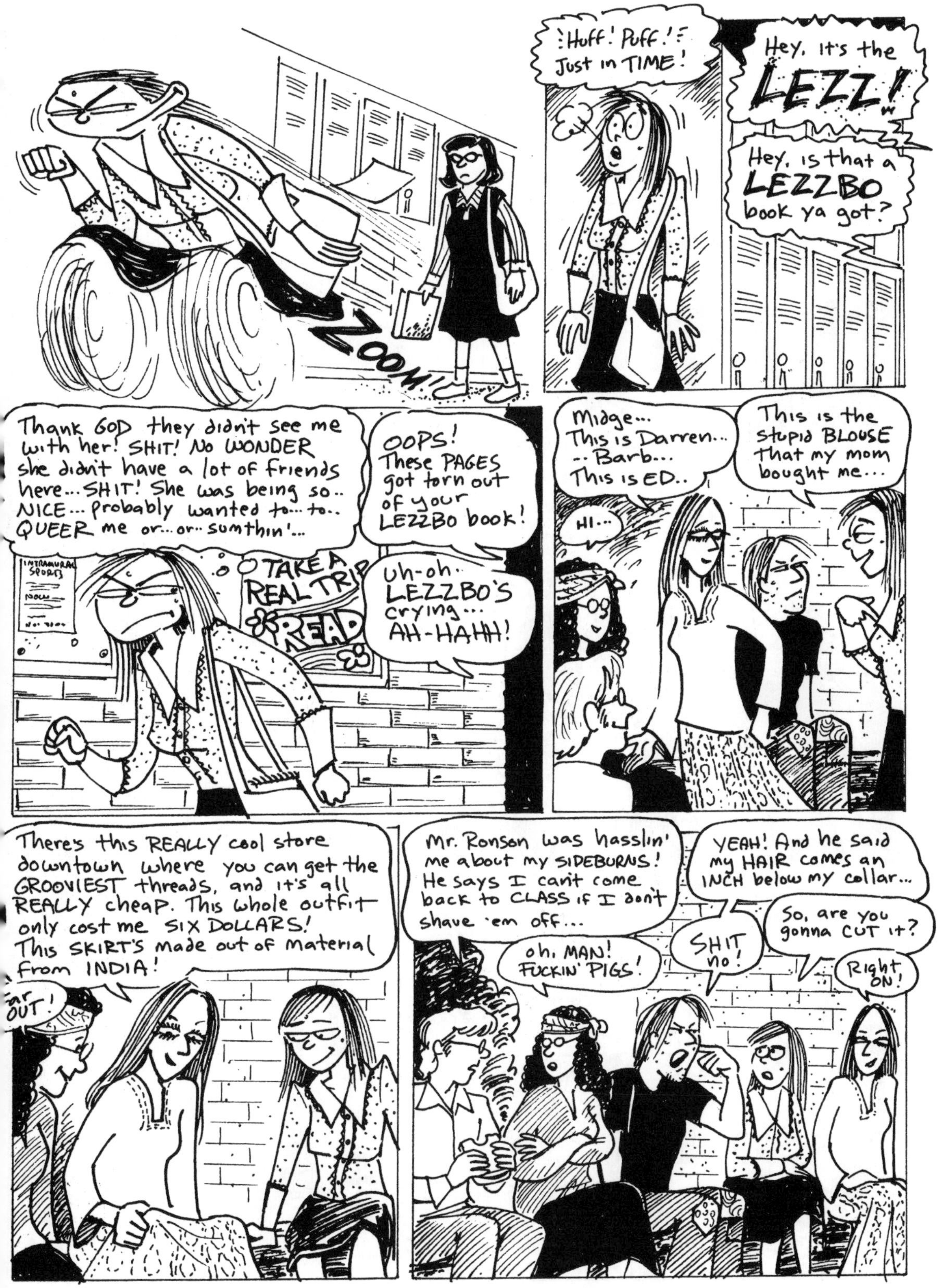

ZOOM!
Huff! Puff! Just in TIME!
Hey, it's the LEZZ!
Hey, is that a LEZZBO book ya got?
Thank GOD they didn't see me with her! SHIT! No WONDER she didn't have a lot of friends here... SHIT! She was being so.. NICE... probably wanted to... to.. QUEER me or... or.. sumthin'...
OOPS! These PAGES got torn out of your LEZZBO book!
Uh-oh.. LEZZBO'S crying... AH-HAHH!
TAKE A REAL TRIP READ
Midge... This is Darren... .. Barb... This is ED..
HI...
This is the stupid BLOUSE that my mom bought me...
There's this REALLY cool store downtown where you can get the GROOVIEST threads, and it's all REALLY cheap. This whole outfit only cost me SIX DOLLARS! This SKIRT'S made out of material from INDIA!
Far OUT!
Mr. Ronson was hasslin' me about my SIDEBURNS! He says I can't come back to CLASS if I don't shave 'em off...
oh, MAN! FUCKIN' PIGS!
YEAH! And he said my HAIR comes an INCH below my collar...
SHIT no!
So, are you gonna CUT it?
Right ON!

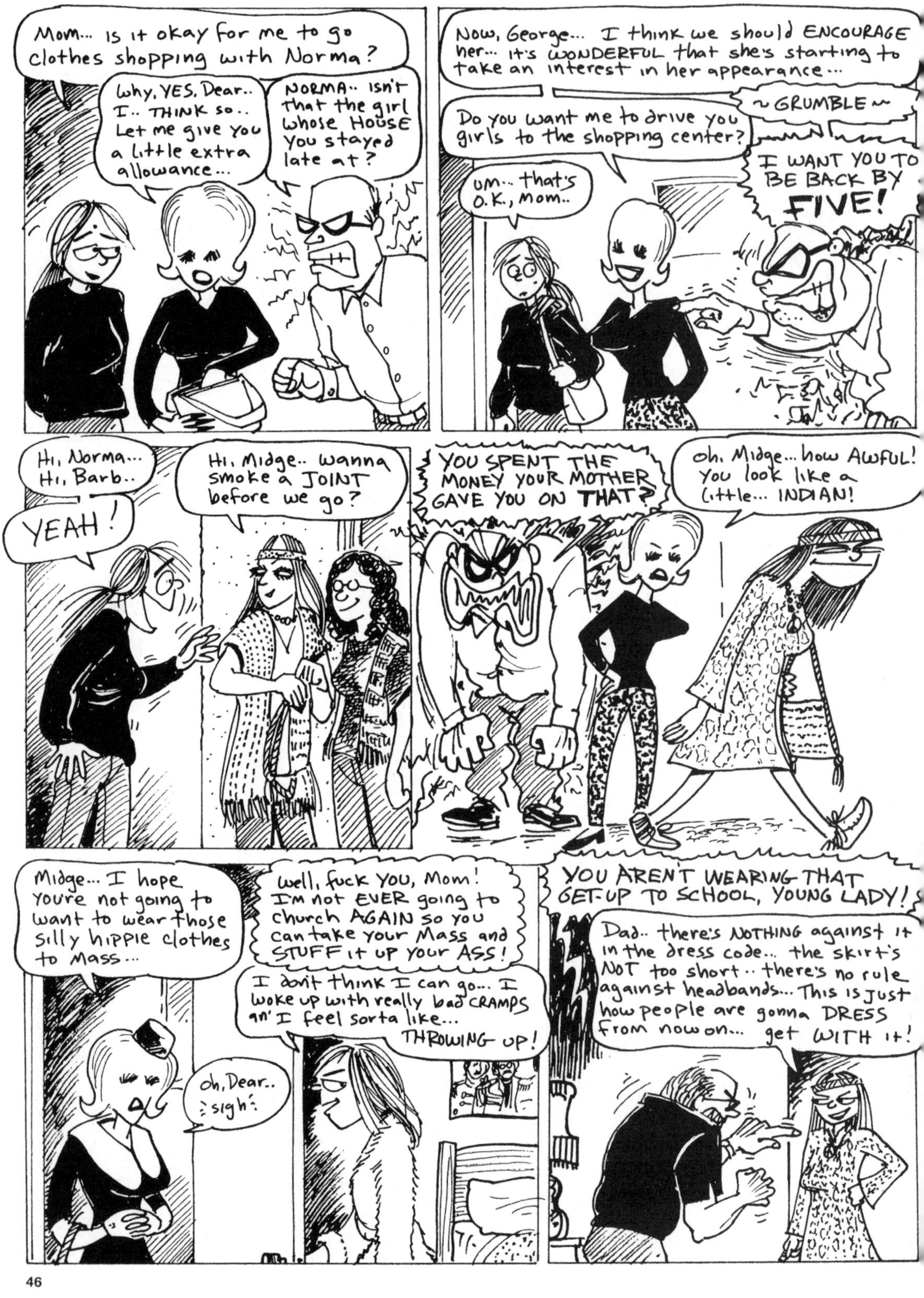
Mom... is it okay for me to go clothes shopping with Norma?
Why, YES, Dear.. I.. THINK so.. Let me give you a little extra allowance...
NORMA.. isn't that the girl whose HOUSE you stayed late at?
Now, George... I think we should ENCOURAGE her... it's WONDERFUL that she's starting to take an interest in her appearance...
~GRUMBLE~
Do you want me to drive you girls to the shopping center?
I WANT YOU TO BE BACK BY FIVE!
um.. that's O.K., Mom..
Hi, Norma... Hi, Barb..
YEAH!
Hi, Midge.. wanna smoke a JOINT before we go?
YOU SPENT THE MONEY YOUR MOTHER GAVE YOU ON THAT?
oh, Midge... how AWFUL! You look like a little... INDIAN!
Midge... I hope you're not going to want to wear those silly hippie clothes to Mass...
Well, fuck YOU, Mom! I'm not EVER going to church AGAIN so you can take your Mass and STUFF it up your ASS!
I don't think I can go... I woke up with really bad CRAMPS an' I feel sorta like... THROWING up!
oh, Dear.. :sigh:
YOU AREN'T WEARING THAT GET-UP TO SCHOOL, YOUNG LADY!
Dad.. there's NOTHING against it in the dress code... the skirt's NOT too short.. there's no rule against headbands... This is just how people are gonna DRESS from now on... get WITH it!

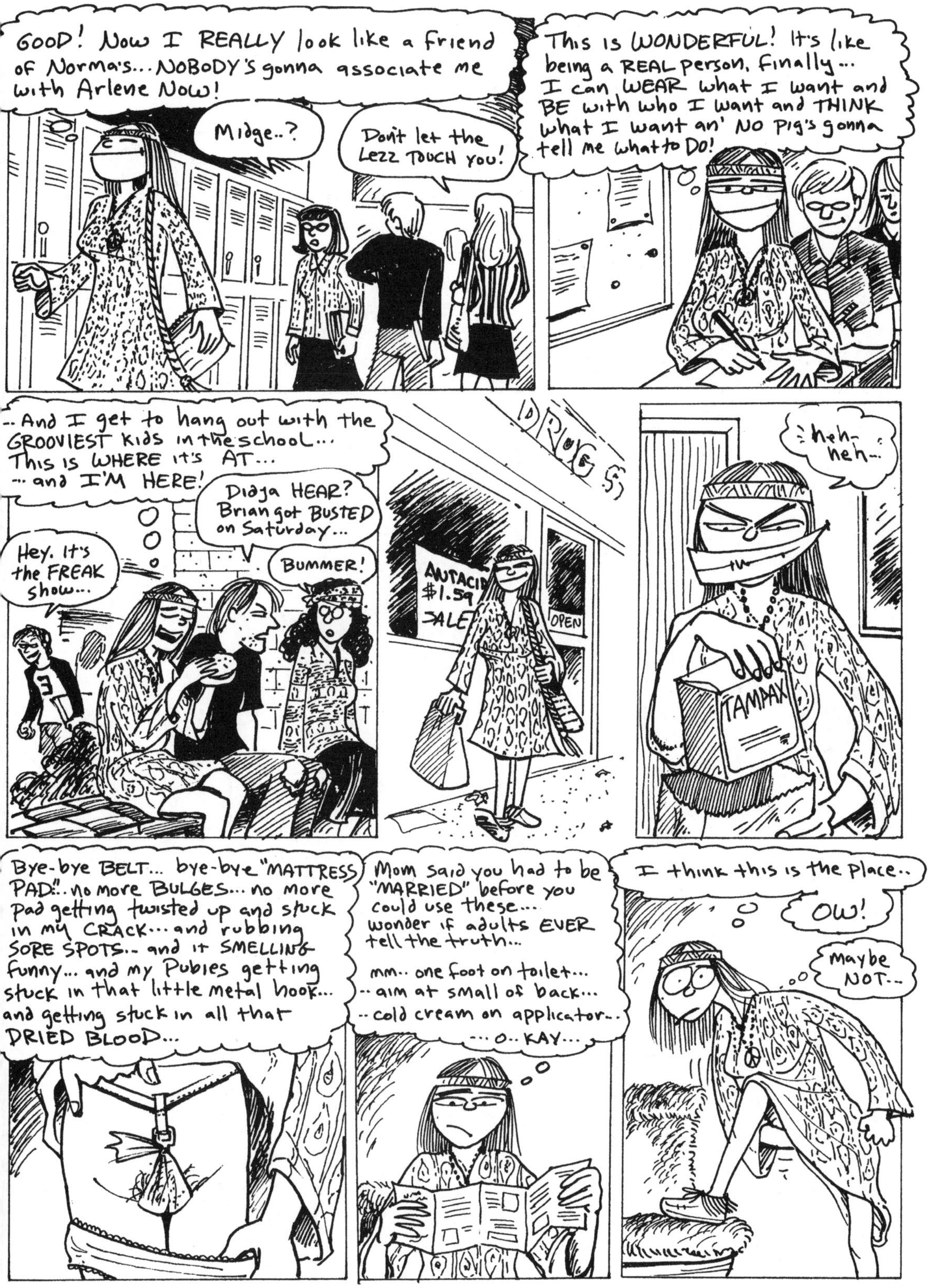

GOOD! Now I REALLY look like a friend of Norma's... NOBODY'S gonna associate me with Arlene NOW!
Midge..?
Don't let the Lezz TOUCH you!
This is WONDERFUL! It's like being a REAL person, finally... I can WEAR what I want and BE with who I want and THINK what I want an' NO pig's gonna tell me what to DO!
..And I get to hang out with the GROOVIEST kids in the school... This is WHERE it's AT... ...and I'M HERE!
Hey. It's the FREAK show...
Didja HEAR? Brian got BUSTED on Saturday...
BUMMER!
DRUGS
ANTACID $1.59 SALE
OPEN
heh-heh-
TAMPAX
Bye-bye BELT... bye-bye "MATTRESS PAD"!..no more BULGES... no more pad getting twisted up and stuck in my CRACK... and rubbing SORE SPOTS.. and it SMELLING funny... and my pubies getting stuck in that little metal hook... and getting stuck in all that DRIED BLOOD...
Mom said you had to be "MARRIED" before you could use these... wonder if adults EVER tell the truth...
mm.. one foot on toilet... ..aim at small of back... ..cold cream on applicator.. ...O..KAY...
I think this is the place..
OW!
Maybe NOT..

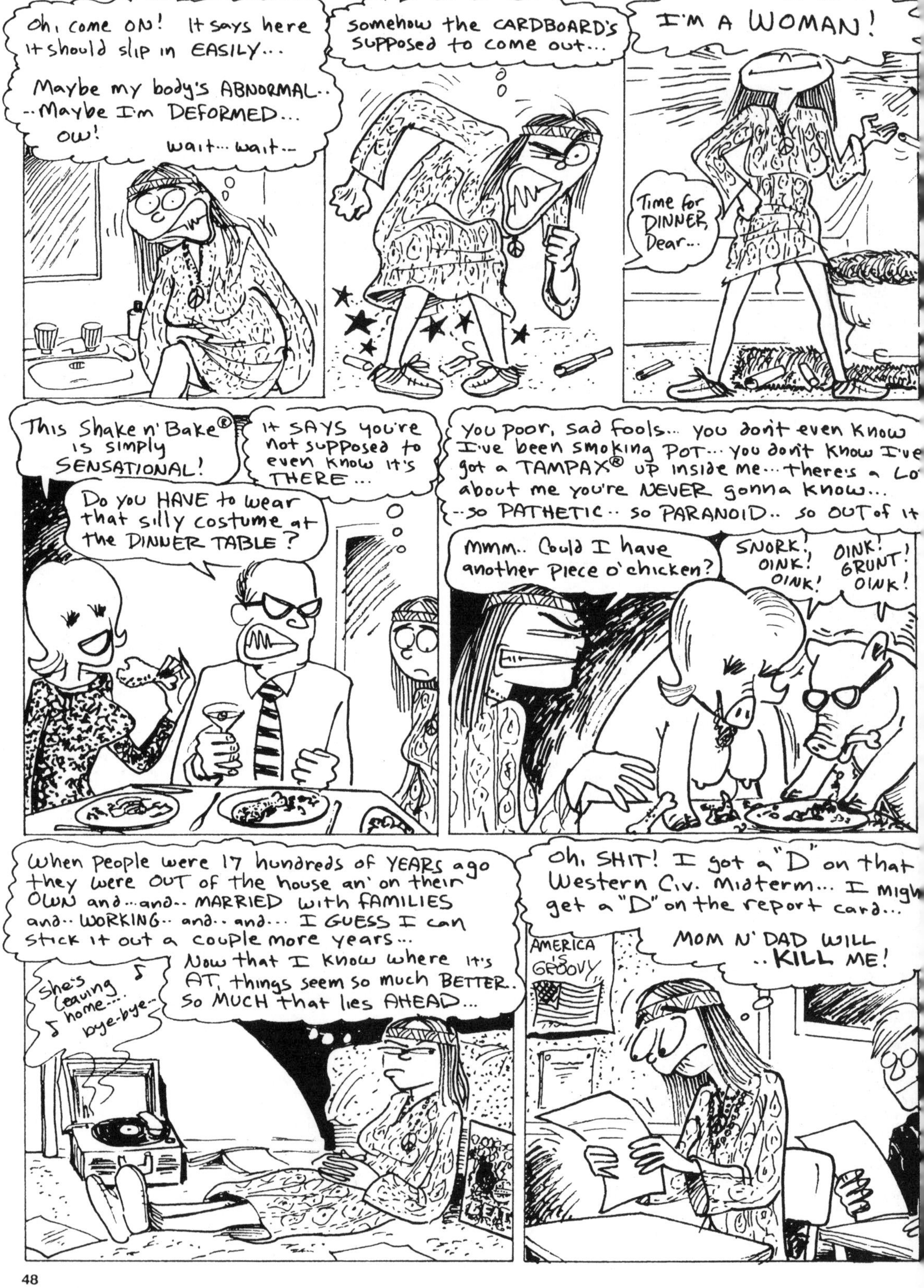

Oh, come ON! It says here it should slip in EASILY...
Maybe my body's ABNORMAL.. ..Maybe I'm DEFORMED... OW! wait... wait...
Somehow the CARDBOARD's supposed to come out...
I'M A WOMAN!
Time for DINNER, Dear...
This Shake n' Bake® is simply SENSATIONAL!
It SAYS you're not supposed to even know it's THERE...
Do you HAVE to wear that silly costume at the DINNER TABLE?
You poor, sad fools... you don't even know I've been smoking POT... you don't know I've got a TAMPAX® up inside me... there's a LO about me you're NEVER gonna know... ..so PATHETIC.. so PARANOID.. so OUT of it
Mmm.. Could I have another piece o'chicken?
SNORK! OINK! OINK!
OINK! GRUNT! OINK!
When people were 17 hundreds of YEARS ago they were OUT of the house an' on their OWN and...and.. MARRIED with FAMILIES and.. WORKING.. and.. and... I GUESS I can stick it out a couple more years...
Now that I know where it's AT, things seem so much BETTER. So MUCH that lies AHEAD...
She's leaving home... bye-bye...
Oh, SHIT! I got a "D" on that Western Civ. Midterm... I migh get a "D" on the report card...
MOM N' DAD WILL ..KILL ME!
AMERICA IS GROOVY

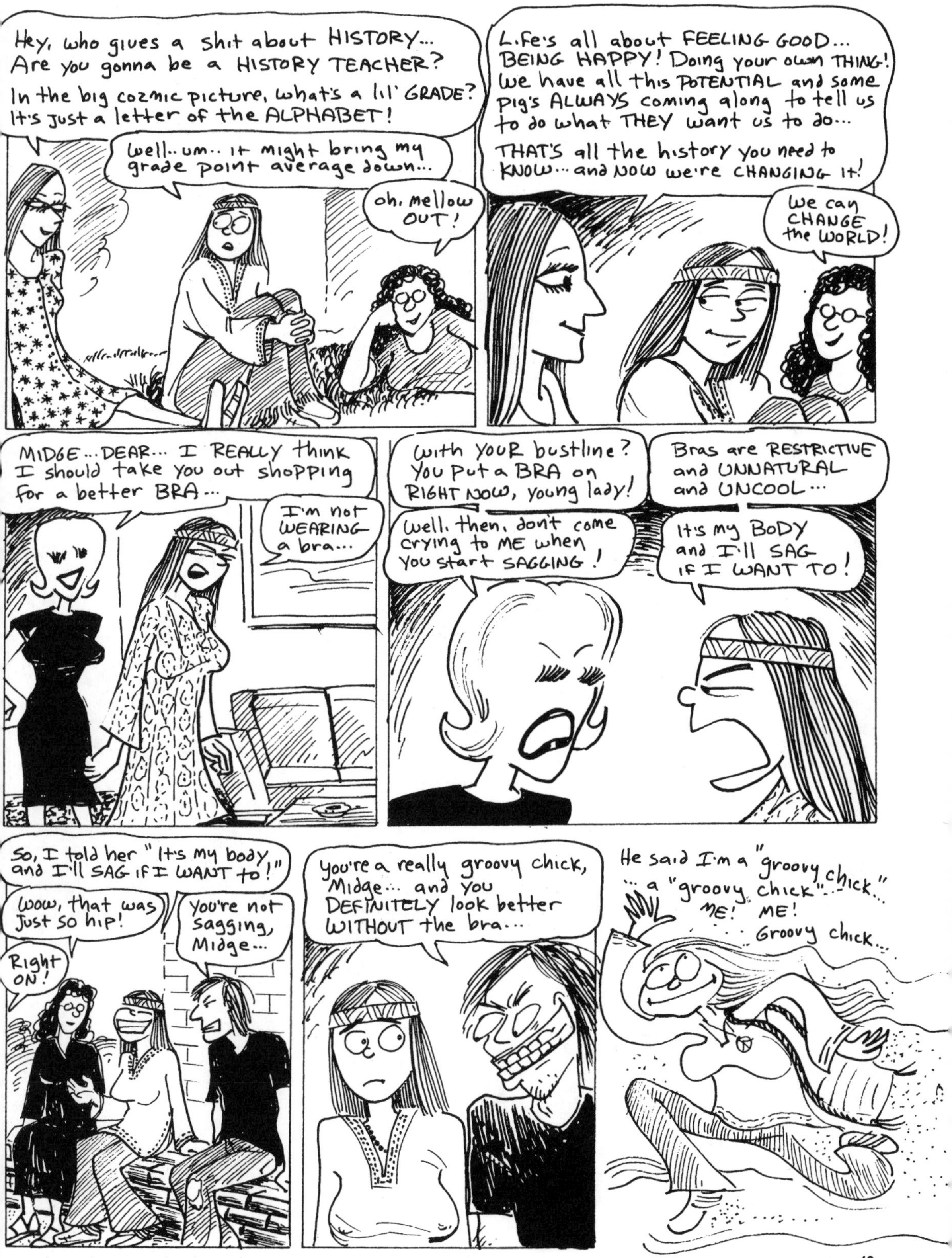
Hey, who gives a shit about HISTORY... Are you gonna be a HISTORY TEACHER?
In the big cozmic picture, what's a lil' GRADE? It's just a letter of the ALPHABET!
Well.. um.. it might bring my grade point average down...
oh, mellow OUT!
Life's all about FEELING GOOD... BEING HAPPY! Doing your own THING! We have all this POTENTIAL and some pig's ALWAYS coming along to tell us to do what THEY want us to do...
THAT'S all the history you need to KNOW... and NOW we're CHANGING it!
We can CHANGE the WORLD!
MIDGE... DEAR... I REALLY think I should take you out shopping for a better BRA...
I'm not WEARING a bra...
With YOUR bustline? You put a BRA on RIGHT NOW, young lady!
Bras are RESTRICTIVE and UNNATURAL and UNCOOL...
Well, then, don't come crying to ME when you start SAGGING!
It's my BODY and I'll SAG if I WANT TO!
So, I told her "It's my body and I'll SAG if I WANT to!"
Wow, that was just so hip!
You're not sagging, Midge...
Right ON!
You're a really groovy chick, Midge... and you DEFINITELY look better WITHOUT the bra...
He said I'm a "groovy chick" ... a "groovy chick"... ME! ME! Groovy chick...

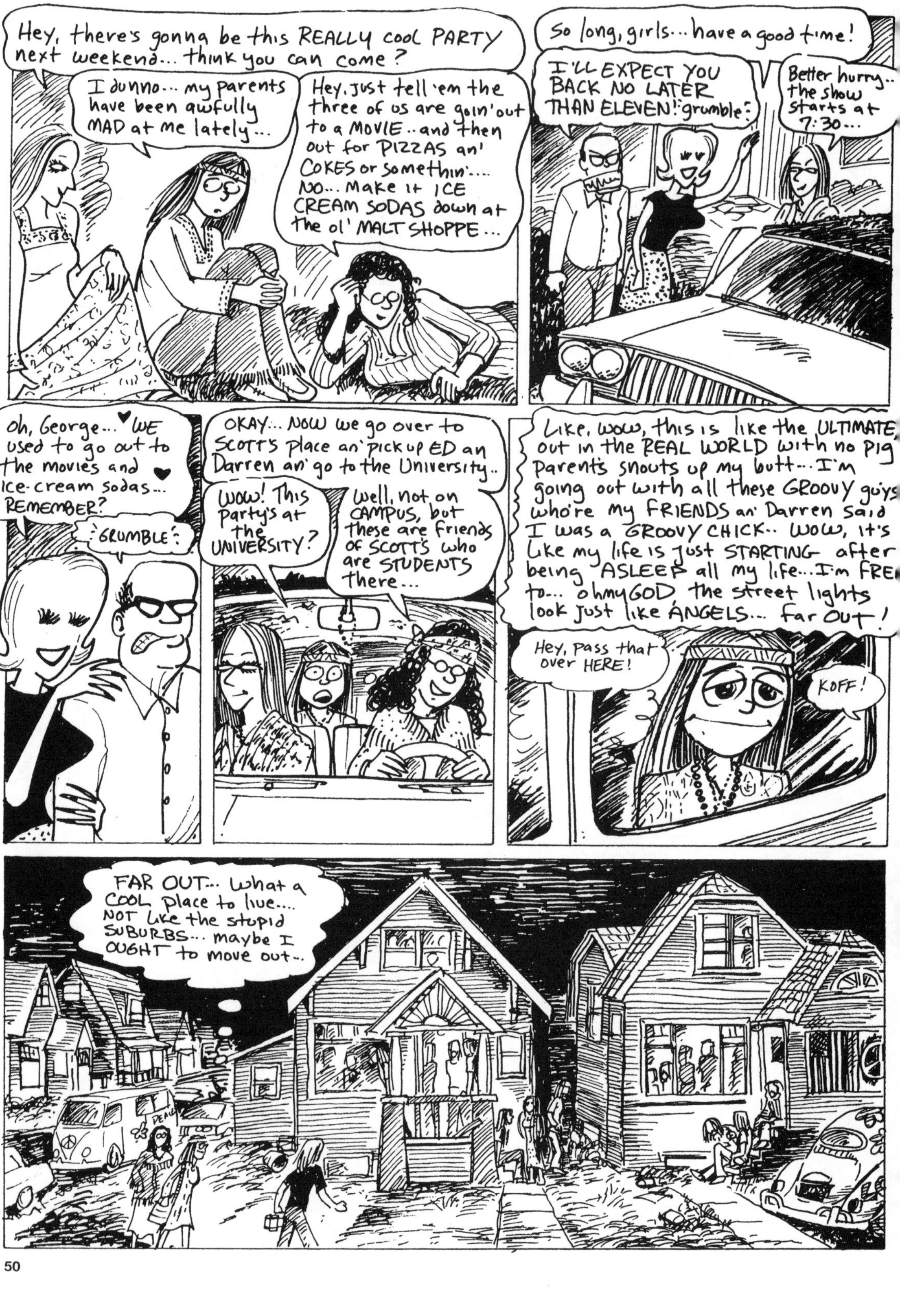
Hey, there's gonna be this REALLY cool PARTY next weekend... think you can come?
I dunno... my parents have been awfully MAD at me lately...
Hey, just tell 'em the three of us are goin' out to a MOVIE.. and then out for PIZZAS an' COKES or somethin'.... NO... Make it ICE CREAM SODAS down at the ol' MALT SHOPPE...
So long, girls... have a good time!
I'LL EXPECT YOU BACK NO LATER THAN ELEVEN! grumble
Better hurry.. the show starts at 7:30...
oh, George... WE used to go out to the movies and ice-cream sodas... REMEMBER?
GRUMBLE
OKAY... NOW we go over to SCOTT'S place an' pick up ED an Darren an' go to the University..
WOW! This party's at the UNIVERSITY?
Well, not on CAMPUS, but these are friends of SCOTT'S who are STUDENTS there...
Like, wow, this is like the ULTIMATE out in the REAL WORLD with no pig parents snouts up my butt... I'm going out with all these GROOVY guys who're my FRIENDS an' Darren said I was a GROOVY CHICK.. WOW, it's like my life is just STARTING after being ASLEEP all my life... I'm FREE to... ohmyGOD the street lights look just like ANGELS... far out!
Hey, pass that over HERE!
KOFF!
FAR OUT... What a COOL place to live.... NOT like the stupid SUBURBS... maybe I OUGHT to move out..
PEACE

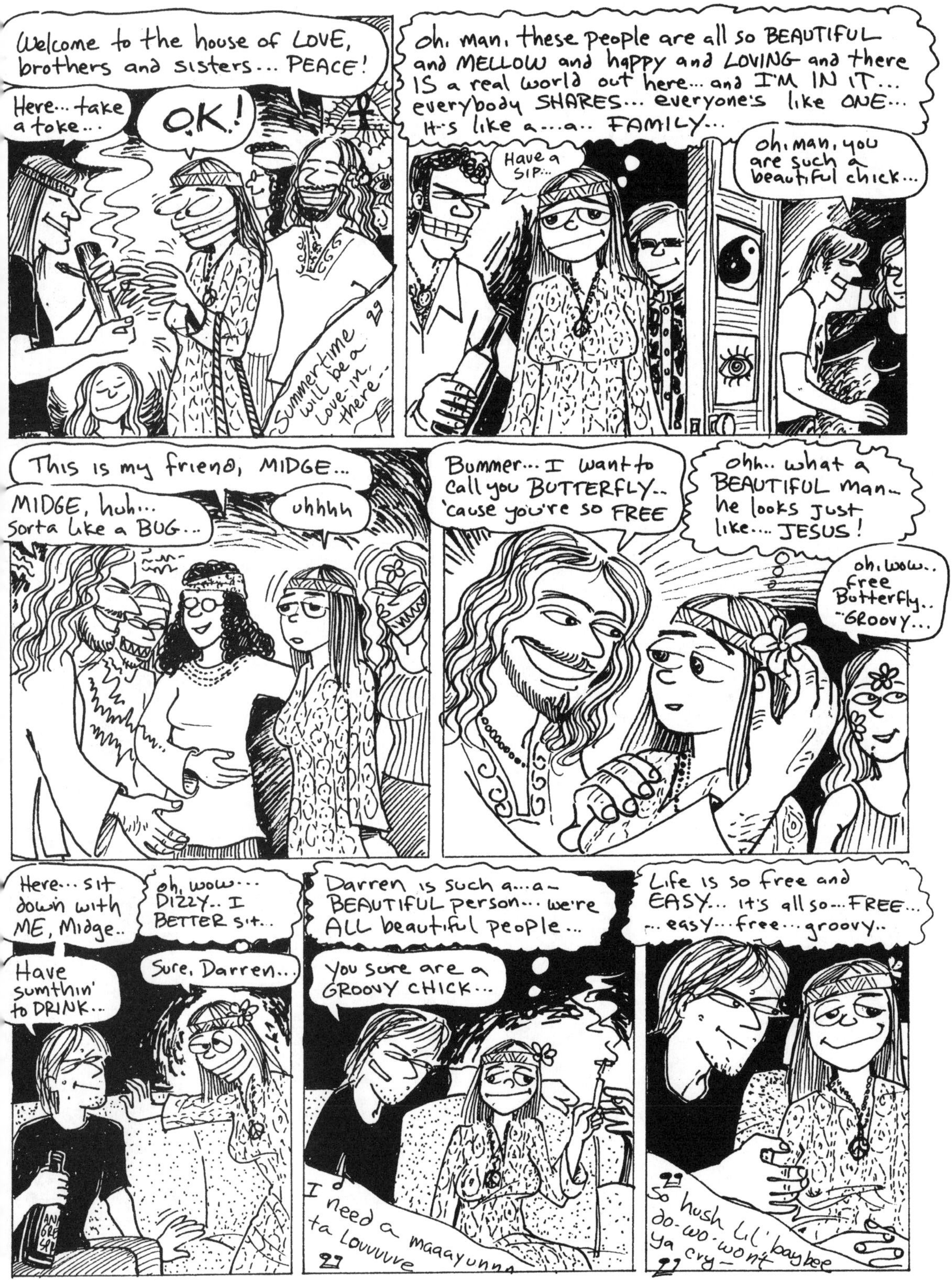
Welcome to the house of LOVE, brothers and sisters... PEACE!
Here... take a toke...
OK!
Summertime will be a love-in there...
oh, man, these people are all so BEAUTIFUL and MELLOW and happy and LOVING and there IS a real world out here... and I'M IN IT... everybody SHARES... everyone's like ONE... It's like a...a.. FAMILY...
Have a SIP...
oh, man, you are such a beautiful chick...
This is my friend, MIDGE...
MIDGE, huh... Sorta like a BUG...
ohhhh
Bummer... I want to call you BUTTERFLY.. 'cause you're so FREE
ohh.. what a BEAUTIFUL man.. he looks just like.... JESUS!
oh, wow.. free Butterfly.. ..GROOVY...
Here... sit down with ME, Midge..
oh, wow... DIZZY.. I BETTER sit...
Have sumthin' to DRINK...
Sure, Darren...
Darren is such a...a.. BEAUTIFUL person... we're ALL beautiful people...
You sure are a GROOVY CHICK...
I need a maaayunn ta Louuuuve
Life is so free and EASY... it's all so...FREE... ...easy...free...groovy..
So hush lil' baybee do-wo-won't ya cry—

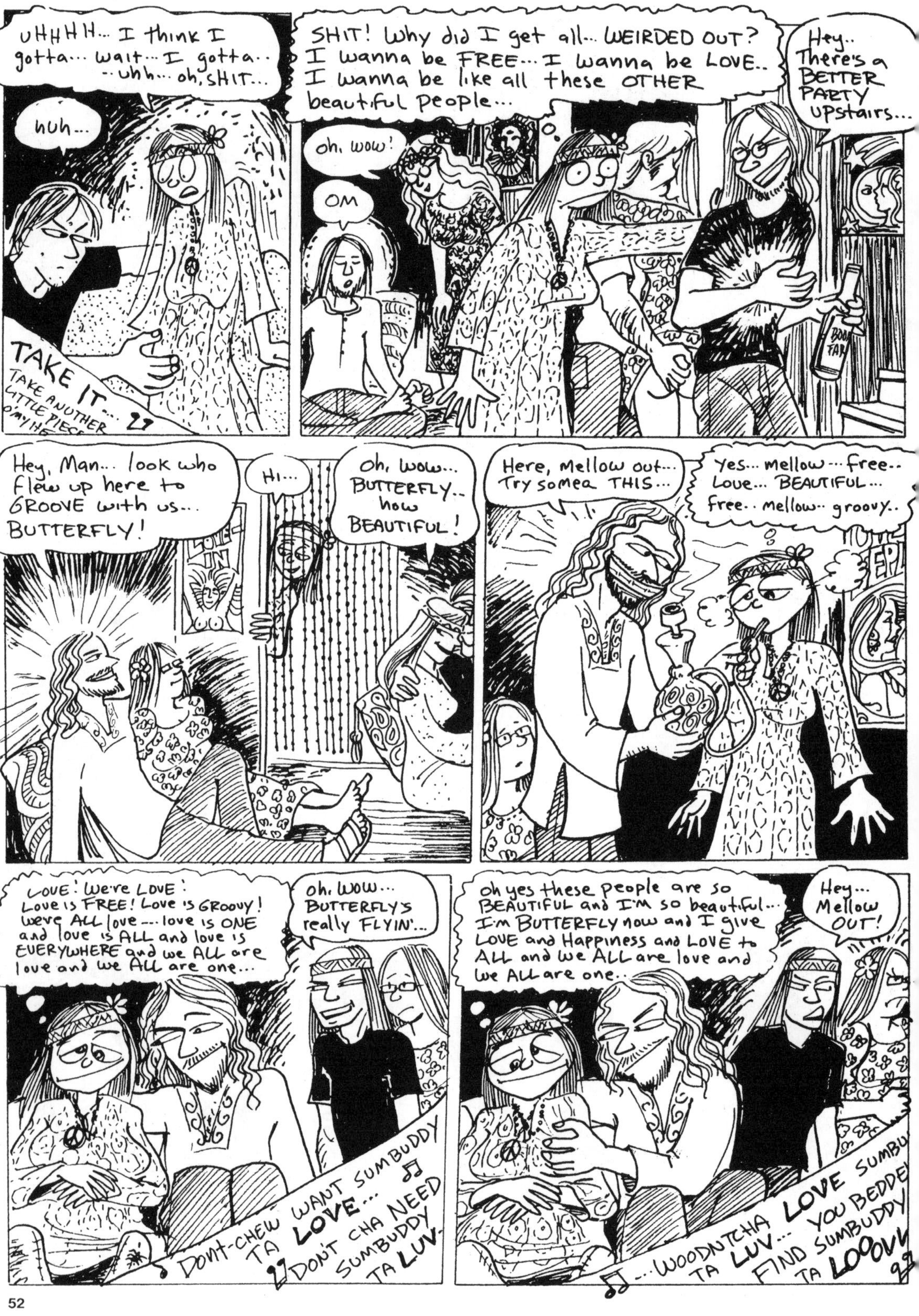
UHHHH... I think I gotta... wait... I gotta... ..uhh... oh, SHIT...
huh...
TAKE IT... TAKE ANOTHER LITTLE PIECE O' MY HE...
SHIT! Why did I get all... WEIRDED OUT? I wanna be FREE... I wanna be LOVE.. I wanna be like all these OTHER beautiful people...
oh, wow!
OM
Hey.. There's a BETTER PARTY upstairs...
Hey, Man... look who flew up here to GROOVE with us... BUTTERFLY!
HI...
Oh, wow... BUTTERFLY.. how BEAUTIFUL!
Here, Mellow out... Try somea THIS...
Yes... mellow... free.. Love... BEAUTIFUL... free.. mellow.. groovy..
LOVE! We're LOVE! Love is FREE! Love is GROOVY! We're ALL love... love is ONE and love is ALL and love is EVERYWHERE and we ALL are love and we ALL are one...
oh, wow... BUTTERFLY's really FLYIN'...
DON'T-CHEW WANT SUMBUDDY TA LOVE... DON'T CHA NEED SUMBUDDY TA LUV.
oh yes these people are so BEAUTIFUL and I'M so beautiful... I'M BUTTERFLY now and I give LOVE and Happiness and LOVE to ALL and we ALL are love and we ALL are one...
Hey... Mellow OUT!
...WOODNTCHA LOVE SUMBU... TA LUV... YOU BEDDER FIND SUMBUDDY TA LOOVV

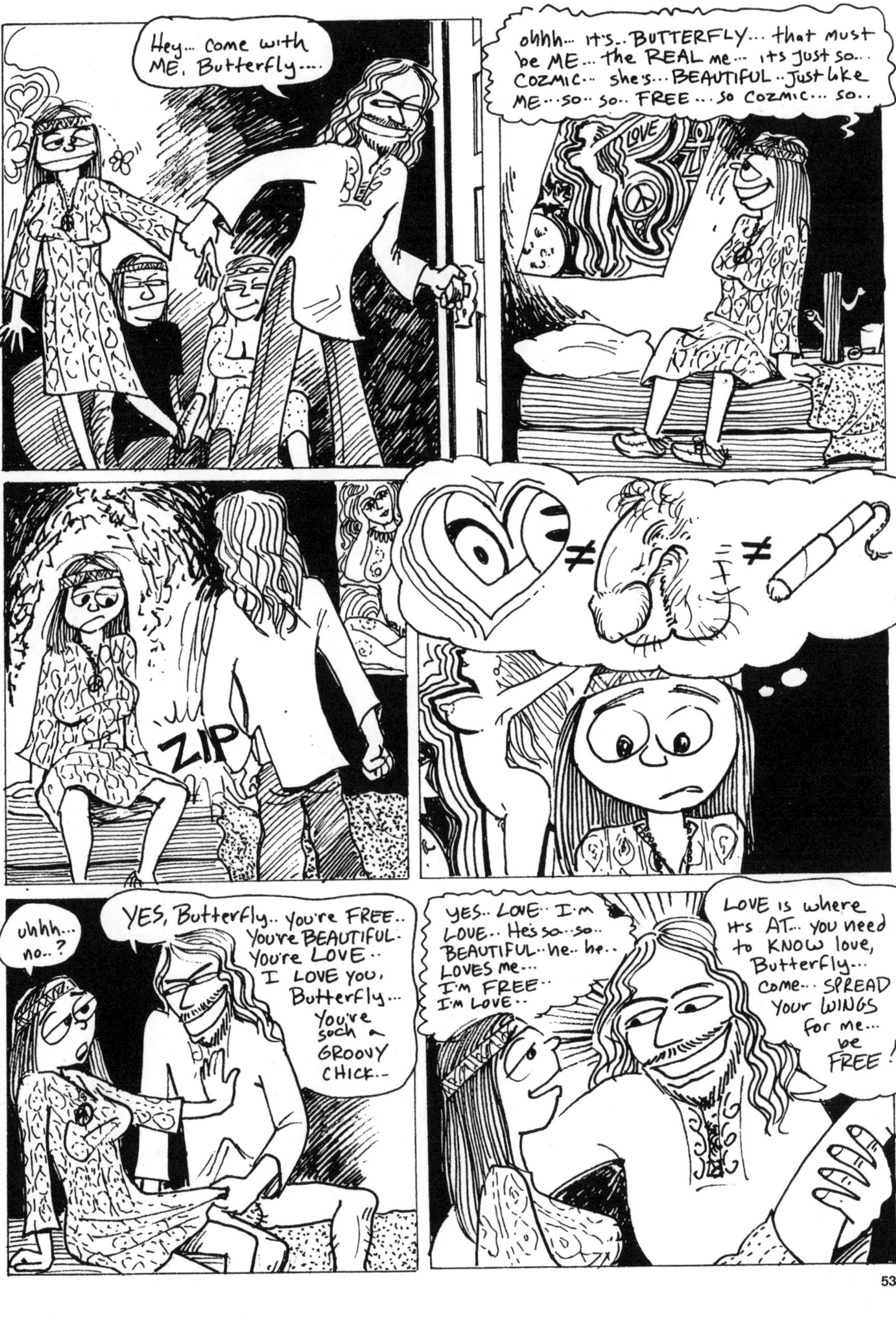
Hey... come with ME, Butterfly....
ohhh... it's.. BUTTERFLY... that must be ME... the REAL me... its just so... COZMIC... she's... BEAUTIFUL.. just like ME... so.. so.. FREE... so COZMIC... so..
LOVE
ZIP
uhhh... no..?
YES, Butterfly.. you're FREE.. You're BEAUTIFUL. You're LOVE.. I LOVE you, Butterfly... You're such a GROOVY CHICK..
YES.. LOVE.. I'm LOVE.. He's so.. so.. BEAUTIFUL.. he.. he.. LOVES me... I'M FREE.. I'M LOVE..
LOVE is where it's AT.. you need to KNOW love, Butterfly... Come... SPREAD your WINGS for me... be FREE!

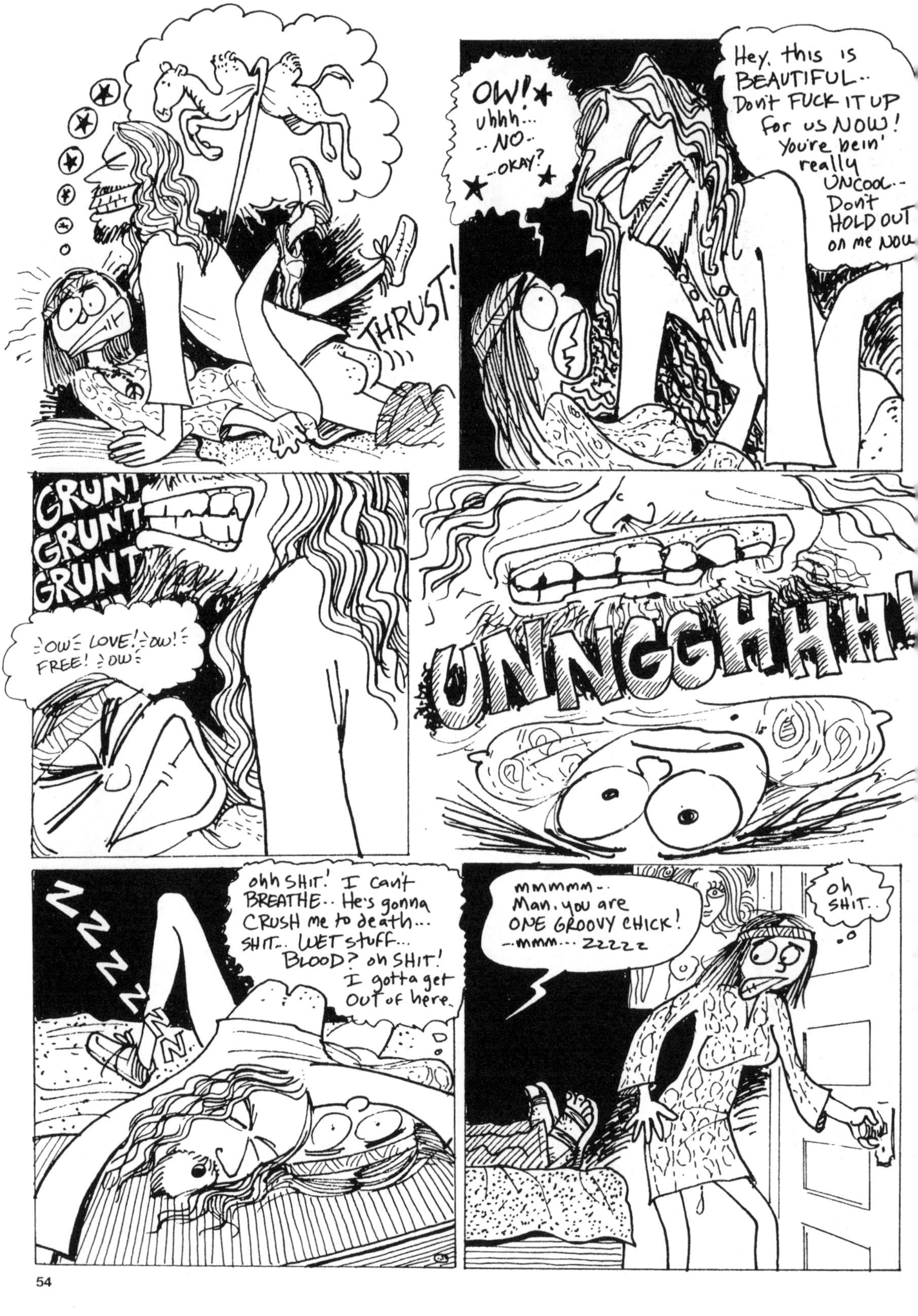
THRUST!
OW! uhhh... --NO-- --OKAY?
Hey, this is BEAUTIFUL.. Don't FUCK IT UP for us NOW! You're bein' really UNCOOL.. Don't HOLD OUT on me NOW
GRUNT GRUNT GRUNT
OW LOVE! OW! FREE! OW
UNNGGHHH
ohh SHIT! I can't BREATHE.. He's gonna CRUSH me to death... SHIT.. WET stuff... BLOOD? oh SHIT! I gotta get out of here.
ZZZZZ
mmmmm.. Man, you are ONE GROOVY CHICK! --mmm... zzzzz
oh SHIT..

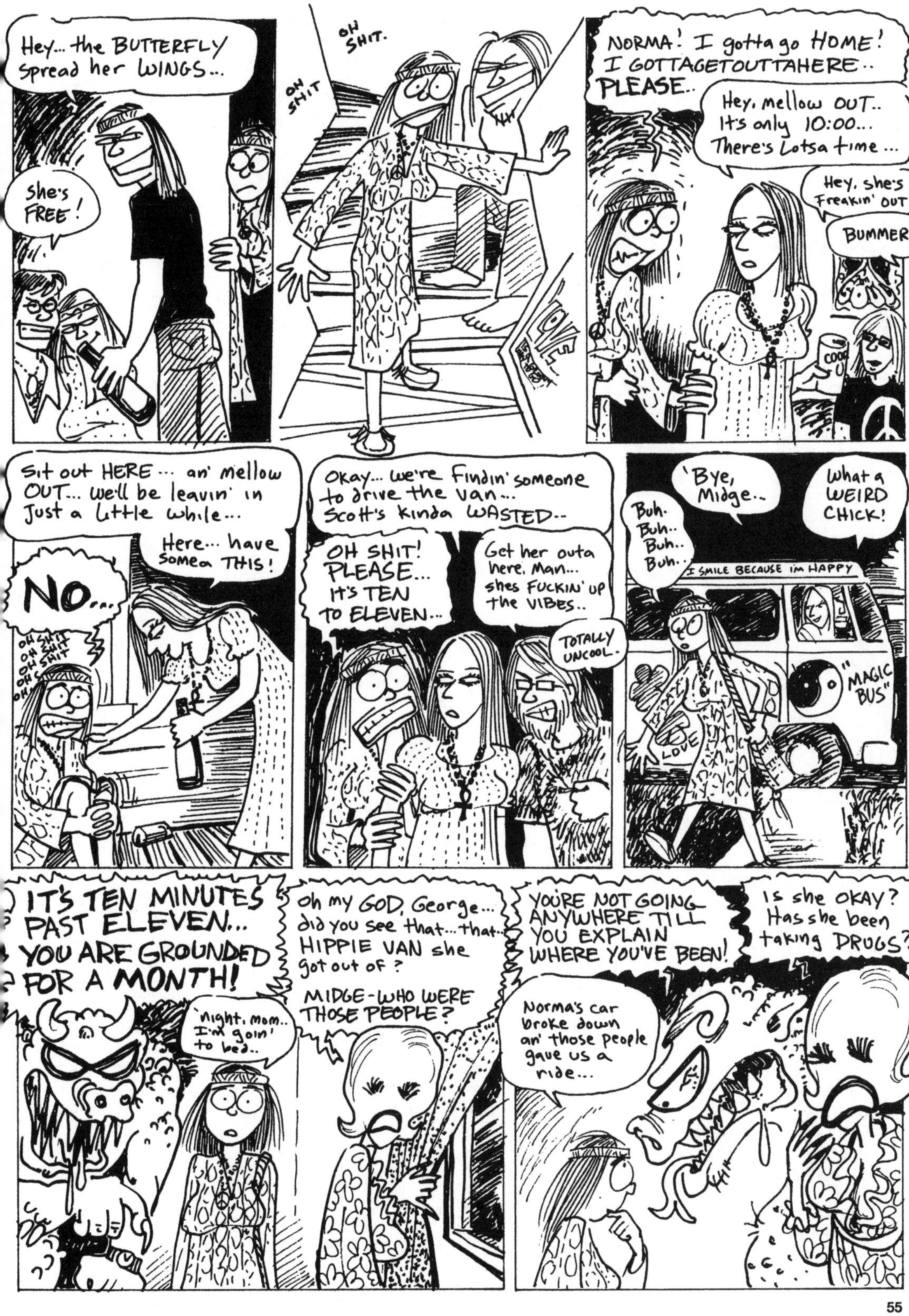
Hey... the BUTTERFLY spread her WINGS...
She's FREE!
OH SHIT.
OH SHIT
NORMA! I gotta go HOME! I GOTTAGETOUTTAHERE.. PLEASE..
Hey, mellow OUT.. It's only 10:00... There's Lotsa time...
Hey, she's Freakin' OUT!
BUMMER!
Sit out HERE... an' mellow OUT... We'll be leavin' in just a little while...
Here... have somea THIS!
NO...
OH SHIT OH SHIT OH SHIT
Okay... we're findin' someone to drive the van... Scott's kinda WASTED..
OH SHIT! PLEASE... IT'S TEN TO ELEVEN...
Get her outa here, man... shes FUCKIN' UP the VIBES..
TOTALLY UNCOOL.
Buh. Buh.. Buh.. Buh..
'Bye, Midge..
What a WEIRD CHICK!
I SMILE BECAUSE IM HAPPY
"MAGIC BUS"
LOVE
IT'S TEN MINUTES PAST ELEVEN... YOU ARE GROUNDED FOR A MONTH!
'night, mom.. I'm goin' to bed..
oh my GOD, George... did you see that... that... HIPPIE VAN she got out of?
MIDGE-WHO WERE THOSE PEOPLE?
YOU'RE NOT GOING ANYWHERE TILL YOU EXPLAIN WHERE YOU'VE BEEN!
Is she OKAY? Has she been taking DRUGS?
Norma's car broke down an' those people gave us a ride...

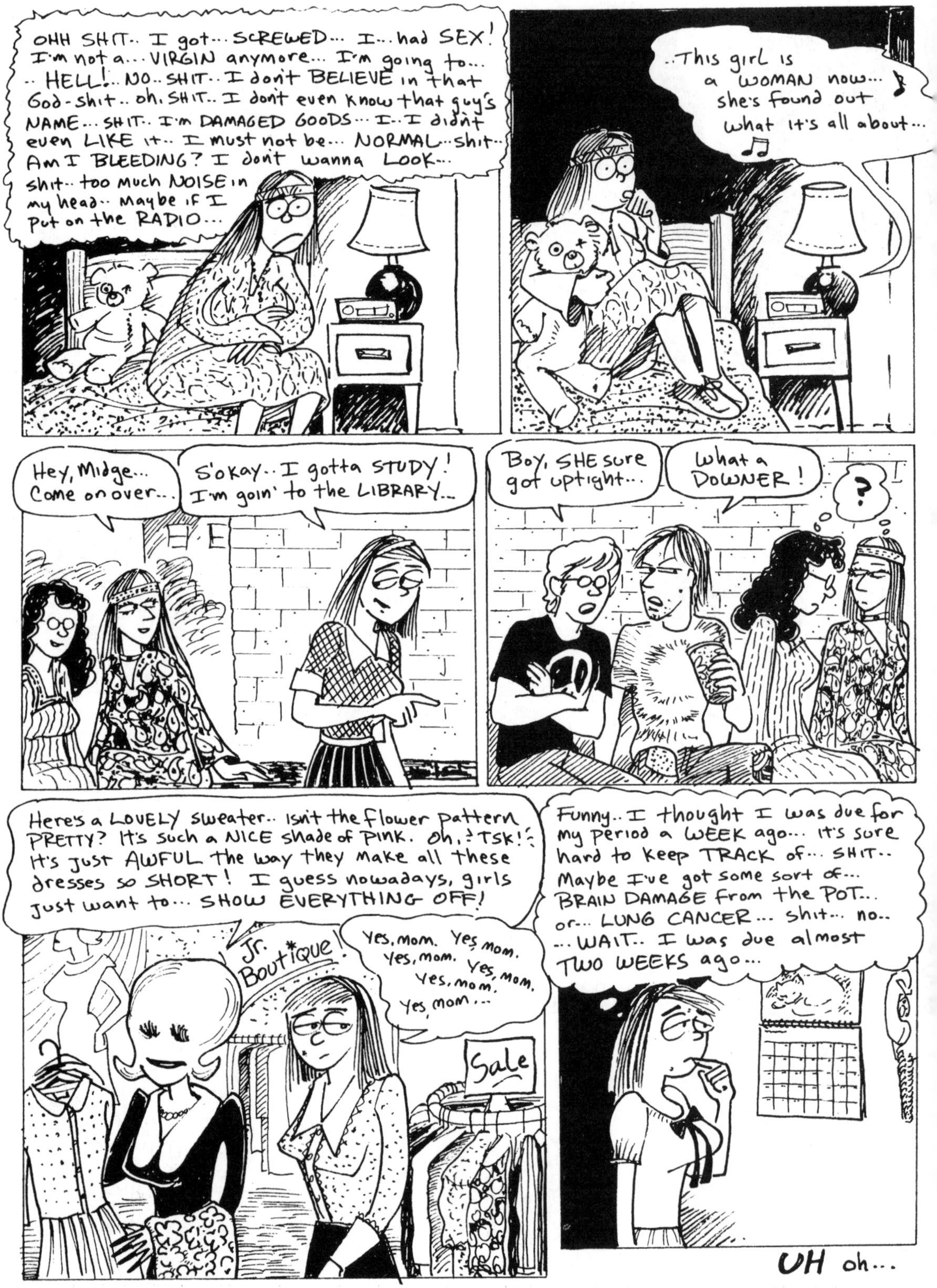
OHH SHIT.. I got... SCREWED... I... had SEX! I'm not a... VIRGIN anymore... I'm going to... .. HELL!.. NO.. SHIT.. I don't BELIEVE in that God-shit.. oh, SHIT.. I don't even know that guy's NAME... SHIT.. I'm DAMAGED GOODS... I.. I didn't even LIKE it.. I must not be... NORMAL.. shit.. Am I BLEEDING? I don't wanna LOOK.. shit.. too much NOISE in my head.. Maybe if I put on the RADIO...
..This girl is a WOMAN now... she's found out what it's all about...
Hey, Midge... Come on over...
S'okay.. I gotta STUDY! I'm goin' to the LIBRARY...
Boy, SHE sure got uptight...
What a DOWNER!
?
Here's a LOVELY sweater.. Isn't the flower pattern PRETTY? It's such a NICE shade of PINK. Oh, ! TSK! It's just AWFUL the way they make all these dresses so SHORT! I guess nowadays, girls just want to... SHOW EVERYTHING OFF!
Jr. Boutique!
Yes, mom. Yes, mom. Yes, mom. Yes, mom. Yes, mom. Yes, mom...
Sale
Funny.. I thought I was due for my period a WEEK ago... It's sure hard to keep TRACK of... SHIT.. Maybe I've got some sort of... BRAIN DAMAGE from the POT.. or... LUNG CANCER... shit... no.. ...WAIT.. I was due almost TWO WEEKS ago...
UH oh...

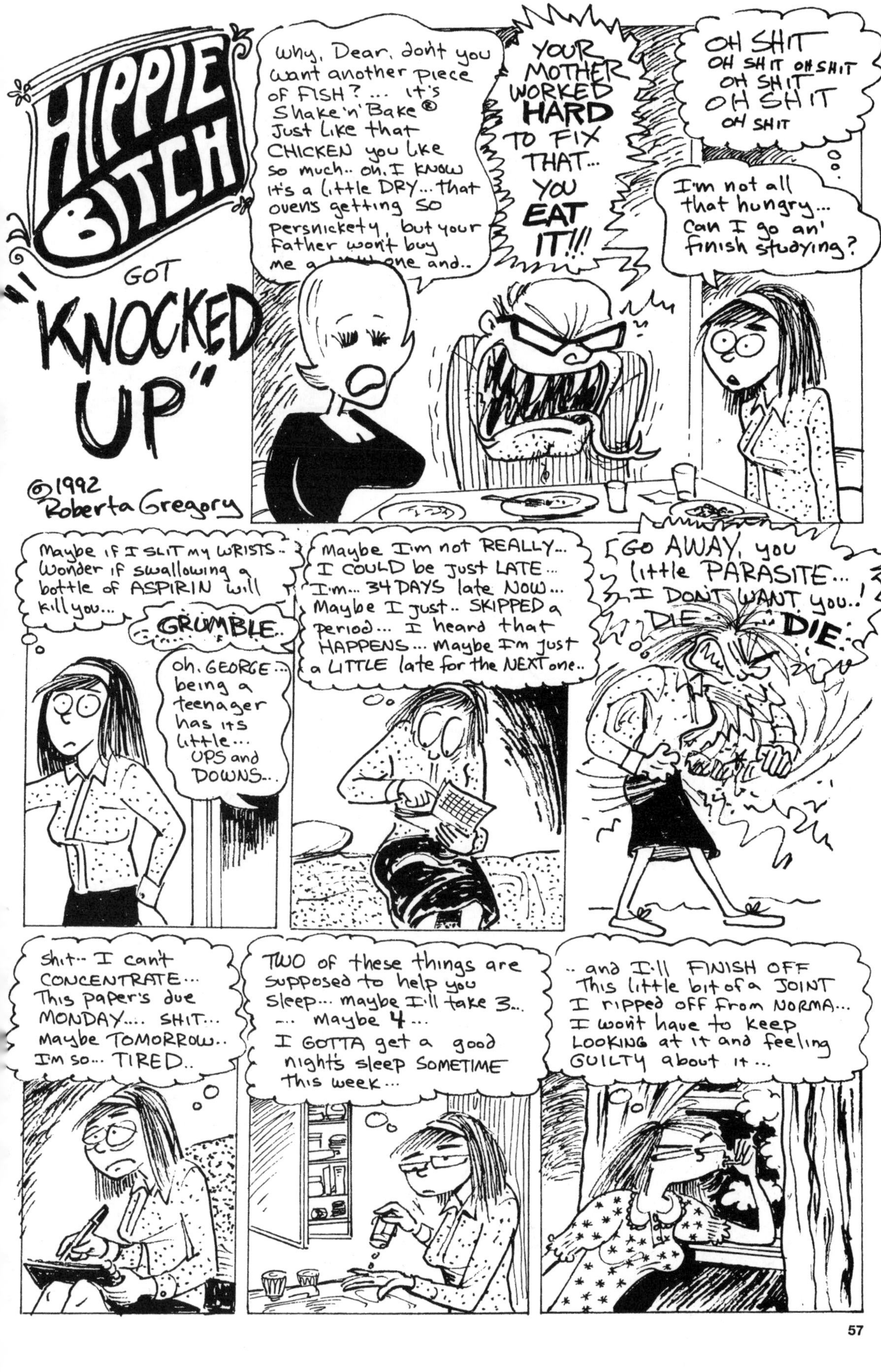

HIPPIE BITCH
GOT "KNOCKED UP"
©1992 Roberta Gregory
Why, Dear, don't you want another piece of FISH? ... It's Shake 'n' Bake® Just like that CHICKEN you like so much.. oh, I KNOW it's a little DRY... that oven's getting SO persnickety, but your Father won't buy me a one and..
YOUR MOTHER WORKED HARD TO FIX THAT... YOU EAT IT!!!
OH SHIT OH SHIT OH SHIT OH SHIT OH SHIT OH SHIT
I'm not all that hungry... Can I go an' finish studying?
Maybe if I SLIT MY WRISTS.. Wonder if swallowing a bottle of ASPIRIN will kill you...
GRUMBLE
oh, GEORGE... being a teenager has its little... UPS and DOWNS...
Maybe I'm not REALLY... I COULD be just LATE... I'm... 34 DAYS late NOW... Maybe I just.. SKIPPED a period... I heard that HAPPENS... Maybe I'm just a LITTLE late for the NEXT one..
GO AWAY, you little PARASITE... I DON'T WANT you..! DIE... DIE
shit.. I can't CONCENTRATE... This paper's due MONDAY.... SHIT... Maybe TOMORROW.. I'm so... TIRED..
TWO of these things are supposed to help you sleep... maybe I'll take 3... ... maybe 4... I GOTTA get a good night's sleep SOMETIME this week...
.. and I'll FINISH OFF This little bit of a JOINT I ripped off from NORMA... I won't have to keep LOOKING at it and feeling GUILTY about it...

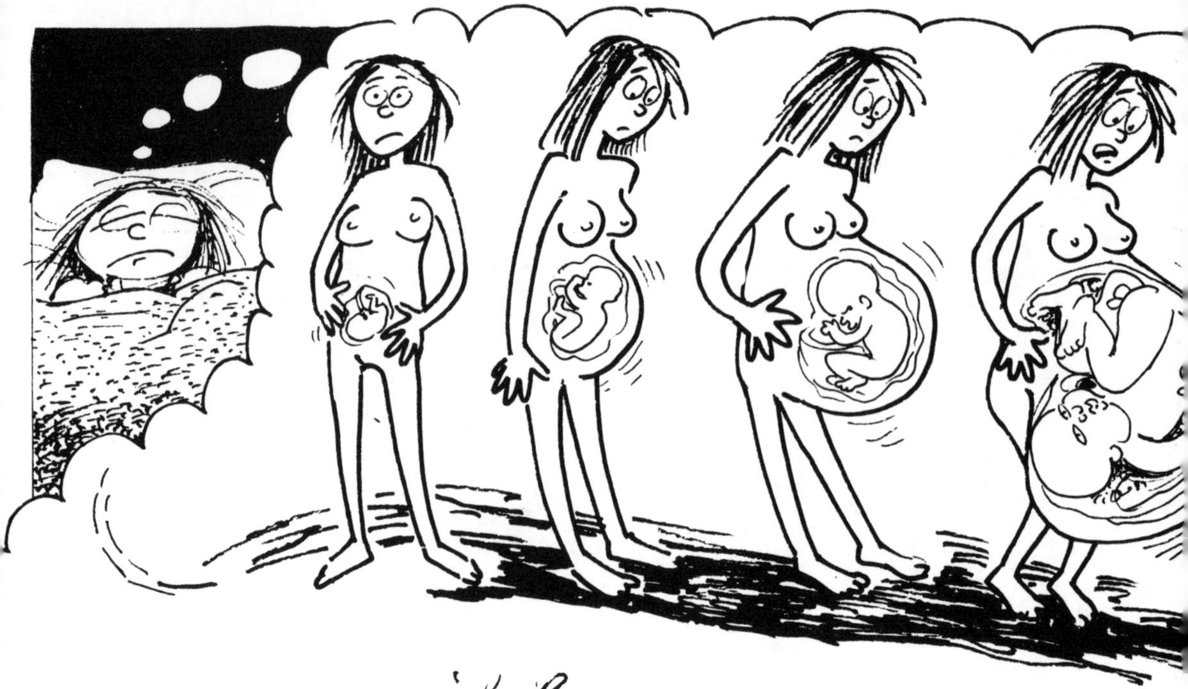

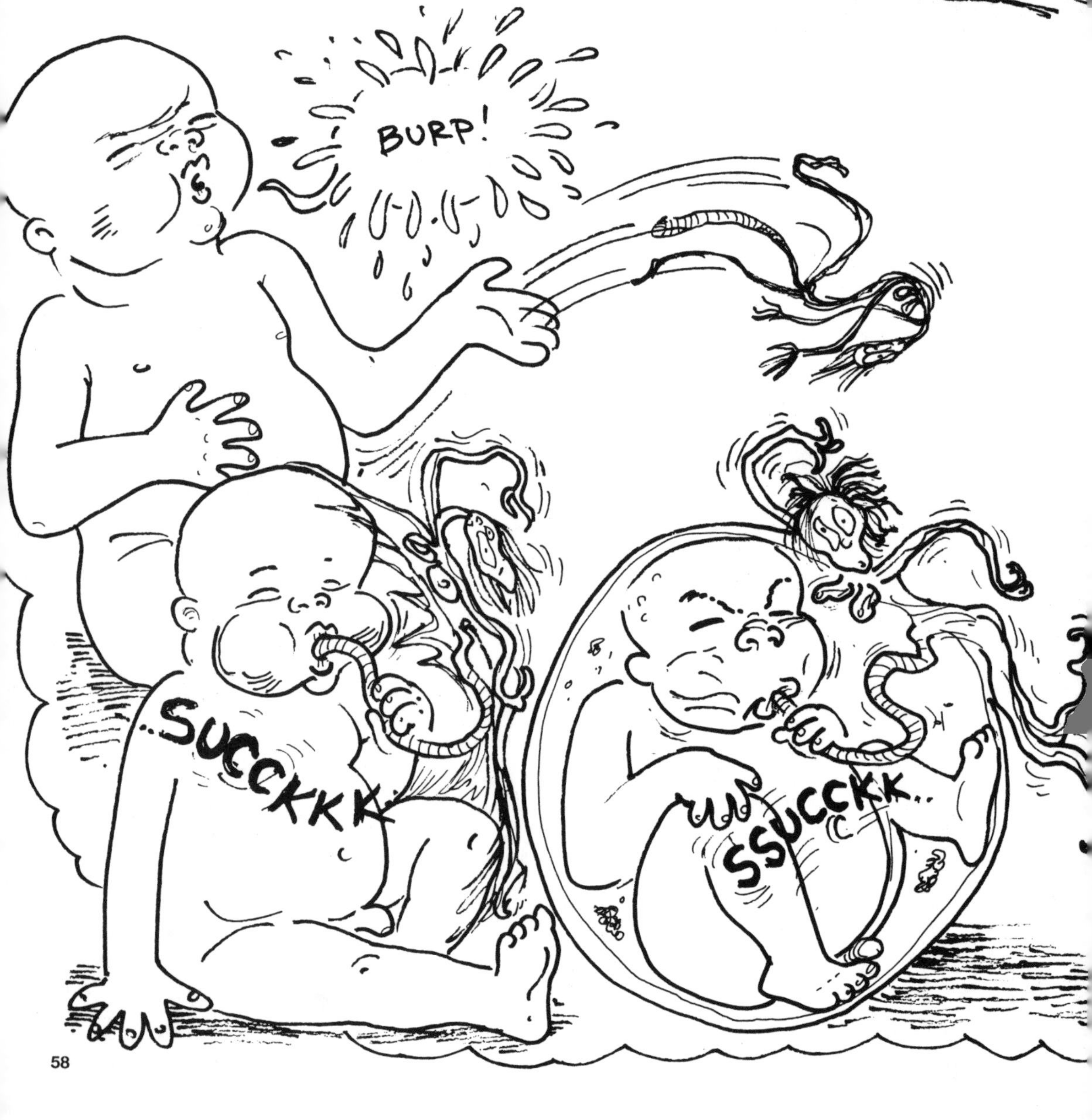
BURP!
SUCCKKK...
SSUCCKK...

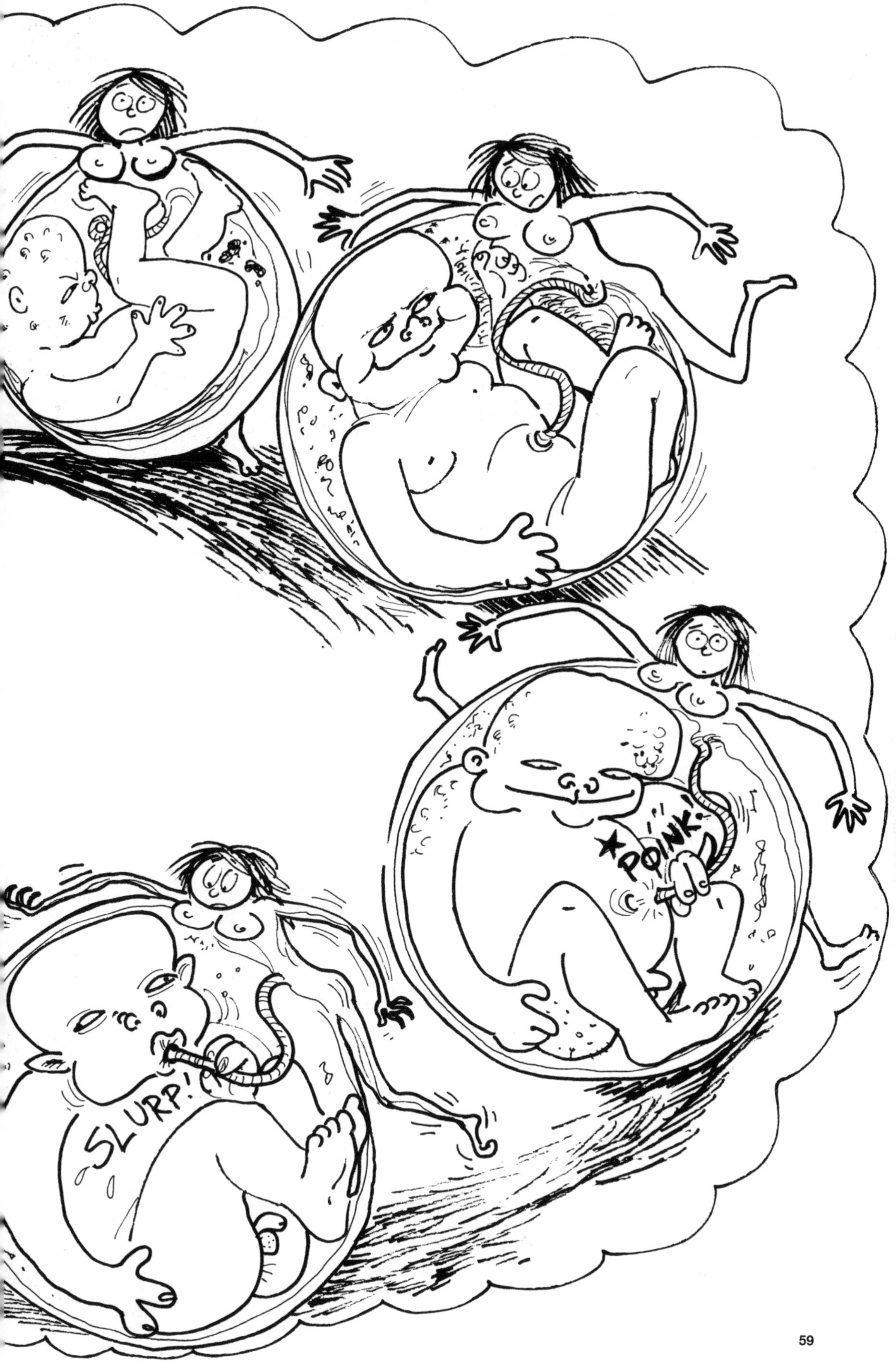
POINK!
SLURP!

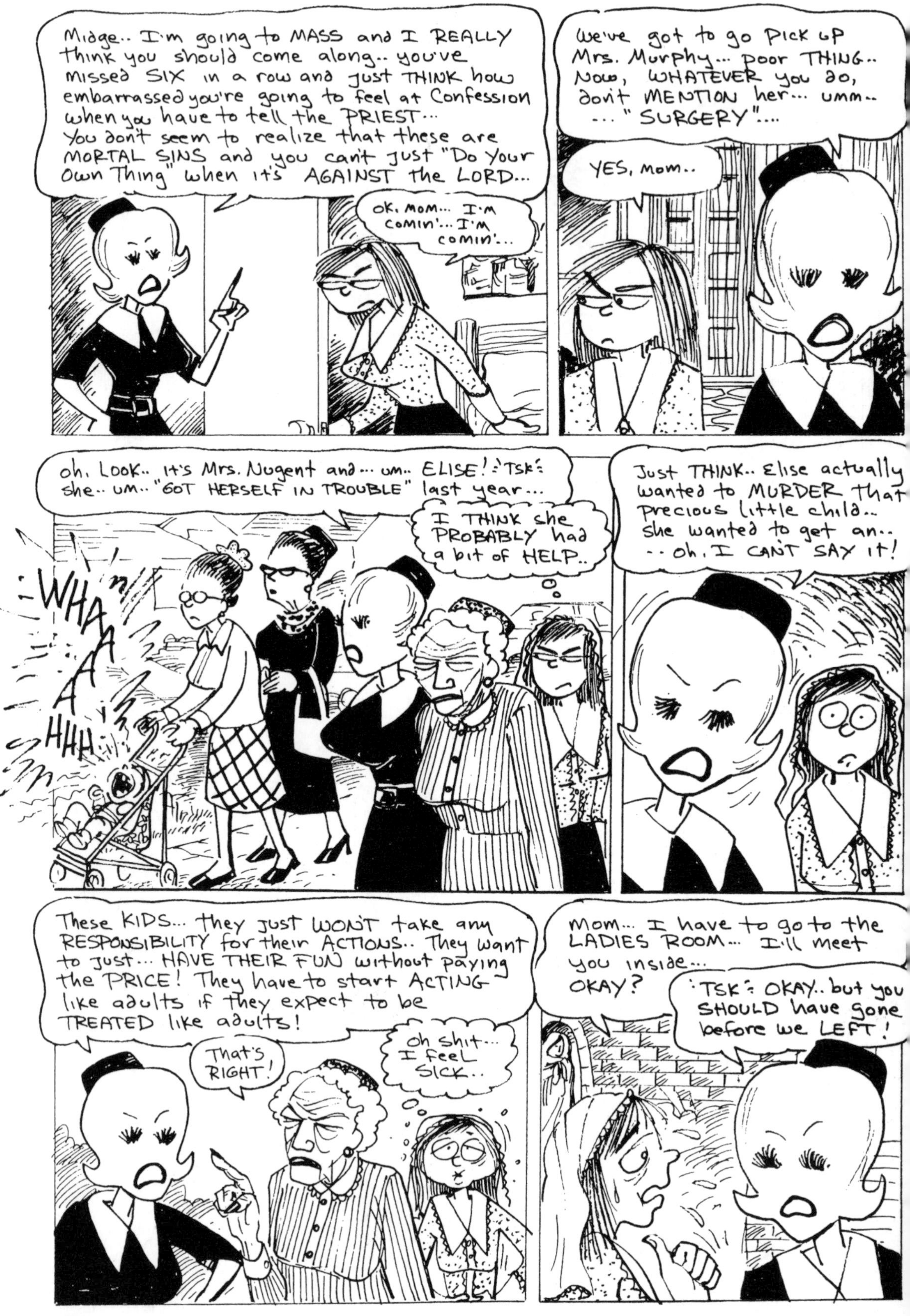
Midge.. I'm going to MASS and I REALLY think you should come along.. you've missed SIX in a row and just THINK how embarrassed you're going to feel at Confession when you have to tell the PRIEST... You don't seem to realize that these are MORTAL SINS and you can't just "Do Your Own Thing" when it's AGAINST the LORD...
OK, MOM... I'M COMIN'... I'M COMIN'...
We've got to go pick up Mrs. Murphy... poor THING.. Now, WHATEVER you do, don't MENTION her... umm.. ... "SURGERY"....
YES, mom..
oh, LOOK.. it's Mrs. Nugent and... um.. ELISE! :TSK: she.. um.. "GOT HERSELF IN TROUBLE" last year...
I THINK she PROBABLY had a bit of HELP..
WHAAAAHHH
Just THINK.. Elise actually wanted to MURDER that precious little child.. she wanted to get an.. ..oh, I CAN'T SAY it!
These KIDS... they just WON'T take any RESPONSIBILITY for their ACTIONS.. They want to just... HAVE THEIR FUN without paying the PRICE! They have to start ACTING like adults if they expect to be TREATED like adults!
That's RIGHT!
oh shit... I feel SICK..
Mom... I have to go to the LADIES ROOM... I'll meet you inside... OKAY?
:TSK: OKAY.. but you SHOULD have gone before we LEFT!

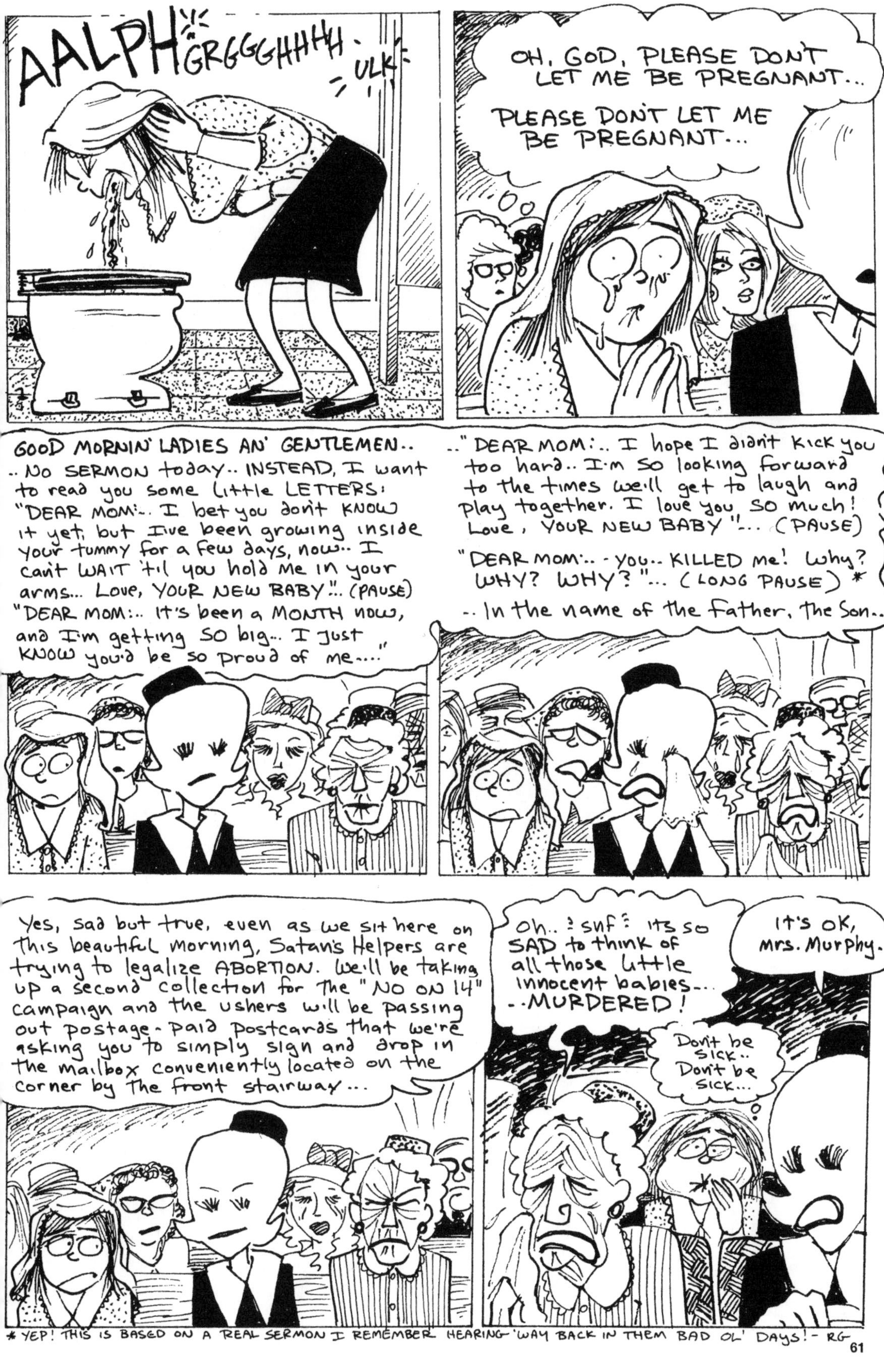
AALPH GRGGGHHHH
ULK
OH, GOD, PLEASE DON'T LET ME BE PREGNANT...
PLEASE DON'T LET ME BE PREGNANT...
GOOD MORNIN' LADIES AN' GENTLEMEN.. ..No SERMON today.. INSTEAD, I want to read you some little LETTERS: "DEAR MOM:.. I bet you don't KNOW it yet, but Ive been growing inside your tummy for a few days, now.. I can't WAIT 'til you hold me in your arms... Love, YOUR NEW BABY"!.. (PAUSE) "DEAR MOM:.. It's been a MONTH now, and I'm getting SO big... I just KNOW you'd be so proud of me...."
.."DEAR MOM:.. I hope I didn't kick you too hard.. I'm so looking forward to the times we'll get to laugh and play together. I love you so much! Love, YOUR NEW BABY"... (PAUSE)
"DEAR MOM:.. - You.. KILLED me! Why? WHY? WHY?"... (LONG PAUSE) *
.. In the name of the Father, the Son..
Yes, sad but true, even as we sit here on this beautiful morning, Satan's Helpers are trying to legalize ABORTION. We'll be taking up a second collection for the "NO ON 14" campaign and the ushers will be passing out postage-paid postcards that we're asking you to simply sign and drop in the mailbox conveniently located on the corner by the front stairway...
Oh.. :snf: its so SAD to think of all those little innocent babies... ..MURDERED!
It's OK, Mrs. Murphy.
Don't be sick.. Don't be sick...

* YEP! THIS IS BASED ON A REAL SERMON I REMEMBER HEARING 'WAY BACK IN THEM BAD OL' DAYS! - RG

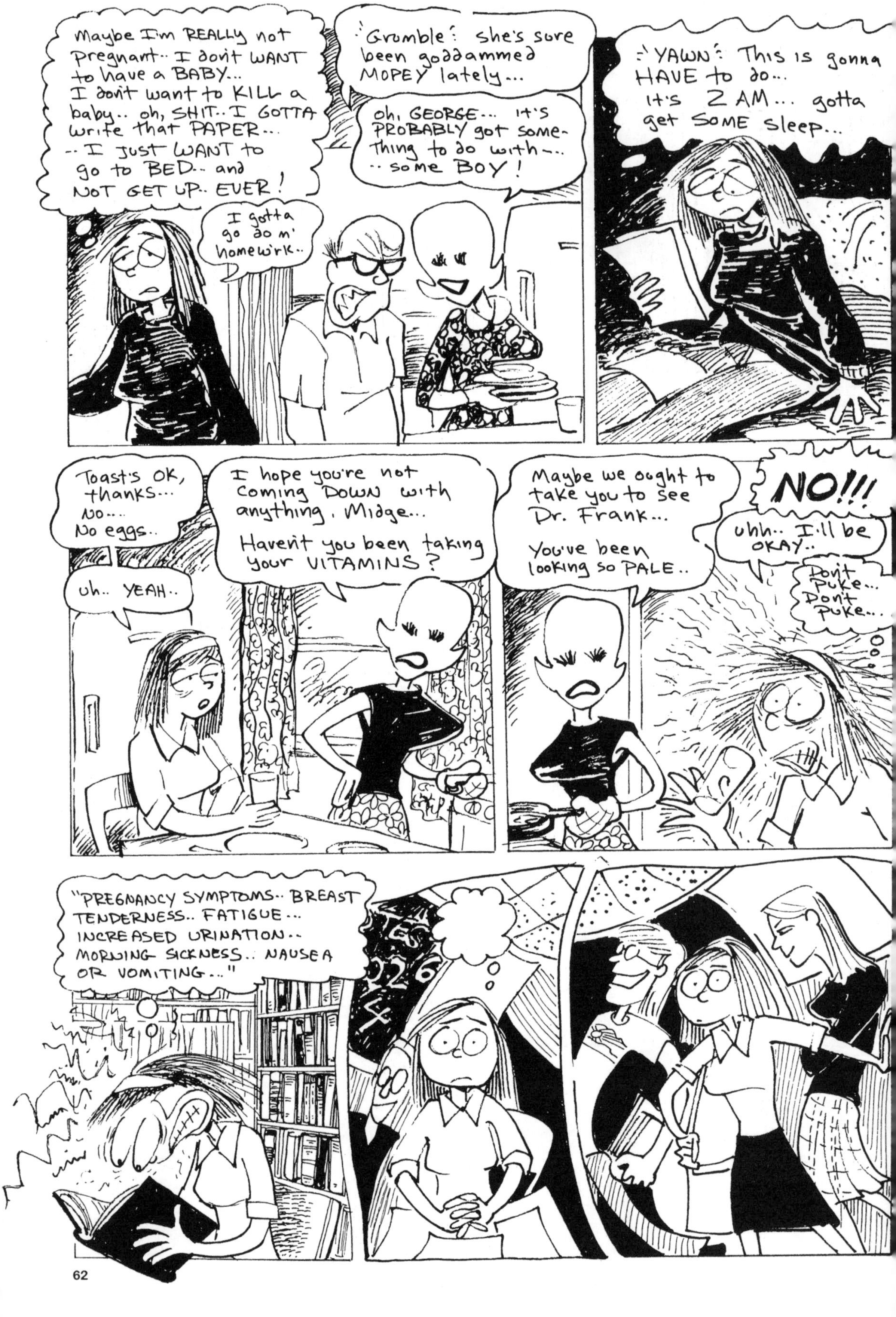
Maybe I'm REALLY not pregnant.. I don't WANT to have a BABY... I don't want to KILL a baby.. oh, SHIT.. I GOTTA write that PAPER... ..I JUST WANT to go to BED.. and NOT GET UP.. EVER!
I gotta go do m' homewirk..
:Grumble: she's sure been goddammed MOPEY lately...
oh, GEORGE... it's PROBABLY got something to do with... ..some BOY!
:YAWN: This is gonna HAVE to do... it's 2 AM... gotta get SOME sleep...
Toast's OK, thanks... No... No eggs..
I hope you're not coming DOWN with anything, Midge... Haven't you been taking your VITAMINS?
uh.. YEAH..
Maybe we ought to take you to see Dr. Frank... You've been looking so PALE..
NO!!!
uhh.. I'll be OKAY..
Don't puke... Don't puke...
"PREGNANCY SYMPTOMS.. BREAST TENDERNESS.. FATIGUE... INCREASED URINATION.. MORNING SICKNESS.. NAUSEA OR VOMITING..."

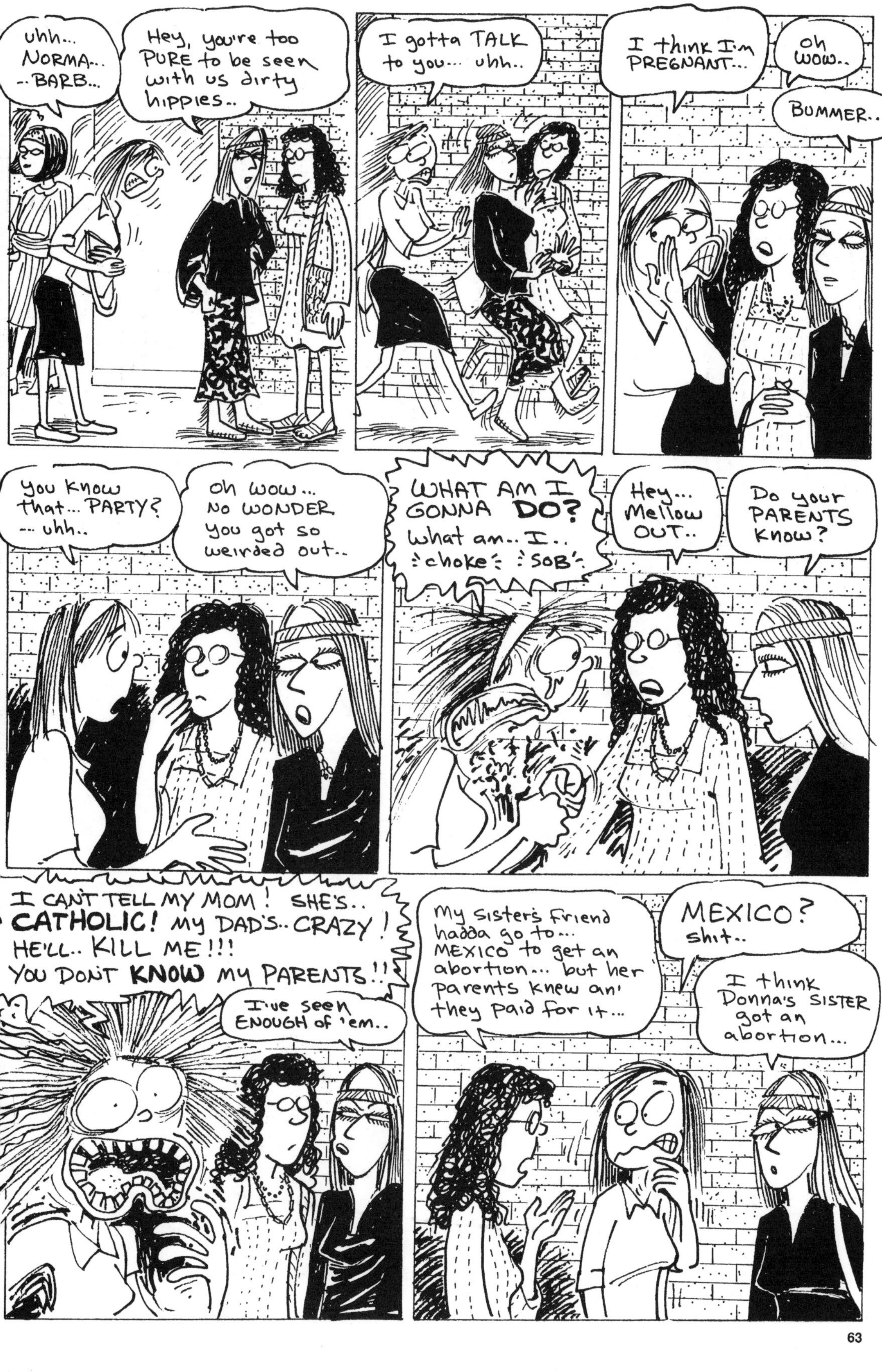
uhh... NORMA... --BARB...
Hey, you're too PURE to be seen with us dirty hippies..
I gotta TALK to you... uhh..
I think I'm PREGNANT...
oh wow..
BUMMER..
you know that... PARTY? -- uhh..
oh wow... No WONDER you got so weirded out..
WHAT AM I GONNA DO? what am.. I.. :choke: :SOB:
Hey... Mellow OUT..
Do your PARENTS know?
I CAN'T TELL MY MOM! SHE'S.. CATHOLIC! MY DAD'S.. CRAZY! HE'LL.. KILL ME!!! YOU DON'T KNOW MY PARENTS!!
I've seen ENOUGH of 'em..
My sister's friend hadda go to... MEXICO to get an abortion... but her parents knew an' they paid for it...
MEXICO? shit..
I think Donna's SISTER got an abortion...

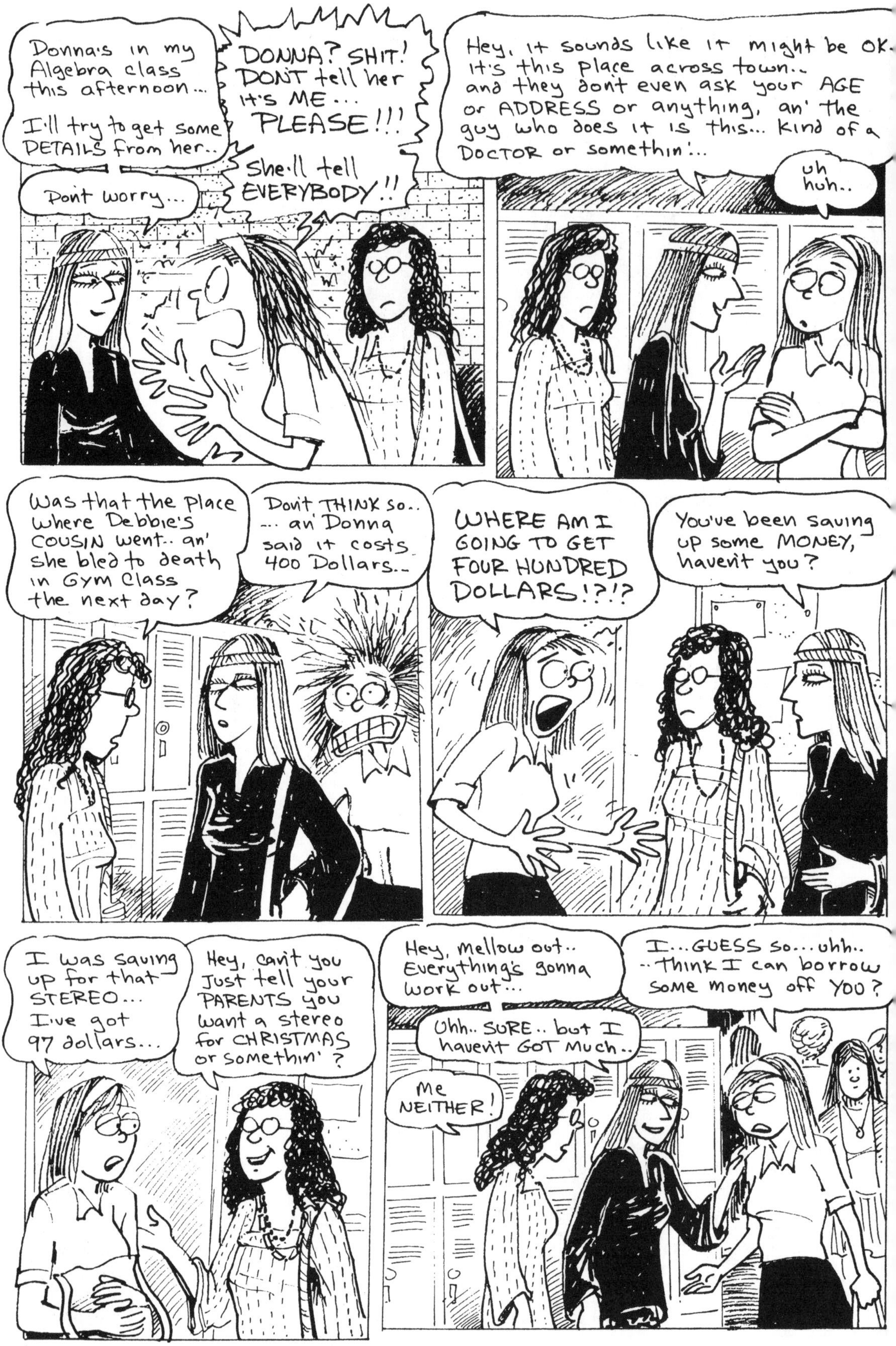
Donna's in my Algebra class this afternoon... I'll try to get some DETAILS from her..
Dont worry...
DONNA? SHIT! DONT tell her it's ME... PLEASE!!!
She'll tell EVERYBODY!!
Hey, it sounds like it might be OK. It's this place across town.. and they dont even ask your AGE or ADDRESS or anything, an' the guy who does it is this... kind of a DOCTOR or somethin'...
uh huh..
Was that the place where Debbie's COUSIN went.. an' she bled to death in GYM Class the next day?
Dont THINK so.. ... an' Donna said it costs 400 Dollars..
WHERE AM I GOING TO GET FOUR HUNDRED DOLLARS!?!?
You've been saving up some MONEY, havent you?
I was saving up for that STEREO... I've got 97 dollars...
Hey, cant you just tell your PARENTS you want a stereo for CHRISTMAS or somethin'?
Hey, mellow out.. Everything's gonna work out...
I...GUESS so...uhh.. ..think I can borrow some money off YOU?
Uhh.. SURE.. but I havent GOT much..
Me NEITHER!

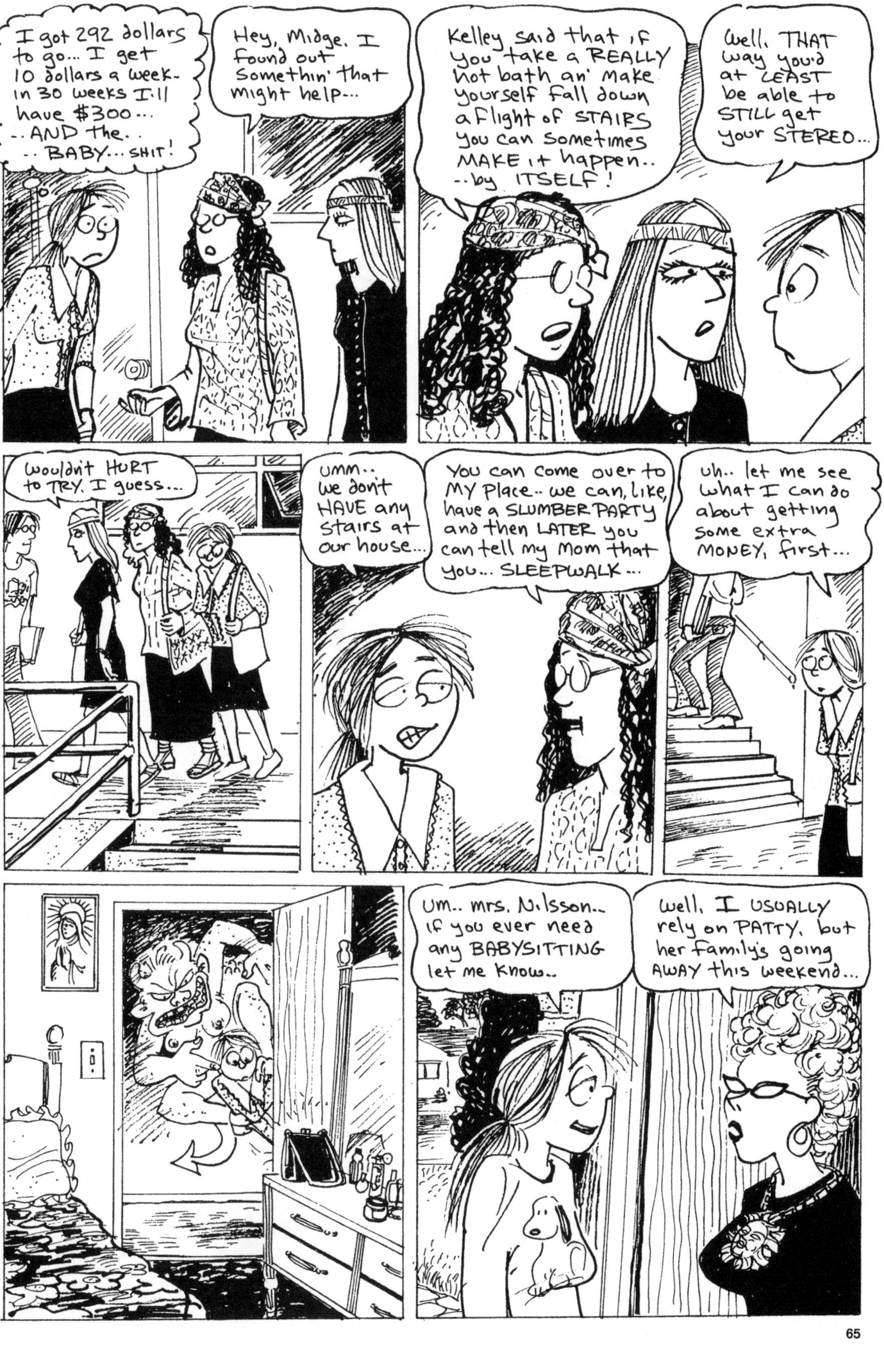
I got 292 dollars to go... I get 10 dollars a week- in 30 weeks I'll have $300... ..AND the.. ..BABY... SHIT!
Hey, Midge. I found out somethin' that might help...
Kelley said that, if you take a REALLY hot bath an' make yourself fall down a flight of STAIRS you can sometimes MAKE it happen.. ..by ITSELF!
Well, THAT way you'd at LEAST be able to STILL get your STEREO...
Wouldn't HURT to TRY, I guess...
umm.. we don't HAVE any stairs at our house...
You can come over to MY place.. we can, like, have a SLUMBER PARTY and then LATER you can tell my Mom that you... SLEEPWALK...
uh.. let me see what I can do about getting some extra MONEY, first...
Um.. mrs. Nilsson.. if you ever need any BABYSITTING let me know..
Well, I USUALLY rely on PATTY, but her family's going AWAY this weekend...

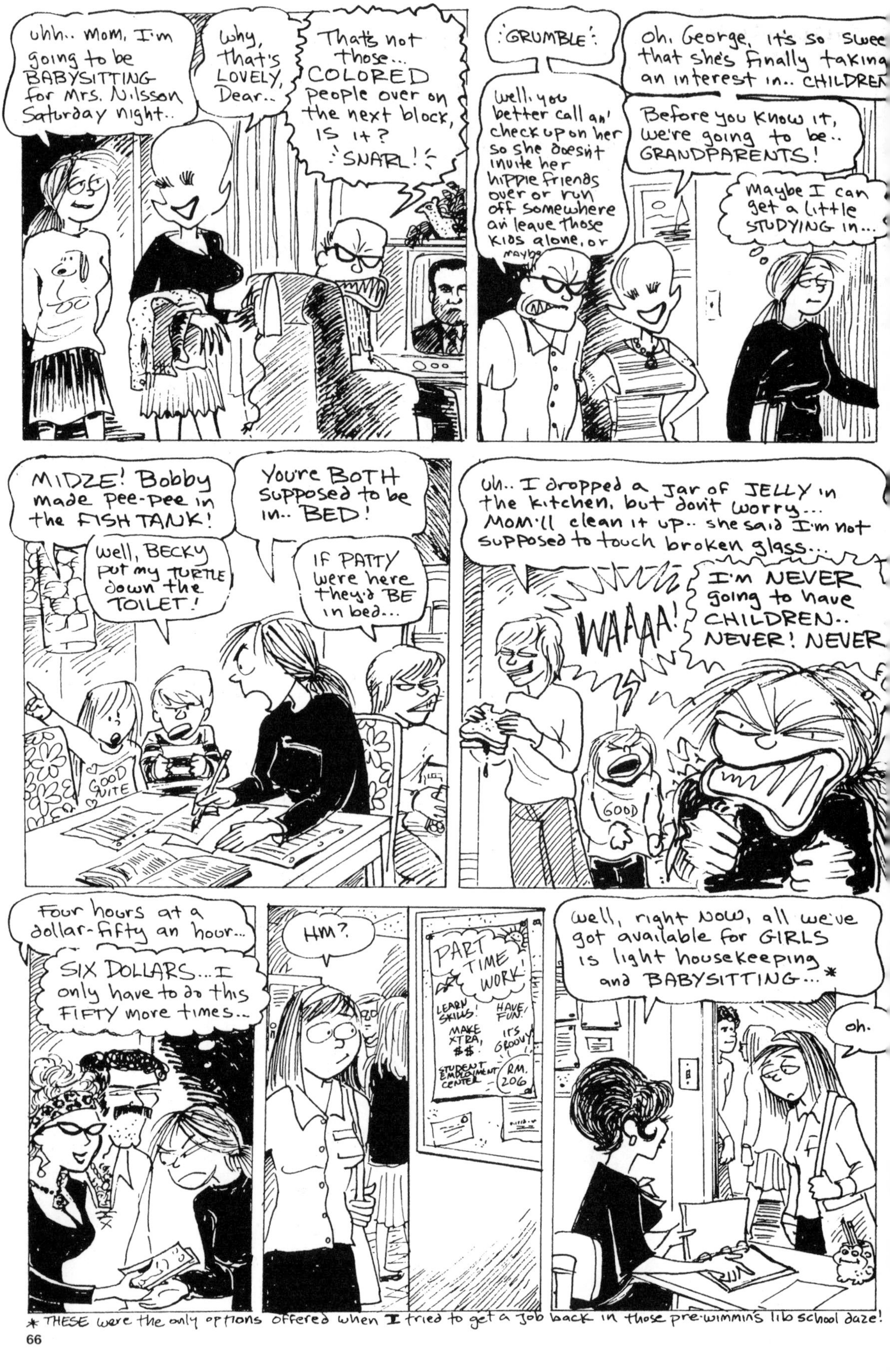
uhh.. MOM, I'm going to be BABYSITTING for Mrs. Nilsson Saturday night..
Why, that's LOVELY, Dear..
That's not those... COLORED people over on the next block, IS it?
SNARL!
GRUMBLE
Oh, George, it's so swee that she's finally taking an interest in.. CHILDRE
Well, you better call an' check up on her so she doesn't invite her hippie friends over or run off somewhere an leave those kids alone, or maybe
Before you know it, we're going to be.. GRANDPARENTS!
Maybe I can get a little STUDYING in...
MIDZE! Bobby made pee-pee in the FISH TANK!
Well, BECKY put my TURTLE down the TOILET!
You're BOTH supposed to be in.. BED!
IF PATTY were here they'd BE in bed...
GOOD
Uh.. I dropped a jar of JELLY in the kitchen, but don't worry... MOM'll clean it up.. she said I'm not supposed to touch broken glass...
WAAAA!
I'M NEVER going to have CHILDREN.. NEVER! NEVER
GOOD
Four hours at a dollar-fifty an hour...
SIX DOLLARS... I only have to do this FIFTY more times...
HM?
PART TIME WORK!
LEARN SKILLS! HAVE FUN! MAKE XTRA $$ IT'S GROOVY
STUDENT EMPLOYMENT CENTER RM. 206
Well, right now, all we've got available for GIRLS is light housekeeping and BABYSITTING...*
Oh.
* THESE were the only options offered when I tried to get a job back in those pre-wimmin's lib school daze!

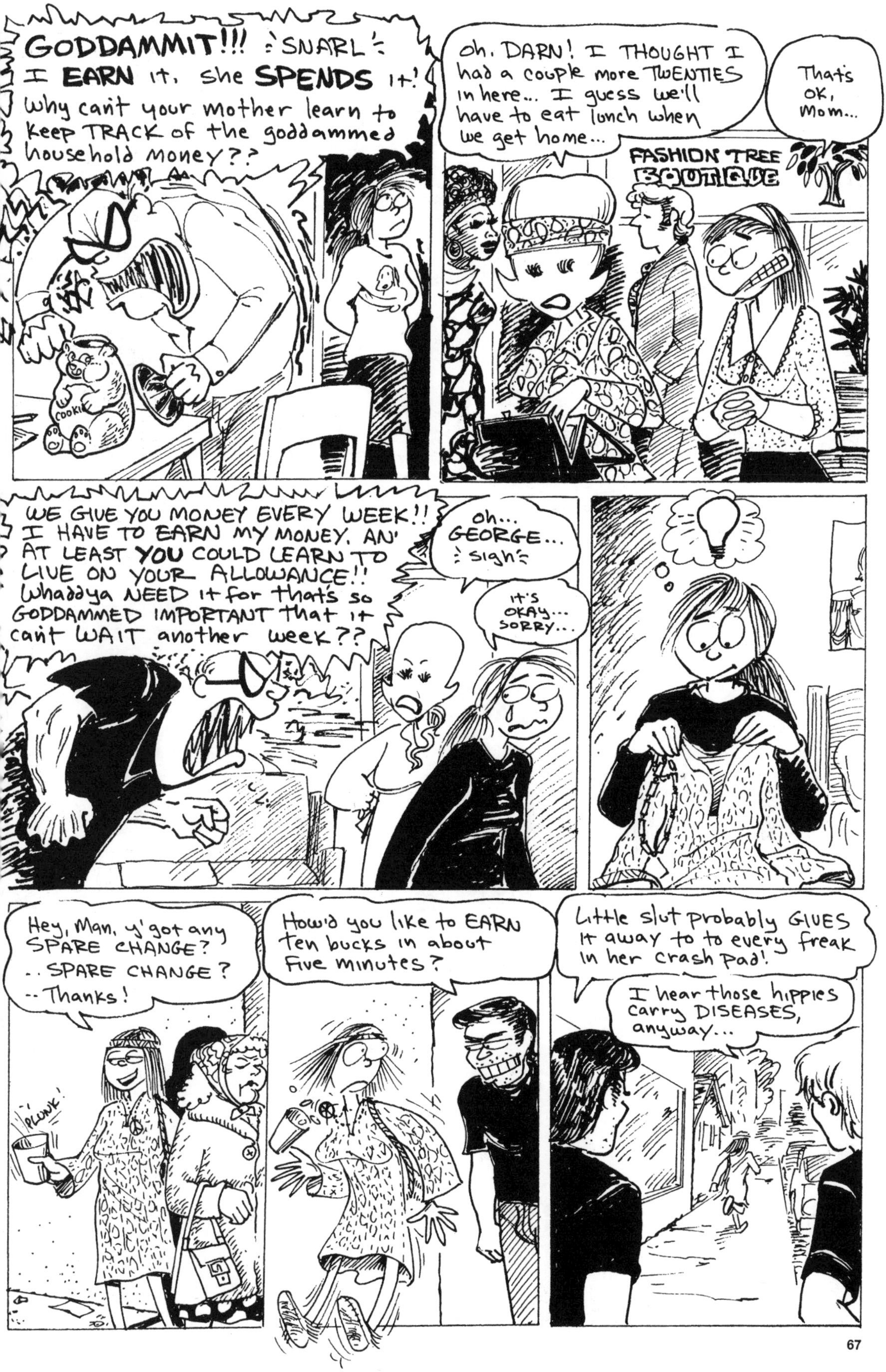
GODDAMMIT!!! :SNARL:
I EARN it, she SPENDS it! Why can't your mother learn to keep TRACK of the goddammed household money??
Oh, DARN! I THOUGHT I had a couple more TWENTIES in here... I guess we'll have to eat lunch when we get home...
That's ok, Mom...
FASHION TREE BOUTIQUE
WE GIVE YOU MONEY EVERY WEEK!! I HAVE TO EARN MY MONEY, AN' AT LEAST YOU COULD LEARN TO LIVE ON YOUR ALLOWANCE!! Whaddya NEED it for that's so GODDAMMED IMPORTANT that it can't WAIT another week??
Oh... GEORGE... :sigh:
It's okay... sorry...
Hey, Man, y'got any SPARE CHANGE? ..SPARE CHANGE? ..Thanks!
PLUNK!
How'd you like to EARN ten bucks in about five minutes?
Little slut probably GIVES it away to to every freak in her crash pad!
I hear those hippies carry DISEASES, anyway...

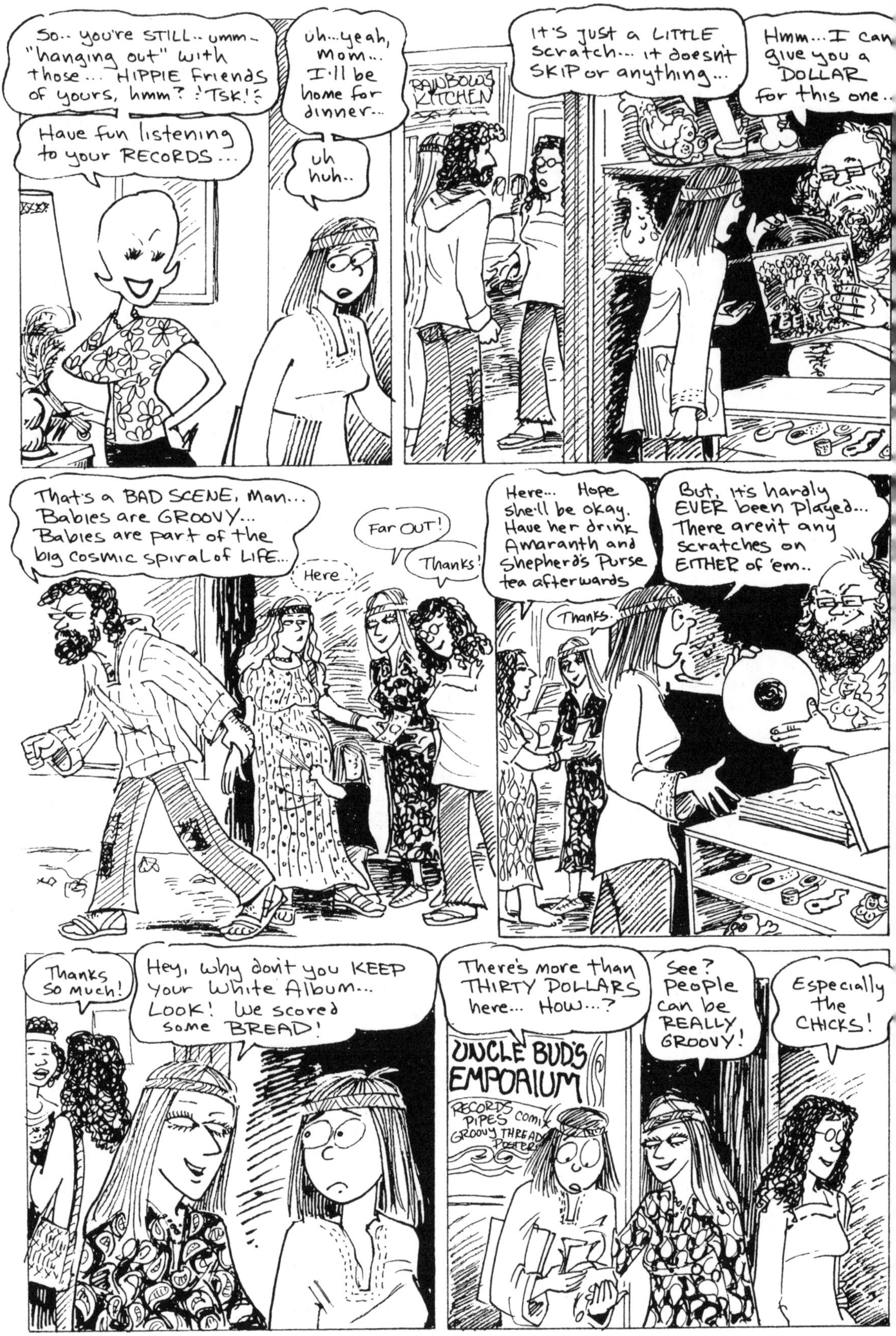
So.. you're STILL.. umm.. "hanging out" with those... HIPPIE friends of yours, hmm? TSK!
uh...yeah, mom... I'll be home for dinner...
Have fun listening to your RECORDS...
uh huh..
RAINBOW'S KITCHEN
It'S JUST a LITTLE Scratch... it doesn't SKIP or anything...
Hmm... I ca give you a DOLLAR for this one...
That's a BAD SCENE, Man... Babies are GROOVY... Babies are part of the big cosmic spiral of LIFE...
Here
Far OUT!
Thanks!
Here... Hope she'll be okay. Have her drink Amaranth and Shepherd's Purse tea afterwards
But, it's hardly EVER been played... There aren't any scratches on EITHER of 'em..
Thanks.
Thanks so much!
Hey, why don't you KEEP your White Album... Look! We scored some BREAD!
There's more than THIRTY DOLLARS here... How...?
See? People can be REALLY GROOVY!
Especially the CHICKS!
UNCLE BUD'S EMPORIUM
RECORDS PIPES COMIX GROOVY THREADS POSTERS

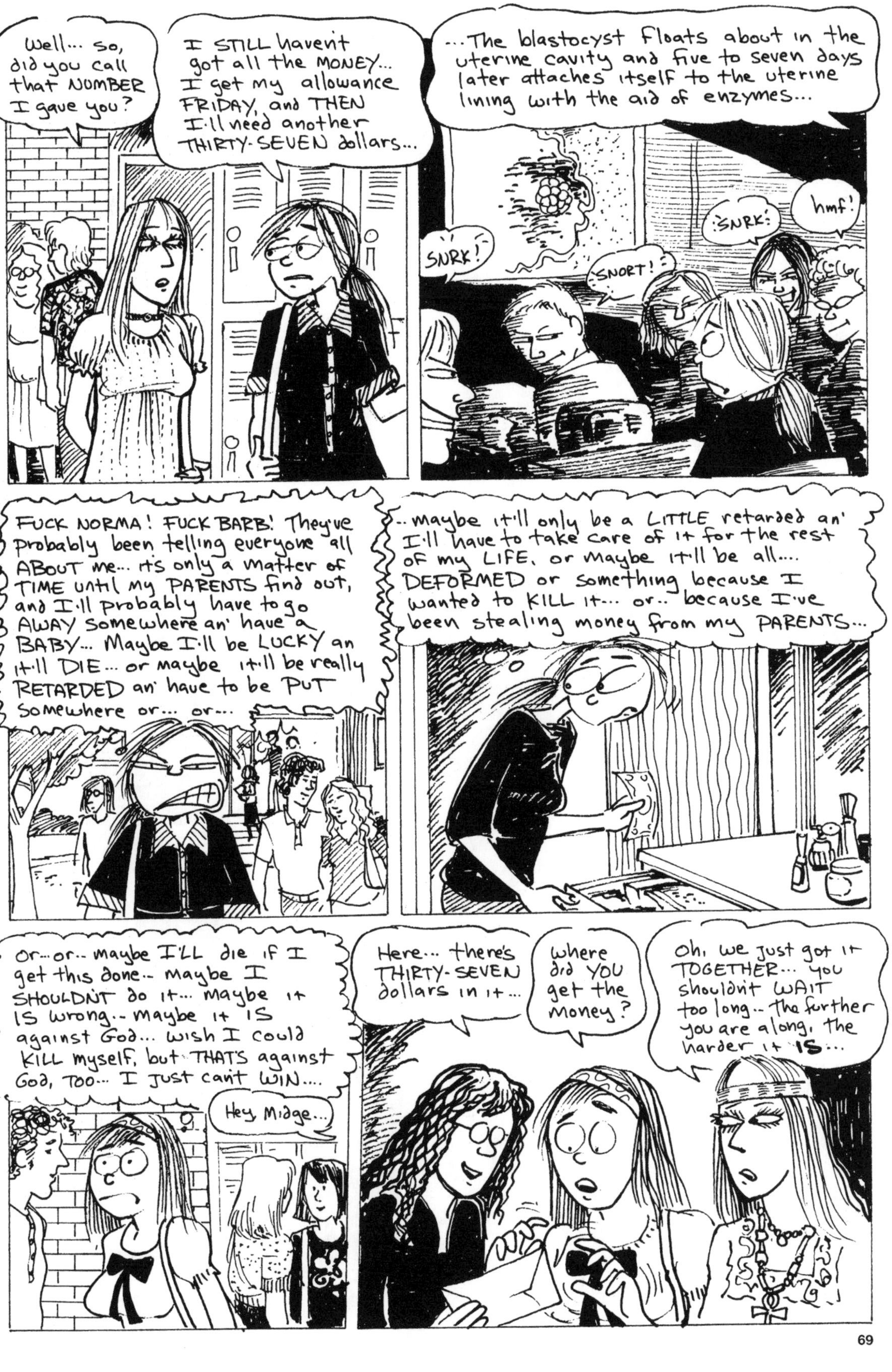
Well... so, did you call that NUMBER I gave you?
I STILL haven't got all the MONEY... I get my allowance FRIDAY, and THEN I'll need another THIRTY-SEVEN dollars...
...The blastocyst floats about in the uterine cavity and five to seven days later attaches itself to the uterine lining with the aid of enzymes...
SNRK!
SNORT!
SNRK
hmf!
FUCK NORMA! FUCK BARB! They've probably been telling everyone all ABOUT me... it's only a matter of TIME until my PARENTS find out, and I'll probably have to go AWAY somewhere an' have a BABY... Maybe I'll be LUCKY an it'll DIE... or maybe it'll be really RETARDED an' have to be PUT somewhere or... or...
..maybe it'll only be a LITTLE retarded an' I'll have to take care of it for the rest of my LIFE, or maybe it'll be all.... DEFORMED or something because I wanted to KILL it... or.. because I've been stealing money from my PARENTS...
or..or.. maybe I'LL die if I get this done.. maybe I SHOULDN'T do it... maybe it IS wrong.. maybe it IS against God... wish I could KILL myself, but THAT'S against God, TOO... I just can't WIN....
Hey, Midge...
Here... there's THIRTY-SEVEN dollars in it...
where did YOU get the money?
Oh, we just got it TOGETHER... you shouldn't WAIT too long.. the further you are along, the harder it IS...

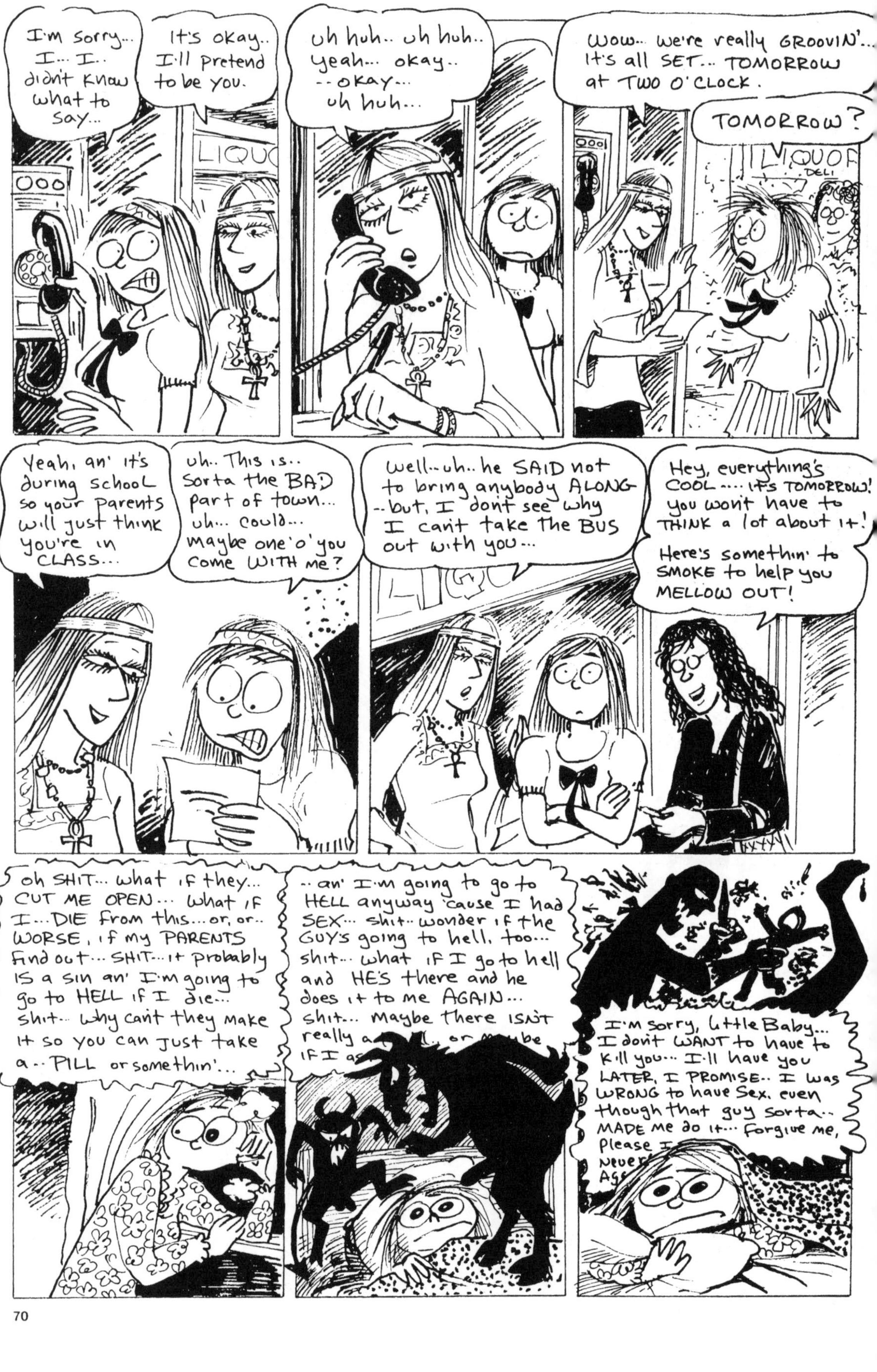
I'm sorry... I... I.. didn't know what to say...
It's okay.. I'll pretend to be you.
LIQU
uh huh.. uh huh.. yeah... okay.. --okay... uh huh...
Wow... we're really GROOVIN'... It's all SET... TOMORROW at TWO O'CLOCK.
TOMORROW?
LIQUOR
DELI
Yeah, an' it's during school so your parents will just think you're in CLASS...
uh.. This is.. Sorta the BAD part of town... uh... could... maybe one 'o' you come WITH me?
Well...uh.. he SAID not to bring anybody ALONG --but, I don't see why I can't take the BUS out with you...
Hey, everything's COOL.... it's TOMORROW! you won't have to THINK a lot about it!
Here's somethin' to SMOKE to help you MELLOW OUT!
oh SHIT... what if they... CUT ME OPEN... what if I...DIE from this...or, or.. WORSE, if my PARENTS find out... SHIT... it probably IS a sin an' I'm going to go to HELL if I die... shit... why can't they make it so you can just take a.. PILL or somethin'...
..an' I'm going to go to HELL anyway 'cause I had SEX... shit.. wonder if the GUY's going to hell, too... shit... what if I go to hell and HE'S there and he does it to me AGAIN... shit... maybe there ISN'T
I'M sorry, Little Baby... I don't WANT to have to kill you... I'll have you LATER, I PROMISE.. I was WRONG to have Sex, even though that guy sorta.. MADE me do it... Forgive me, Please I

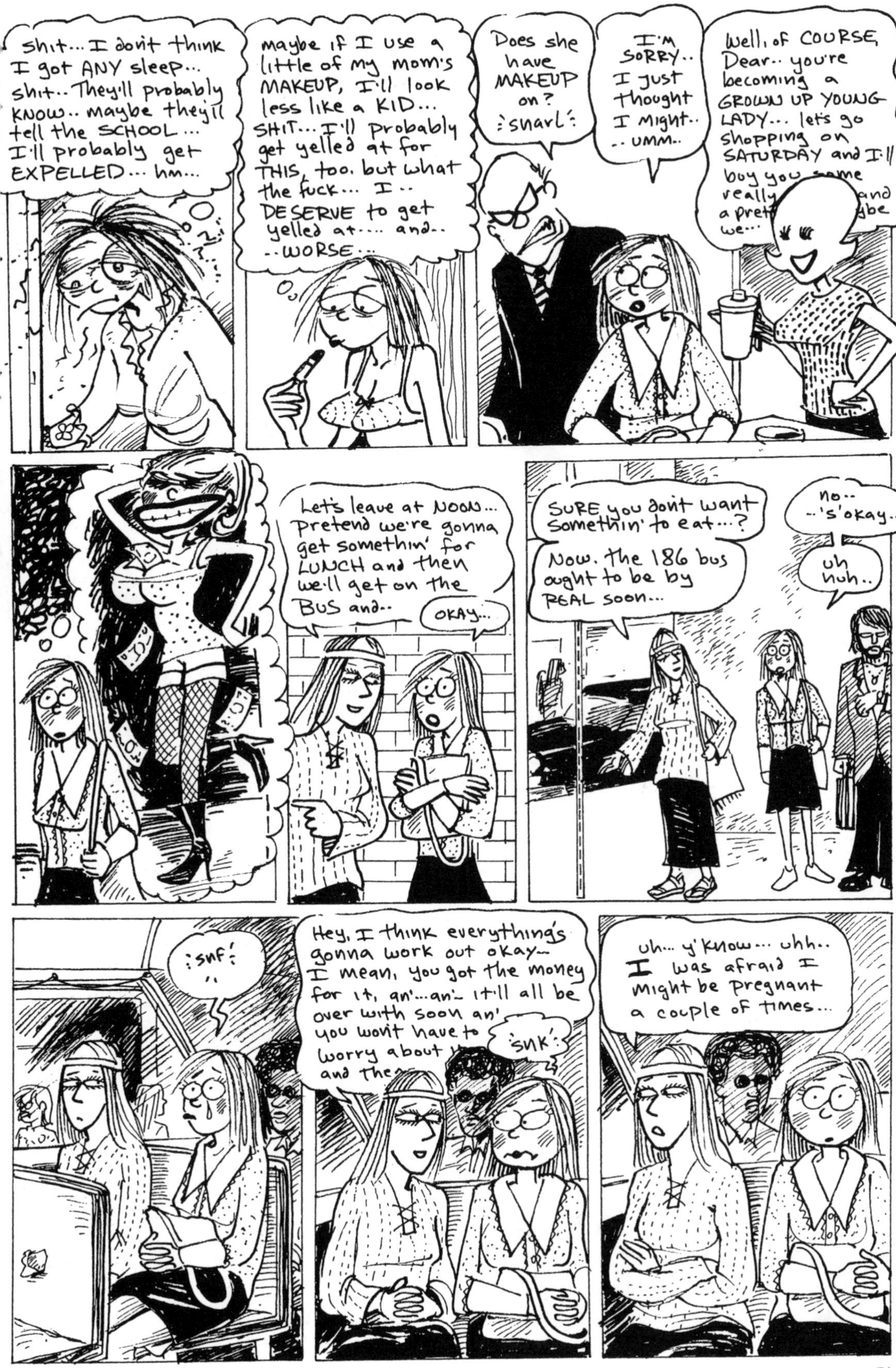
shit... I don't think I got ANY sleep... shit.. They'll probably KNOW.. maybe they'll tell the SCHOOL... I'll probably get EXPELLED... hm...
maybe if I use a little of my mom's MAKEUP, I'll look less like a KID... SHIT... I'll probably get yelled at for THIS, too. but what the fuck... I.. DESERVE to get yelled at.... and.. ..WORSE...
Does she have MAKEUP on? :snarl:
I'M SORRY.. I just thought I might.. ..umm..
Well, of COURSE, Dear.. you're becoming a GROWN UP YOUNG LADY... let's go shopping on SATURDAY and I'll buy you some really
Let's leave at NOON... Pretend we're gonna get somethin' for LUNCH and then we'll get on the BUS and..
OKAY...
SURE you don't want somethin' to eat...?
Now, the 186 bus ought to be by REAL soon...
no.. ..'s'okay..
uh huh..
:snf:
Hey, I think everything's gonna work out okay.. I mean, you got the money for it, an'...an'.. it'll all be over with soon an' you won't have to worry about
:snk:
uh... y'know... uhh.. I was afraid I might be pregnant a couple of times...

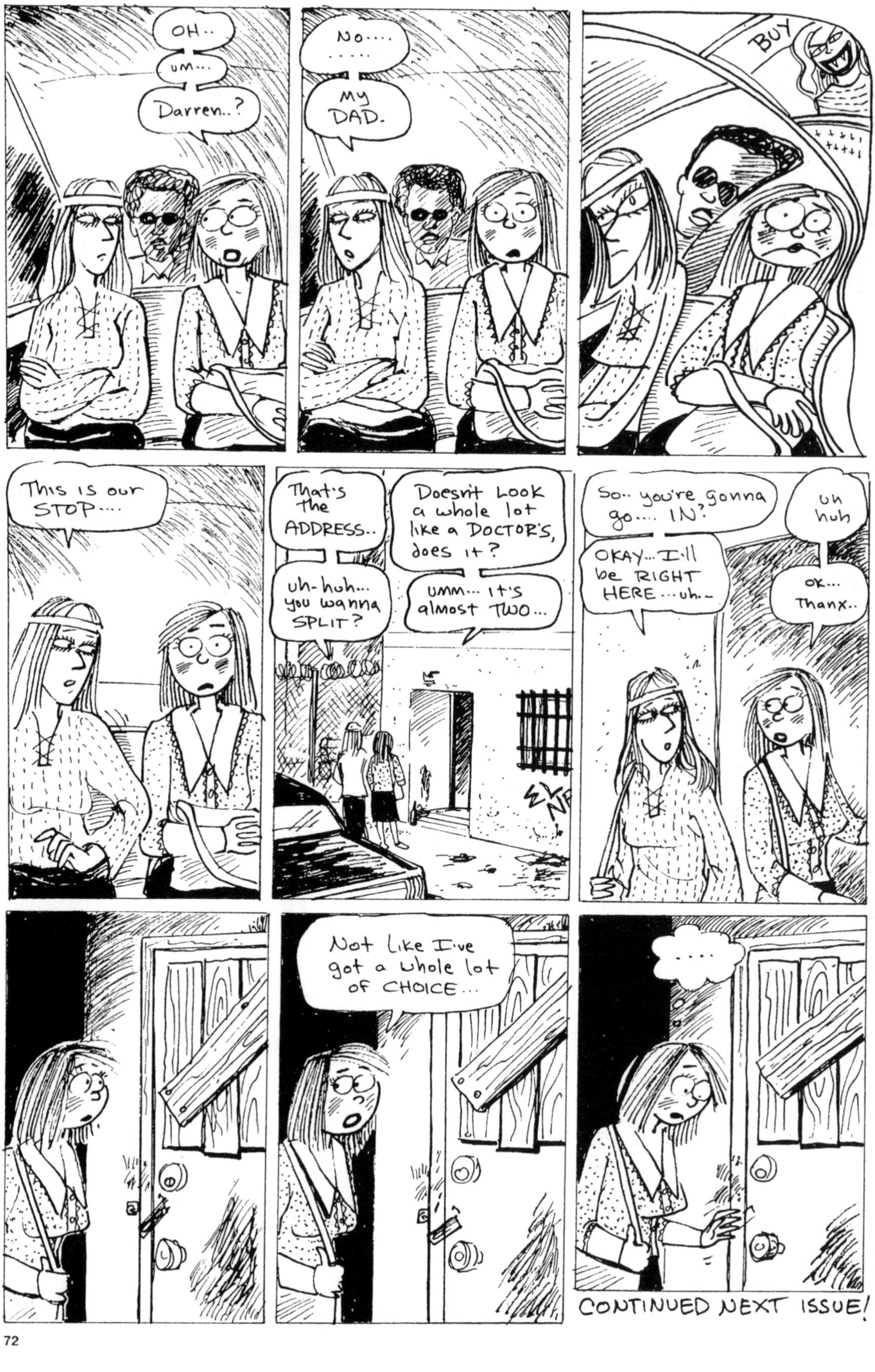
OH..
um...
Darren..?
No....
.....
MY DAD.
BUY
This is our STOP....
That's the ADDRESS..
uh-huh... you wanna SPLIT?
Doesn't Look a whole lot like a DOCTOR'S, does it?
umm... it's almost TWO...
So.. you're gonna go.... IN?
uh huh
OKAY... I'll be RIGHT HERE...uh..
ok... Thanx..
Not like I've got a whole lot of CHOICE...
....
CONTINUED NEXT ISSUE!

HIPPIE BITCH GETS AN ABORTION

©1993 ROBERTA GREGORY

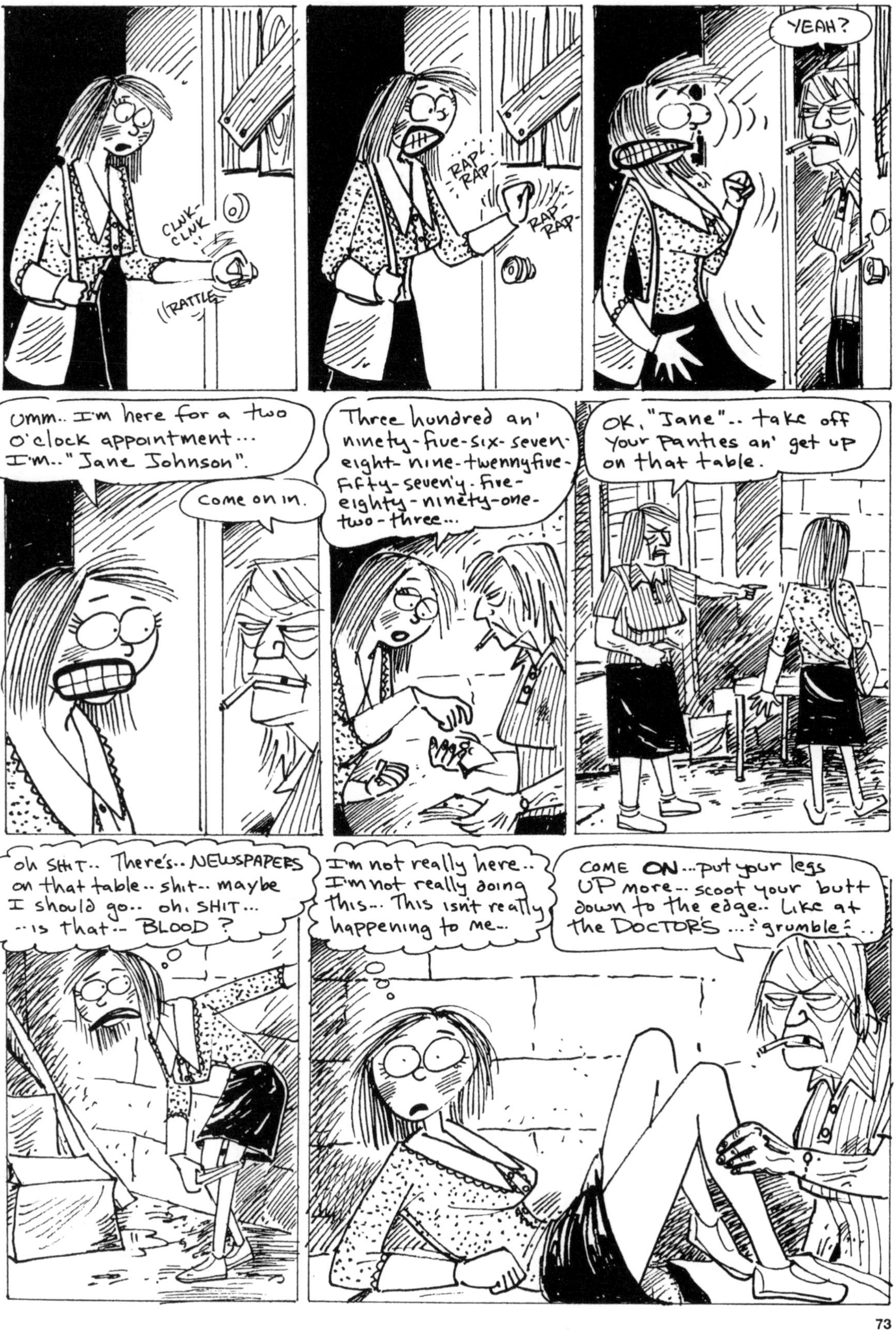
CLNK- CLNK
RATTLE
RAP RAP
RAP RAP
YEAH?
Umm.. I'm here for a two o'clock appointment... I'm.. "Jane Johnson".
Come on in.
Three hundred an' ninety-five-six-seven-eight-nine-twennyfive-fifty-seven'y-five-eighty-ninety-one-two-three...
OK, "Jane".. take off your Panties an' get up on that table.
oh SHIT.. There's.. NEWSPAPERS on that table.. shit.. maybe I should go.. oh, SHIT... ..is that.. BLOOD?
I'm not really here.. I'm not really doing this.. This isn't really happening to me..
COME ON...put your legs UP more.. scoot your butt down to the edge.. Like at the DOCTOR'S ... grumble ...

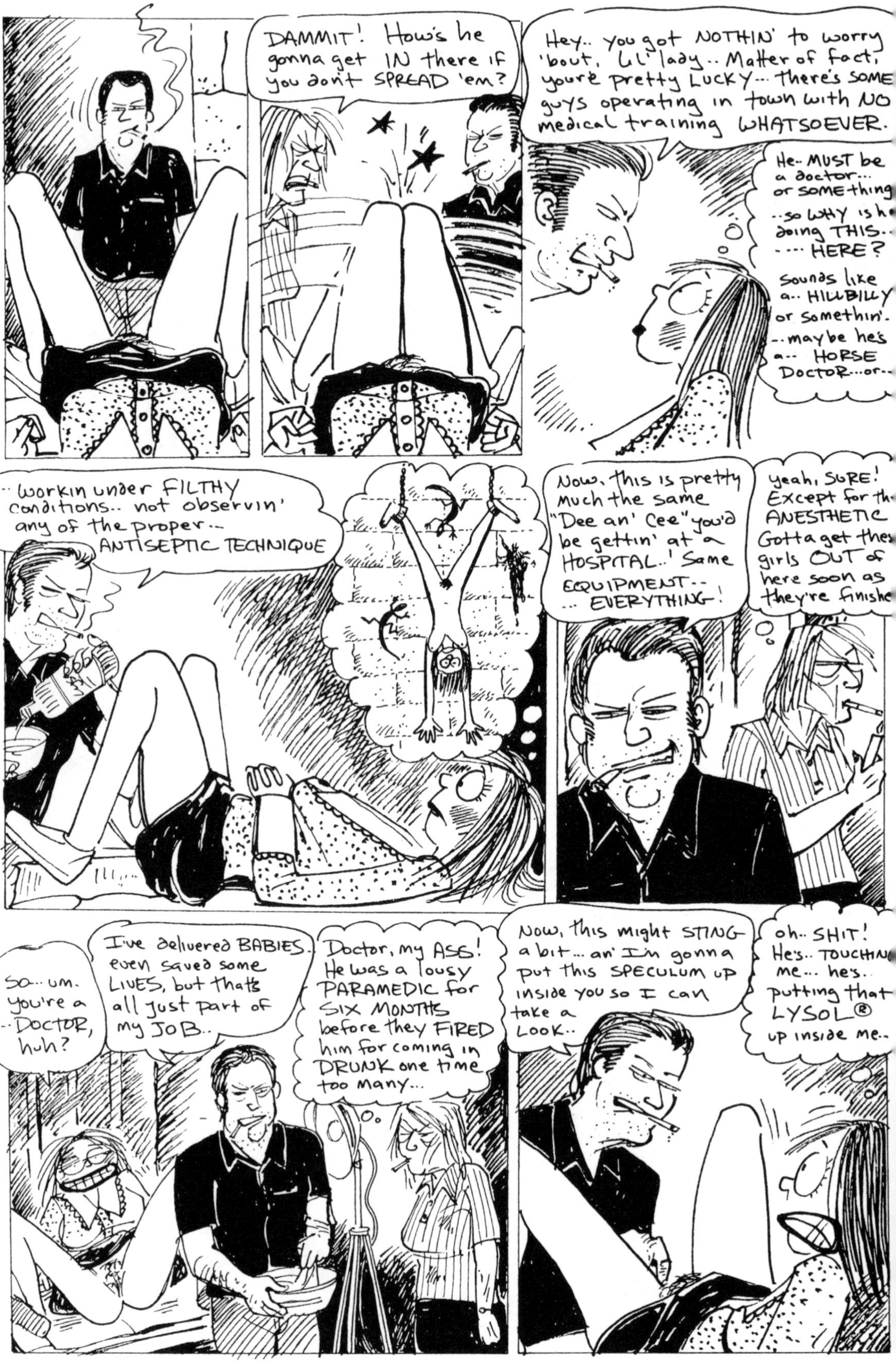
DAMMIT! How's he gonna get IN there if you don't SPREAD 'em?
Hey.. you got NOTHIN' to worry 'bout, lil' lady.. Matter of fact, you're pretty LUCKY... there's SOME guys operating in town with NO medical training WHATSOEVER.
He.. MUST be a doctor... or SOMETHING
..so WHY is h doing THIS.. ....HERE?
Sounds like a.. HILLBILLY or somethin'.. ..maybe he's a.. HORSE DOCTOR...or...
..workin under FILTHY conditions.. not observin' any of the proper.. ANTISEPTIC TECHNIQUE
Now, this is pretty much the same "Dee an' Cee" you'd be gettin' at a HOSPITAL..! Same EQUIPMENT.. ...EVERYTHING!
yeah, SURE! Except for th ANESTHETIC Gotta get thes girls OUT of here soon as they're finishe
So...um.. you're a ..DOCTOR, huh?
I've delivered BABIES.. even saved some LIVES, but that's all just part of my JOB..
Doctor, my ASS! He was a lousy PARAMEDIC for SIX MONTHS before they FIRED him for coming in DRUNK one time too many...
Now, this might STING a bit... an' I'm gonna put this SPECULUM up inside you so I can take a LOOK..
oh.. SHIT! He's.. TOUCHIN me... he's.. putting that LYSOL® up inside me..

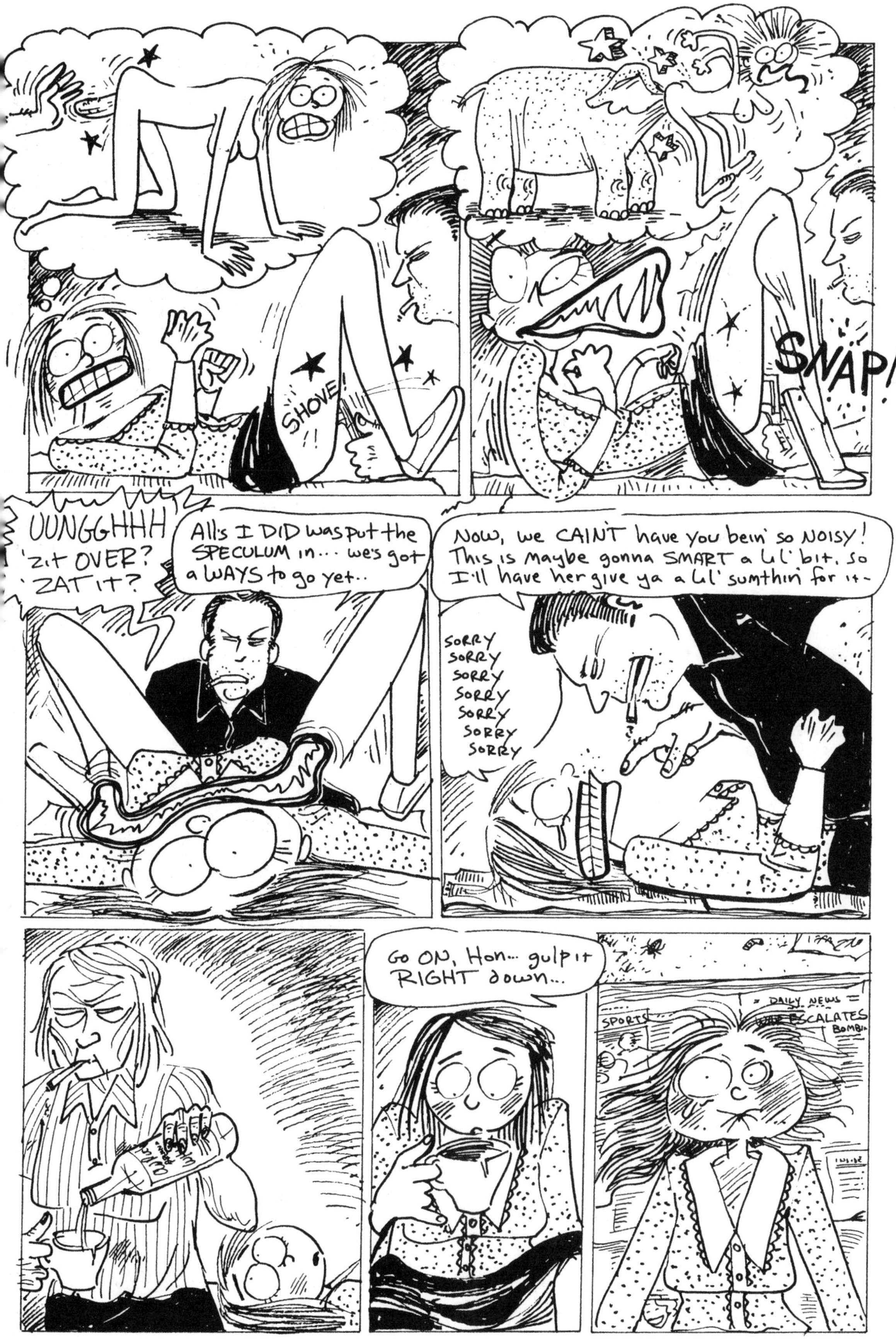
SHOVE!
SNAP!
UUNGGHHH 'zit OVER? 'ZAT IT?
All's I DID was put the SPECULUM in... we's got a WAYS to go yet..
Now, we CAIN'T have you bein' so NOISY! This is maybe gonna SMART a li'l bit, so I'll have her give ya a li'l sumthin' for it-
SORRY SORRY SORRY SORRY SORRY SORRY SORRY
Go ON, Hon... gulp it RIGHT down...
DAILY NEWS
ESCALATES
BOMB
SPORTS

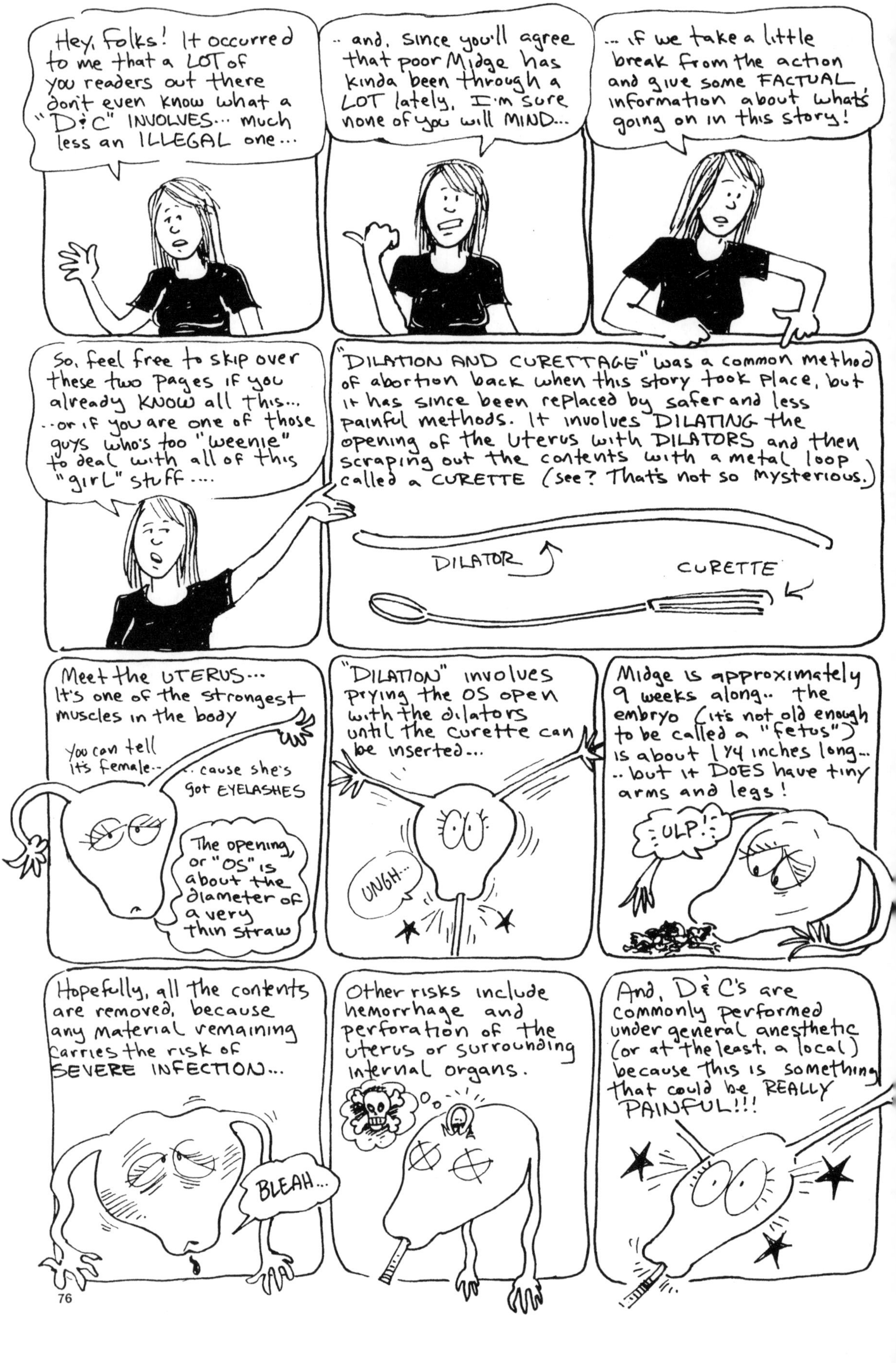
Hey, folks! It occurred to me that a LOT of you readers out there don't even know what a "D&C" INVOLVES... much less an ILLEGAL one...
..and, since you'll agree that poor Midge has kinda been through a LOT lately, I'm sure none of you will MIND...
...if we take a little break from the action and give some FACTUAL information about what's going on in this story!
So, feel free to skip over these two pages if you already KNOW all this... ..or if you are one of those guys who's too "weenie" to deal with all of this "girl" stuff....
"DILATION AND CURETTAGE" was a common method of abortion back when this story took place, but it has since been replaced by safer and less painful methods. It involves DILATING the opening of the uterus with DILATORS and then scraping out the contents with a metal loop called a CURETTE (see? That's not so mysterious.)
DILATOR
CURETTE
Meet the UTERUS... It's one of the strongest muscles in the body
You can tell it's female-
-cause she's got EYELASHES
The opening, or "OS" is about the diameter of a very thin straw
"DILATION" involves prying the OS open with the dilators until the curette can be inserted...
UNGH...
Midge is approximately 9 weeks along.. the embryo (it's not old enough to be called a "fetus") is about 1 1/4 inches long... ..but it DOES have tiny arms and legs!
ULP!
Hopefully, all the contents are removed, because any material remaining carries the risk of SEVERE INFECTION...
BLEAH...
Other risks include hemorrhage and perforation of the uterus or surrounding internal organs.
And, D&C's are commonly performed under general anesthetic (or at the least, a local) because this is something that could be REALLY PAINFUL!!!

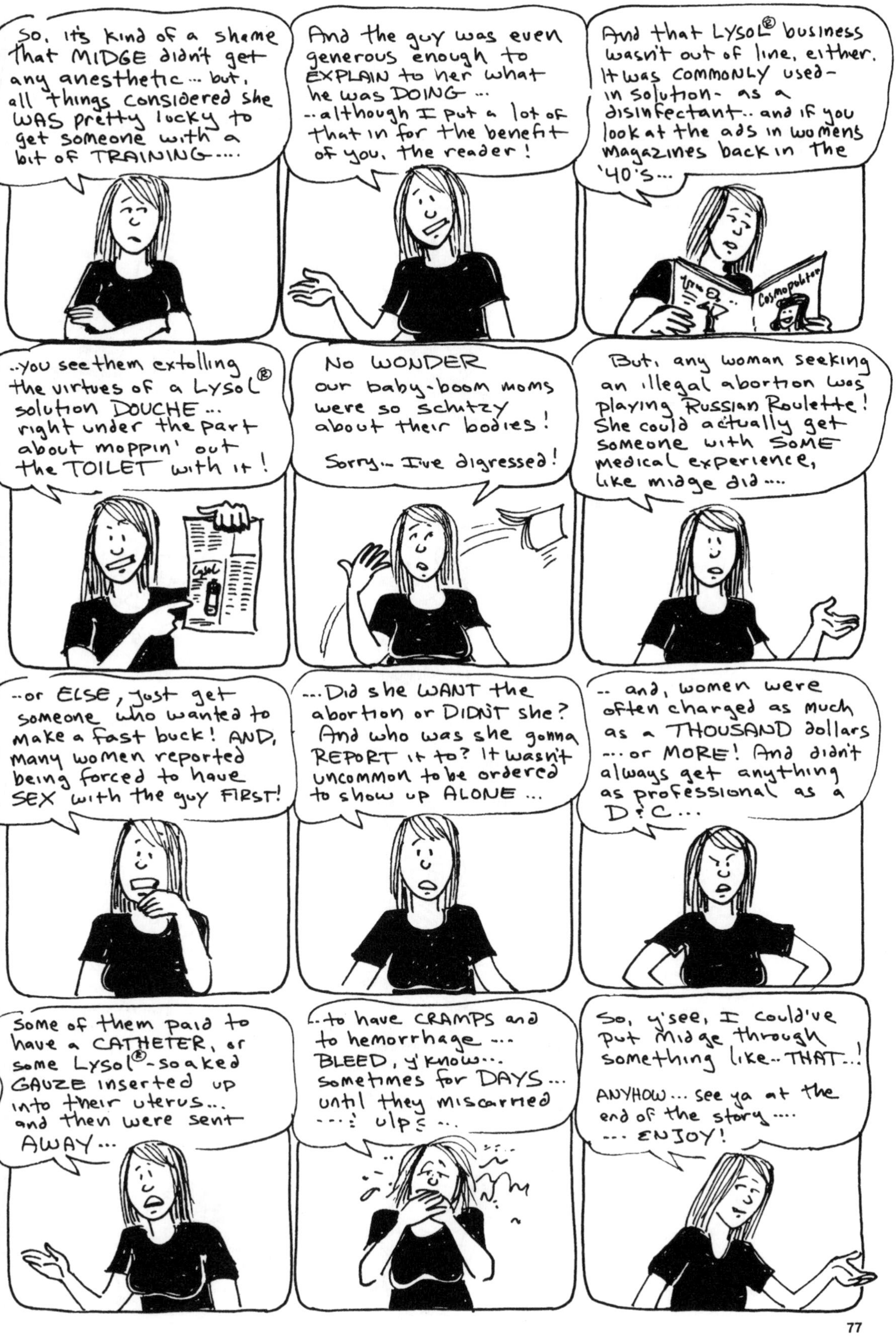

So, it's kind of a shame that MIDGE didn't get any anesthetic... but, all things considered she WAS pretty lucky to get someone with a bit of TRAINING....
And the guy was even generous enough to EXPLAIN to her what he was DOING... ..although I put a lot of that in for the benefit of you, the reader!
And that LYSOL® business wasn't out of line, either. It was COMMONLY used - in solution - as a disinfectant.. and if you look at the ads in womens magazines back in the '40's...
Cosmopolitan
..you see them extolling the virtues of a LYSOL® solution DOUCHE... right under the part about moppin' out the TOILET with it!
Lysol
No WONDER our baby-boom moms were so schitzy about their bodies!
Sorry.. I've digressed!
But, any woman seeking an illegal abortion was playing Russian Roulette! She could actually get someone with SOME medical experience, like midge did....
..or ELSE, just get someone who wanted to make a fast buck! AND, many women reported being forced to have SEX with the guy FIRST!
...Did she WANT the abortion or DIDN'T she? And who was she gonna REPORT it to? It wasn't uncommon to be ordered to show up ALONE...
.. and, women were often charged as much as a THOUSAND dollars ... or MORE! And didn't always get anything as professional as a D&C...
Some of them paid to have a CATHETER, or some Lysol®-soaked GAUZE inserted up into their uterus... and then were sent AWAY...
..to have CRAMPS and to hemorrhage... BLEED, y'know... sometimes for DAYS... until they miscarried ...: ulp:..
So, y'see, I could've put Midge through something like.. THAT..!
ANYHOW... see ya at the end of the story.... ... ENJOY!

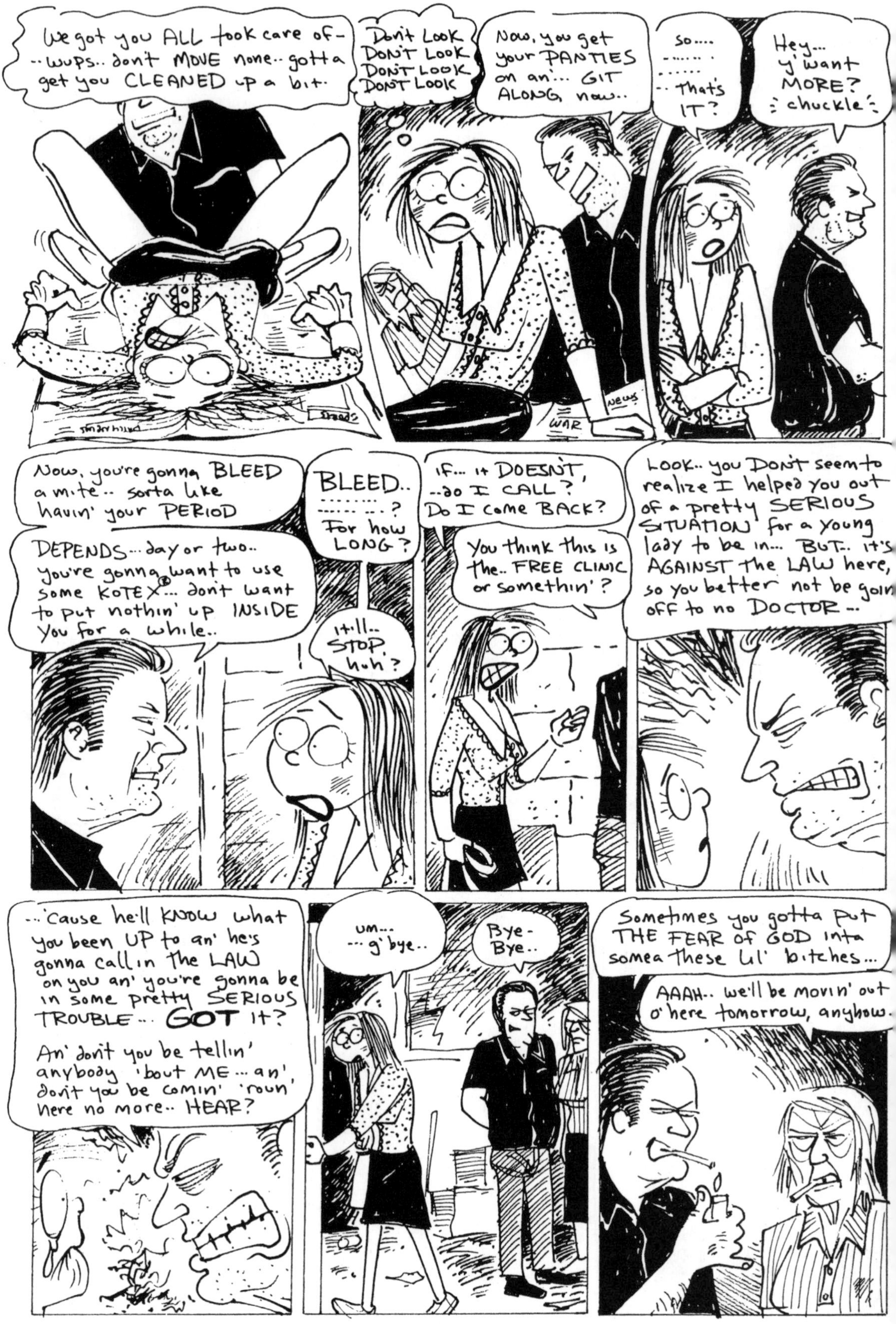
We got you ALL took care of- -- wups.. don't MOVE none.. gotta get you CLEANED up a bit-
Don't LOOK DON'T LOOK DON'T LOOK DON'T LOOK
Now, you get your PANTIES on an'... GIT ALONG, now..
SO.... .... That's IT?
Hey... y' want MORE? chuckle
NEWS
WAR
Now, you're gonna BLEED a mite.. sorta like havin' your PERIOD
DEPENDS... day or two.. you're gonna want to use some KOTEX®... don't want to put nothin' up INSIDE you for a while..
BLEED.. ....? For how LONG?
It'll.. STOP, huh?
IF... it DOESN'T, --do I CALL? Do I come BACK?
You think this is the.. FREE CLINIC or somethin'?
LOOK.. you DON'T seem to realize I helped you out of a pretty SERIOUS SITUATION for a young lady to be in... BUT.. it's AGAINST the LAW here, so you better not be goin off to no DOCTOR..
..'cause he'll KNOW what you been UP to an' he's gonna call in the LAW on you an' you're gonna be in some pretty SERIOUS TROUBLE... GOT it?
An' don't you be tellin' anybody 'bout ME... an', don't you be comin' 'roun here no more.. HEAR?
um... ...g'bye..
Bye-Bye..
Sometimes you gotta put THE FEAR OF GOD inta somea these lil' bitches...
AAAH.. we'll be movin' out o'here tomorrow, anyhow.

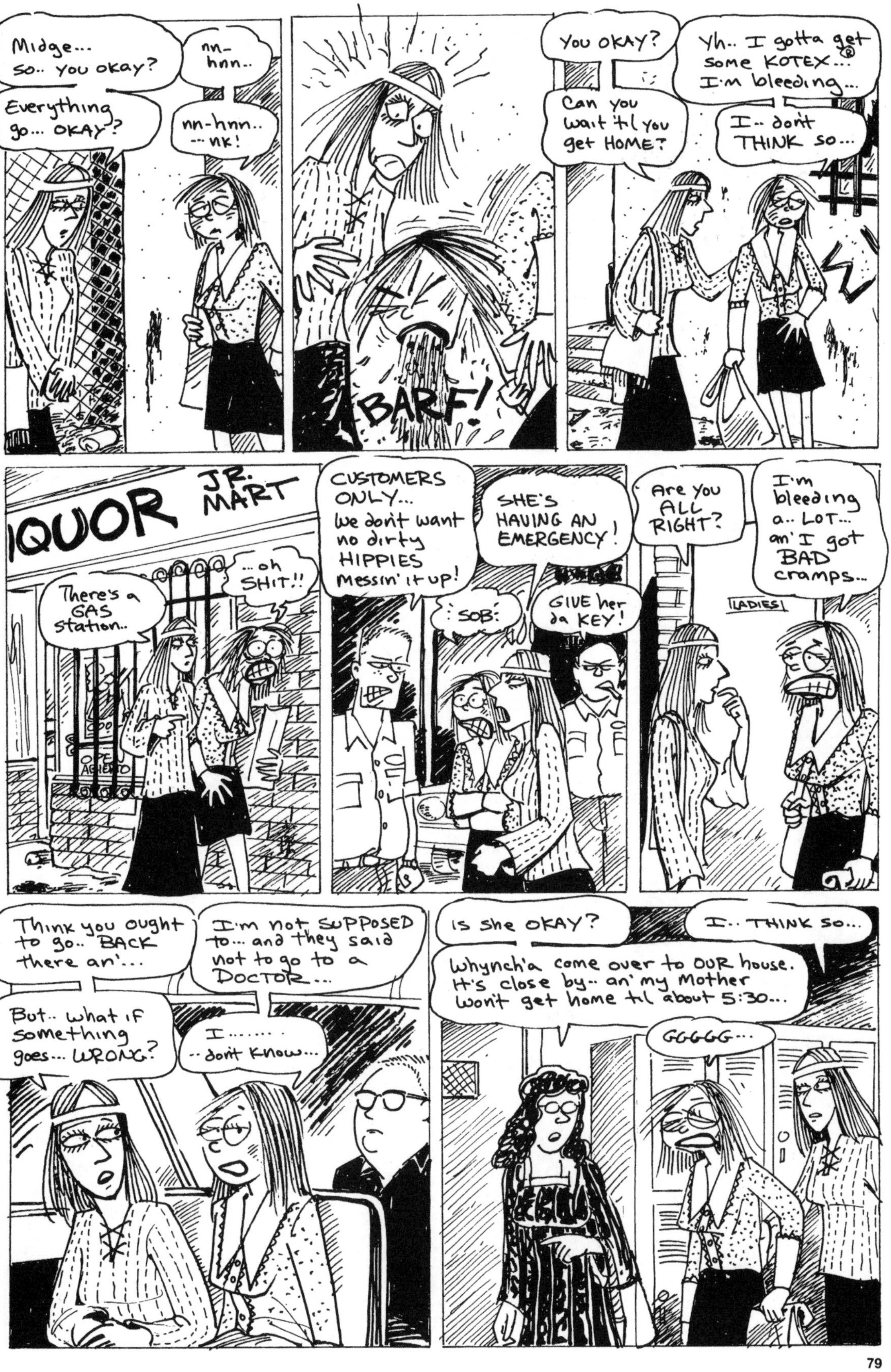
Midge... so.. you okay?
Everything go... OKAY?
nn- hnn..
nn-hnn.. --nk!
BARF!
You OKAY?
Can you wait til you get HOME?
Yh.. I gotta get some KOTEX® .. I'm bleeding...
I.. don't THINK so...
IQUOR
JR. MART
There's a GAS station..
...oh SHIT!!
CUSTOMERS ONLY... We don't want no dirty HIPPIES Messin' it up!
SHE'S HAVING AN EMERGENCY!
SOB
GIVE her da KEY!
Are you ALL RIGHT?
I'm bleeding a.. LOT... an' I got BAD cramps...
LADIES
Think you ought to go.. BACK there an'...
I'm not SUPPOSED to... and they said not to go to a DOCTOR...
But.. what if something goes... WRONG?
I....... --don't know...
Is she OKAY?
I.. THINK so...
Whynch'a come over to OUR house. It's close by.. an' my Mother won't get home til about 5:30...
GGGGG...

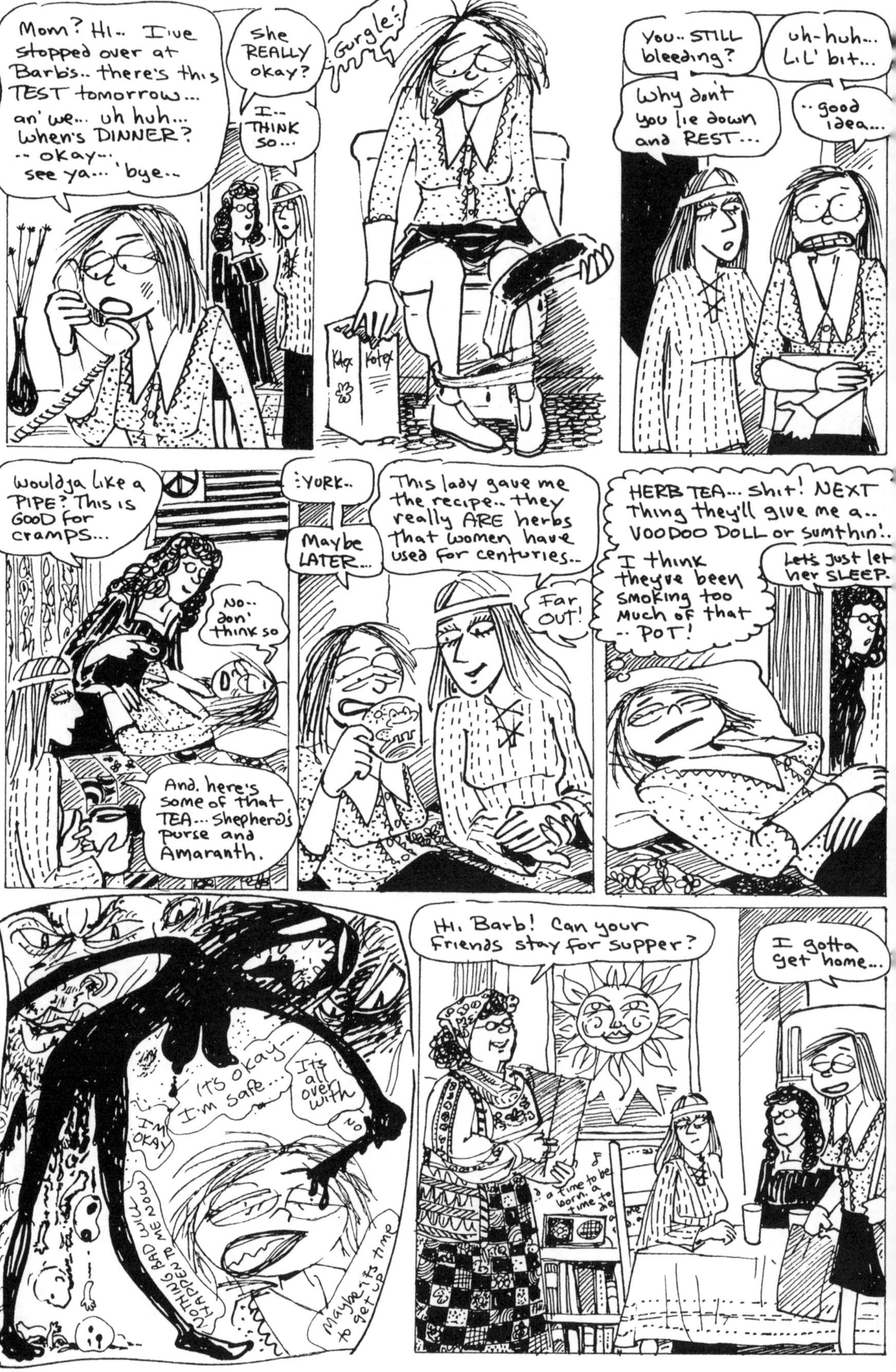
Mom? Hi.. I've stopped over at Barb's.. there's this TEST tomorrow... an' we.. uh huh... when's DINNER? -- okay-- see ya... 'bye..
She REALLY okay?
I-- THINK so...
Gurgle!
You.. STILL bleeding?
uh-huh... Li'l bit...
Why don't you lie down and REST...
..good idea...
Wouldja like a PIPE? This is GOOD for cramps...
No.. don' think so
And. here's some of that TEA... Shepherd's purse and Amaranth.
:YORK..
Maybe LATER...
This lady gave me the recipe.. they really ARE herbs that women have used for centuries..
Far OUT!
HERB TEA... shit! NEXT thing they'll give me a.. VOODOO DOLL or sumthin'..
I think they've been smoking too much of that -- POT!
Let's just let her SLEEP.
I'M OKAY
It's okay-- I'm safe...
It's all over with
NO
NOTHING BAD WILL HAPPEN TO ME NOW
Maybe it's time to get up
Hi, Barb! Can your friends stay for supper?
a time to be born, a time to die
I gotta get home...

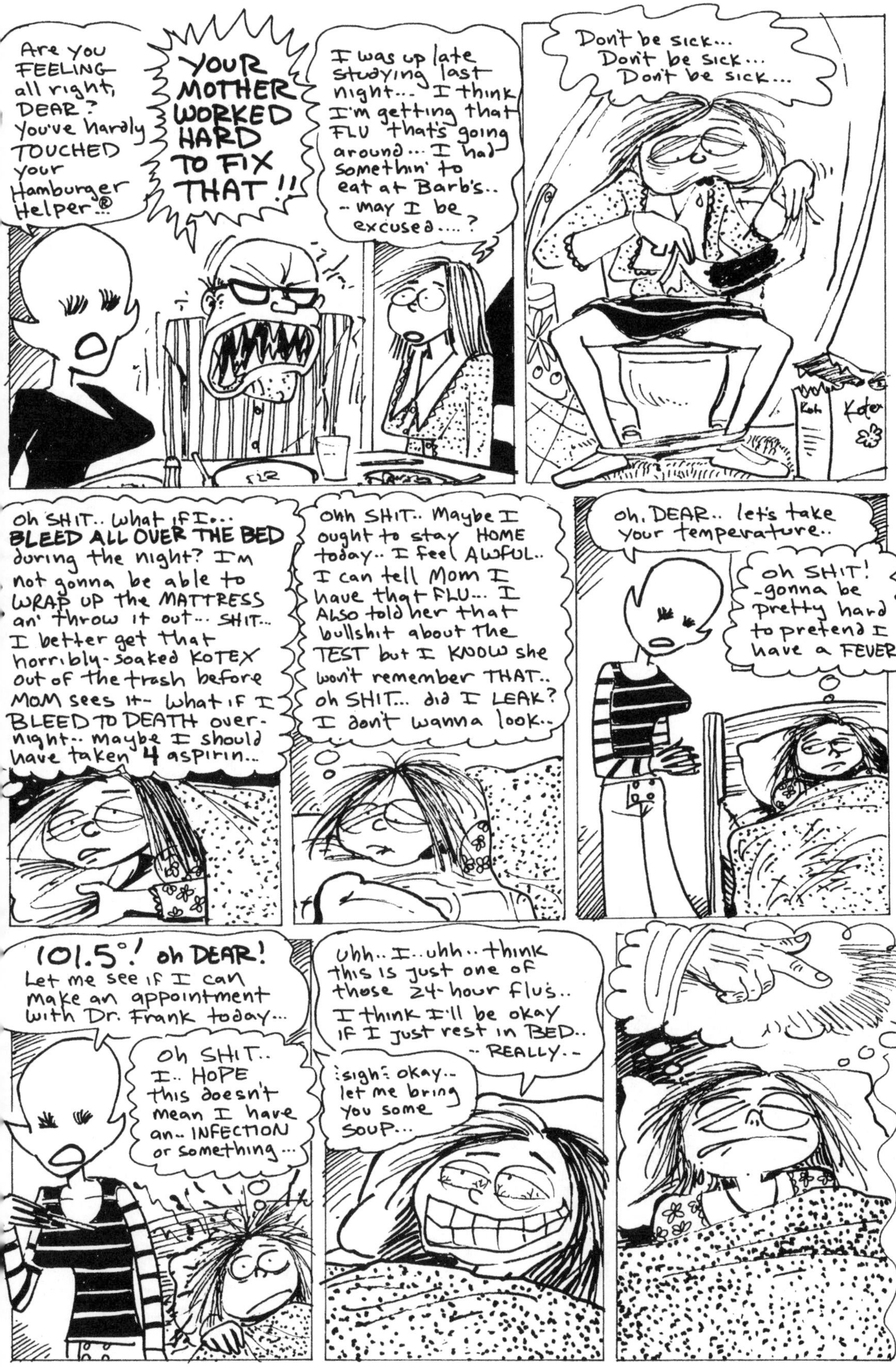

Are you FEELING all right, DEAR? You've hardly TOUCHED your Hamburger Helper®...
YOUR MOTHER WORKED HARD TO FIX THAT!!
I was up late studying last night... I think I'm getting that FLU that's going around... I had somethin' to eat at Barb's.. --may I be excused....?
Don't be sick... Don't be sick... Don't be sick...
Kotex
oh SHIT.. what if I... BLEED ALL OVER THE BED during the night? I'm not gonna be able to WRAP UP the MATTRESS an' throw it out... SHIT... I better get that horribly-soaked KOTEX out of the trash before MOM sees it-- what if I BLEED TO DEATH over-night.. maybe I should have taken 4 aspirin...
Ohh SHIT.. Maybe I ought to stay HOME today.. I feel AWFUL.. I can tell Mom I have that FLU... I Also told her that bullshit about the TEST but I KNOW she won't remember THAT.. oh SHIT... did I LEAK? I don't wanna look..
oh, DEAR.. let's take your temperature..
oh SHIT! -gonna be pretty hard to pretend I have a FEVER..
101.5°! oh DEAR! Let me see if I can make an appointment with Dr. Frank today...
oh SHIT.. I.. HOPE this doesn't mean I have an.. INFECTION or something...
Uhh.. I.. uhh.. think this is just one of those 24-hour flus.. I think I'll be okay if I just rest in BED.. --REALLY.--
:sigh: okay.. let me bring you some SOUP...

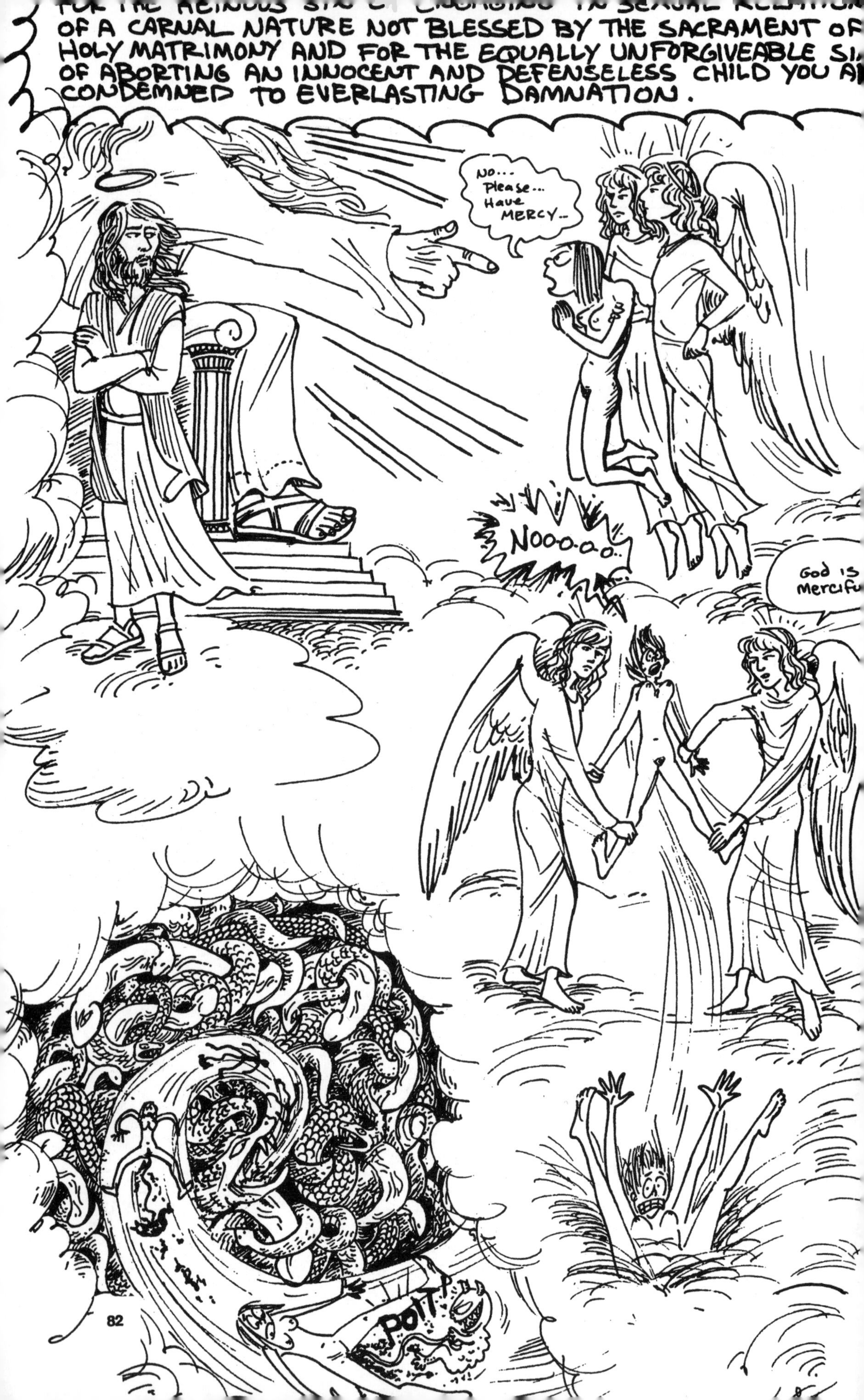

OF A CARNAL NATURE NOT BLESSED BY THE SACRAMENT OF
HOLY MATRIMONY AND FOR THE EQUALLY UNFORGIVEABLE SI
OF ABORTING AN INNOCENT AND DEFENSELESS CHILD YOU A
CONDEMNED TO EVERLASTING DAMNATION.
No... Please... Have MERCY...
NOOO-O-O-O..
God is Mercifu
POIT!

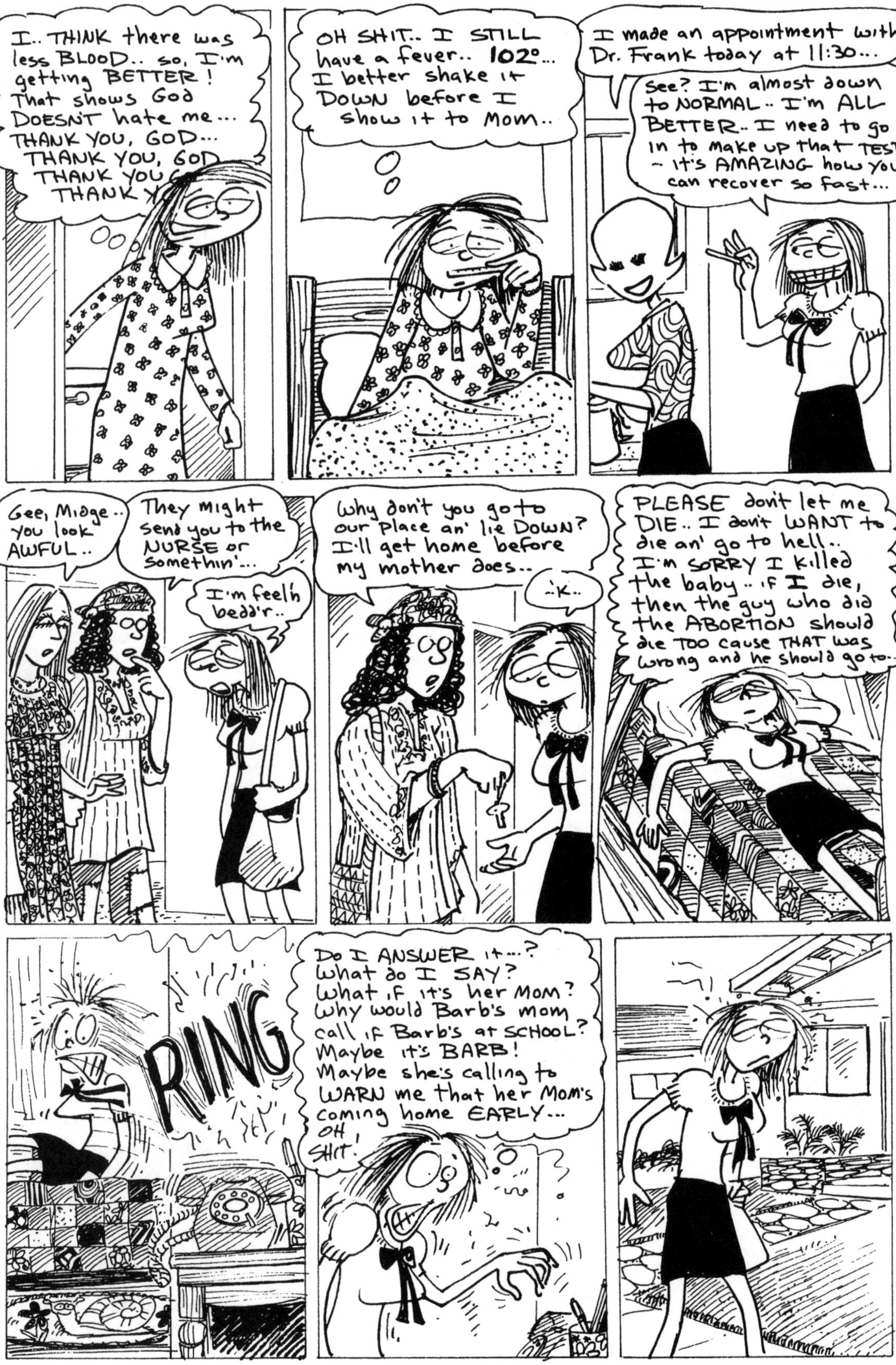
I.. THINK there was less BLOOD.. so, I'm getting BETTER! That shows God DOESN'T hate me... THANK YOU, GOD... THANK YOU, GOD THANK YOU THANK Y
OH SHIT.. I STILL have a fever.. 102°... I better shake it DOWN before I show it to MOM..
I made an appointment with Dr. Frank today at 11:30...
See? I'm almost down to NORMAL.. I'm ALL BETTER.. I need to go in to make up that TEST.. - it's AMAZING how you can recover so fast...
Gee, Midge.. you look AWFUL..
They might send you to the NURSE or somethin'...
I'm feelin bedd'r..
Why don't you go to our place an' lie DOWN? I'll get home before my mother does..
..K..
PLEASE don't let me DIE.. I don't WANT to die an' go to hell.. I'M SORRY I killed the baby.. if I die, then the guy who did the ABORTION should die TOO cause THAT was wrong and he should go to..
RING
Do I ANSWER it...? What do I SAY? What if it's her MOM? Why would Barb's mom call if Barb's at SCHOOL? Maybe it's BARB! Maybe she's calling to WARN me that her Mom's coming home EARLY... OH SHIT!

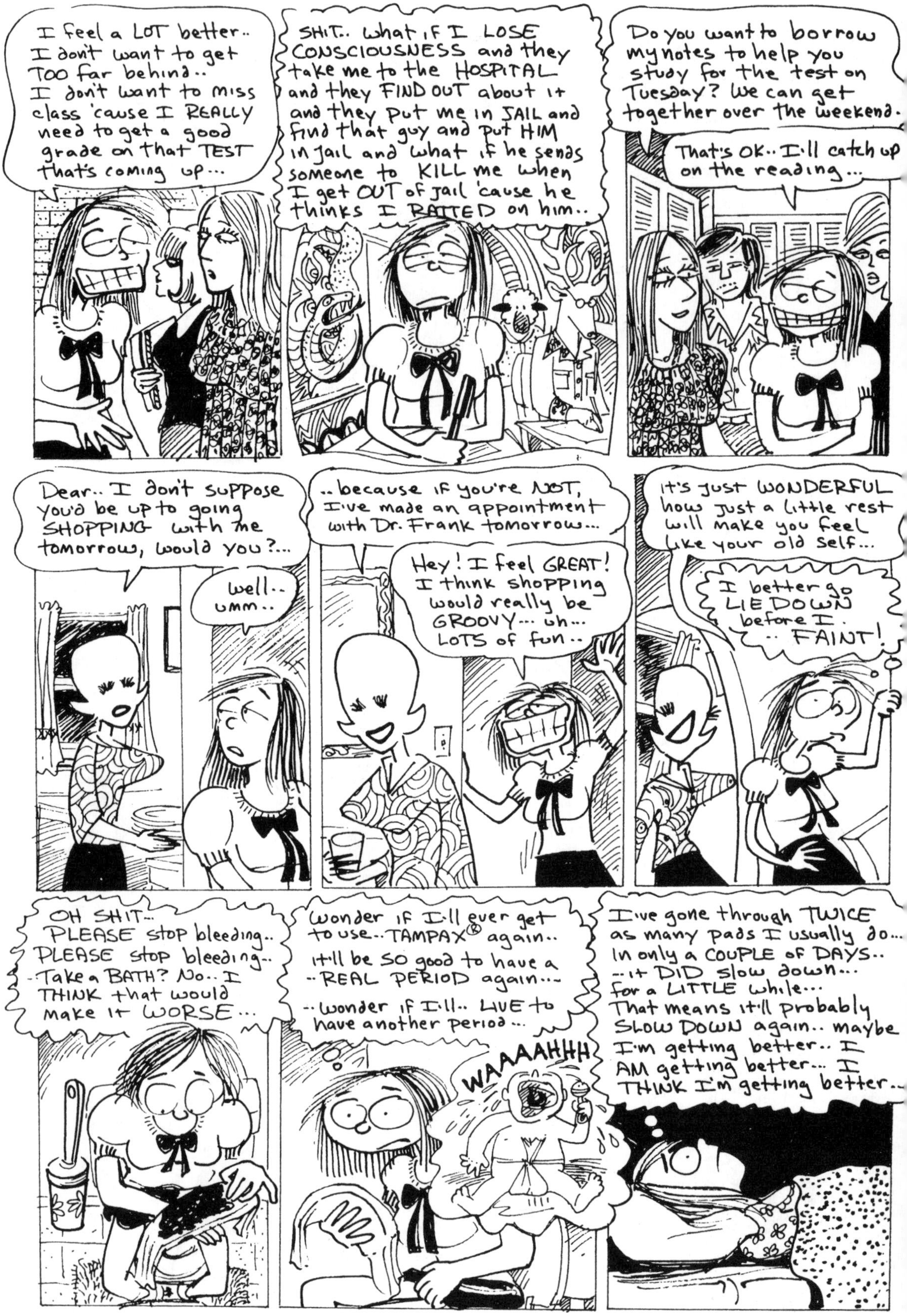
I feel a LOT better.. I don't want to get TOO far behind.. I don't want to miss class 'cause I REALLY need to get a good grade on that TEST that's coming up...
SHIT.. what if I LOSE CONSCIOUSNESS and they take me to the HOSPITAL and they FIND OUT about it and they put me in JAIL and find that guy and put HIM in jail and what if he sends someone to KILL me when I get OUT of jail 'cause he thinks I RATTED on him..
Do you want to borrow my notes to help you study for the test on Tuesday? We can get together over the weekend.
That's OK.. I'll catch up on the reading...
Dear.. I don't suppose you'd be up to going SHOPPING with me tomorrow, would you?...
Well.. umm..
..because if you're NOT, I've made an appointment with Dr. Frank tomorrow...
Hey! I feel GREAT! I think shopping would really be GROOVY... uh... LOTS of fun..
It's just WONDERFUL how just a little rest will make you feel like your old self...
I better go LIE DOWN before I.. FAINT!
OH SHIT.. PLEASE stop bleeding.. PLEASE stop bleeding.. Take a BATH? No.. I THINK that would make it WORSE...
Wonder if I'll ever get to use.. TAMPAX® again..
It'll be SO good to have a REAL PERIOD again...
..wonder if I'll.. LIVE to have another period...
WAAAAHHH
I've gone through TWICE as many pads I usually do... In only a COUPLE of DAYS.. ..it DID slow down... for a LITTLE while... That means it'll probably SLOW DOWN again.. maybe I'm getting better.. I AM getting better... I THINK I'm getting better...

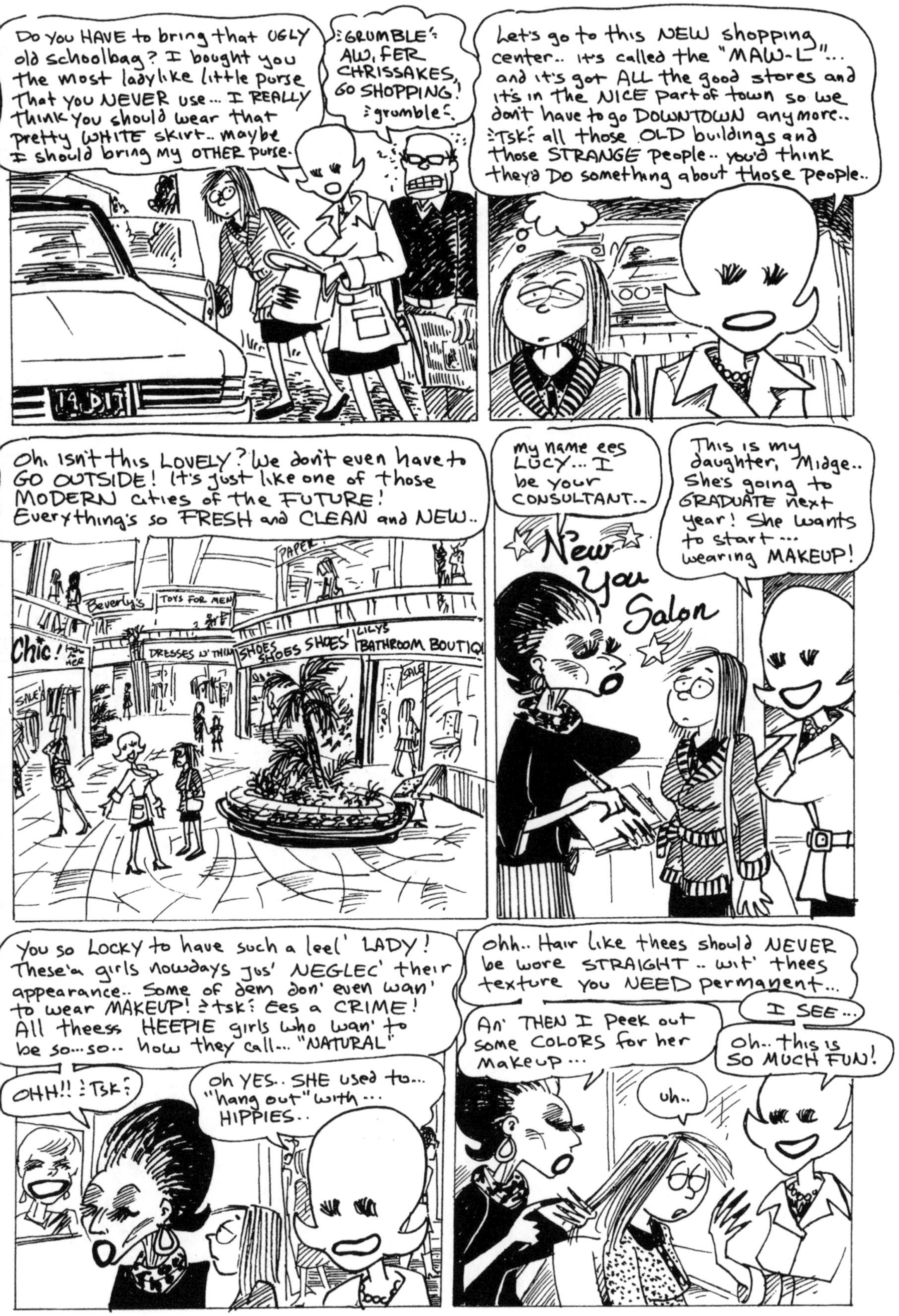
Do you HAVE to bring that UGLY old schoolbag? I bought you the most ladylike little purse That you NEVER use... I REALLY think you should wear that pretty WHITE skirt.. maybe I should bring my OTHER purse..
:GRUMBLE: AW, FER CHRISSAKES, GO SHOPPING! :grumble:
14 DIT
Let's go to this NEW shopping center.. it's called the "MAW-L"... and it's got ALL the good stores and it's in the NICE part of town so we don't have to go DOWNTOWN anymore.. :TSK: all those OLD buildings and those STRANGE people.. you'd think they'd DO something about those people..
Oh, isn't this LOVELY? We don't even have to GO OUTSIDE! It's just like one of those MODERN cities of the FUTURE! Everything's so FRESH and CLEAN and NEW..
PAPER
Beverly's
TOYS FOR MEN
Chic!
DRESSES N' THINGS
SHOES SHOES SHOES
LILY'S BATHROOM BOUTIQ
SALE
my name ees LUCY... I be your CONSULTANT..
This is my daughter, Midge.. She's going to GRADUATE next year! She wants to start... wearing MAKEUP!
New You Salon
You so LOCKY to have such a leel' LADY! These'a girls nowdays jus' NEGLEC' their appearance.. Some of dem don' even wan' to wear MAKEUP! :tsk: Ees a CRIME! All theess HEEPIE girls who wan' to be so...so.. how they call... "NATURAL"
OHH!! :Tsk:
oh YES.. SHE used to... "hang out" with... HIPPIES..
ohh.. Hair like thees should NEVER be wore STRAIGHT.. wit' thees texture you NEED permanent...
I SEE..
An' THEN I peek out some COLORS for her makeup...
oh.. this is SO MUCH FUN!
uh..

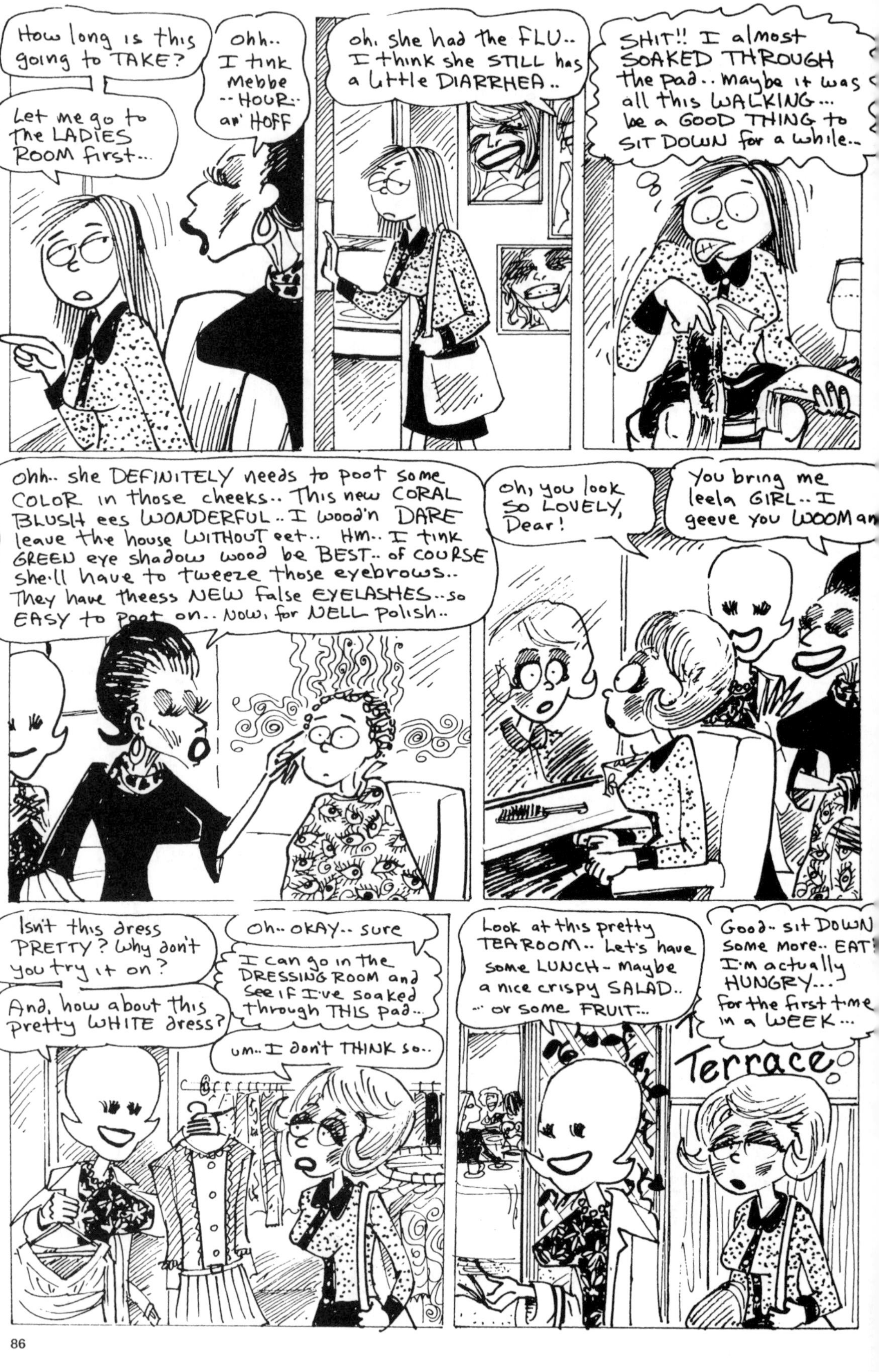
How long is this going to TAKE?
Let me go to the LADIES ROOM first...
Ohh.. I tink Mebbe --HOUR-- an' HOFF
oh, she had the FLU.. I think she STILL has a Little DIARRHEA..
SHIT!! I almost SOAKED THROUGH the pad.. maybe it was all this WALKING... be a GOOD THING to SIT DOWN for a while..
Ohh.. she DEFINITELY needs to poot some COLOR in those cheeks.. This new CORAL BLUSH ees WONDERFUL.. I wood'n DARE leave the house WITHOUT eet.. Hm.. I tink GREEN eye shadow wood be BEST.. of COURSE she'll have to tweeze those eyebrows.. They have theess NEW false EYELASHES..so EASY to poot on.. Now, for NELL polish..
Oh, you look so LOVELY, Dear!
You bring me leela GIRL.. I geeve you WOOMan
Isn't this dress PRETTY? Why don't you try it on?
And, how about this pretty WHITE dress?
Oh.. OKAY.. sure
I can go in the DRESSING ROOM and see if I've soaked through THIS pad..
um.. I don't THINK so..
Look at this pretty TEAROOM.. Let's have some LUNCH - maybe a nice crispy SALAD.. ... or some FRUIT...
Good.. sit DOWN Some more.. EAT! I'm actually HUNGRY... for the first time in a WEEK...
Terrace

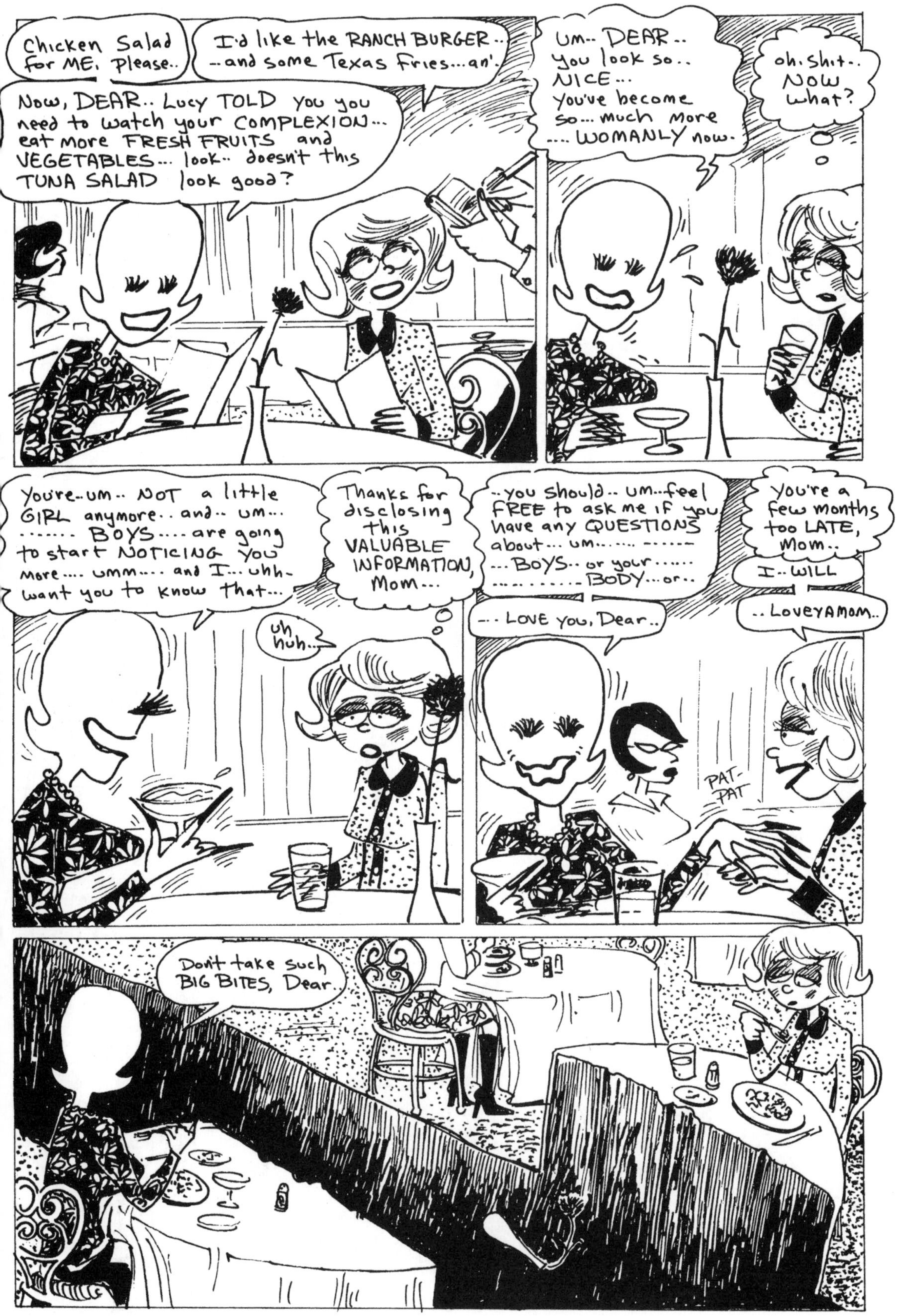
Chicken Salad for ME, please..
I'd like the RANCH BURGER.. ..and some Texas fries...an'.
Now, DEAR.. Lucy TOLD you you need to watch your COMPLEXION... eat more FRESH FRUITS and VEGETABLES... look.. doesn't this TUNA SALAD look good?
Um.. DEAR.. You look so.. NICE... You've become so... much more .... WOMANLY now.
oh.shit.. NOW what?
You're..um.. NOT a little GIRL anymore.. and.. um... .... BOYS.... are going to start NOTICING you more.... umm.... and I... uhh.. want you to know that...
uh huh..
Thanks for disclosing this VALUABLE INFORMATION, Mom...
..you should.. um..feel FREE to ask me if you have any QUESTIONS about... um........ ------ ... BOYS.. or your...... .... BODY... or..
You're a few months too LATE, Mom..
I.. WILL
..LOVEYAMOM..
... LOVE you, Dear..
PAT-PAT
Don't take such BIG BITES, Dear.

Isn't she LOVELY? I took her to "The New You Salon" over in the ... MAW-L.. This is one of her new DRESSES..

Nice to see that SOME of these girls still want to be ...... LADIES!

PLEASE GOD.. LET ME LIVE.. LET ME STOP BLEEDING-- PLEASE GOD.. I KNOW I DID WRONG.. FORGIVE ME.. I'LL NEVER HAVE SEX AGAIN-- I'LL DEVOTE MY LIFE TO YOUR SERVICE-- PLEASE MAKE ME .... EEDING...

There's only a LITTLE bit.. ..Maybe I'm getting BETTER.. THANK YOU, GOD.. and if I'm getting BETTER, it means GOD isn't Punishing me, so maybe it was OKAY what I did.. or maybe it means the... really ISN'T a GOD.. ... CHURCH Say... RONG and I... unished, so

oh, WOW, Midge.. you sure look... DIFFERENT.

So.. are you FEELING any better?

oh, YES.. the cramps are GONE.. and I'm hardly bleeding!

That's groovy! So.. we're going to get together right after school an'..

OH... I think I'll just go home.. take it EASY..

THAT'S MY BAG

Mom and Dad never DID find out about this.. ..I had this BIG PROBLEM and I got it TOGETHER enough to TAKE CARE of The situation... I.. REALLY feel like I.. ACCOMPLISHED something.. feels GOOD! Like.. I'm REALLY a part of the REAL world.. as an ADULT.. Like I've moved on to an.. IMPORTANT place..

-and now I get to hang out with the.. -REALLY important kids in this school-

I thought she was.. YOUR friend..

I.. guess she needs time to get her... HEAD together about what happened to her..

THAT'S MY BAG

88

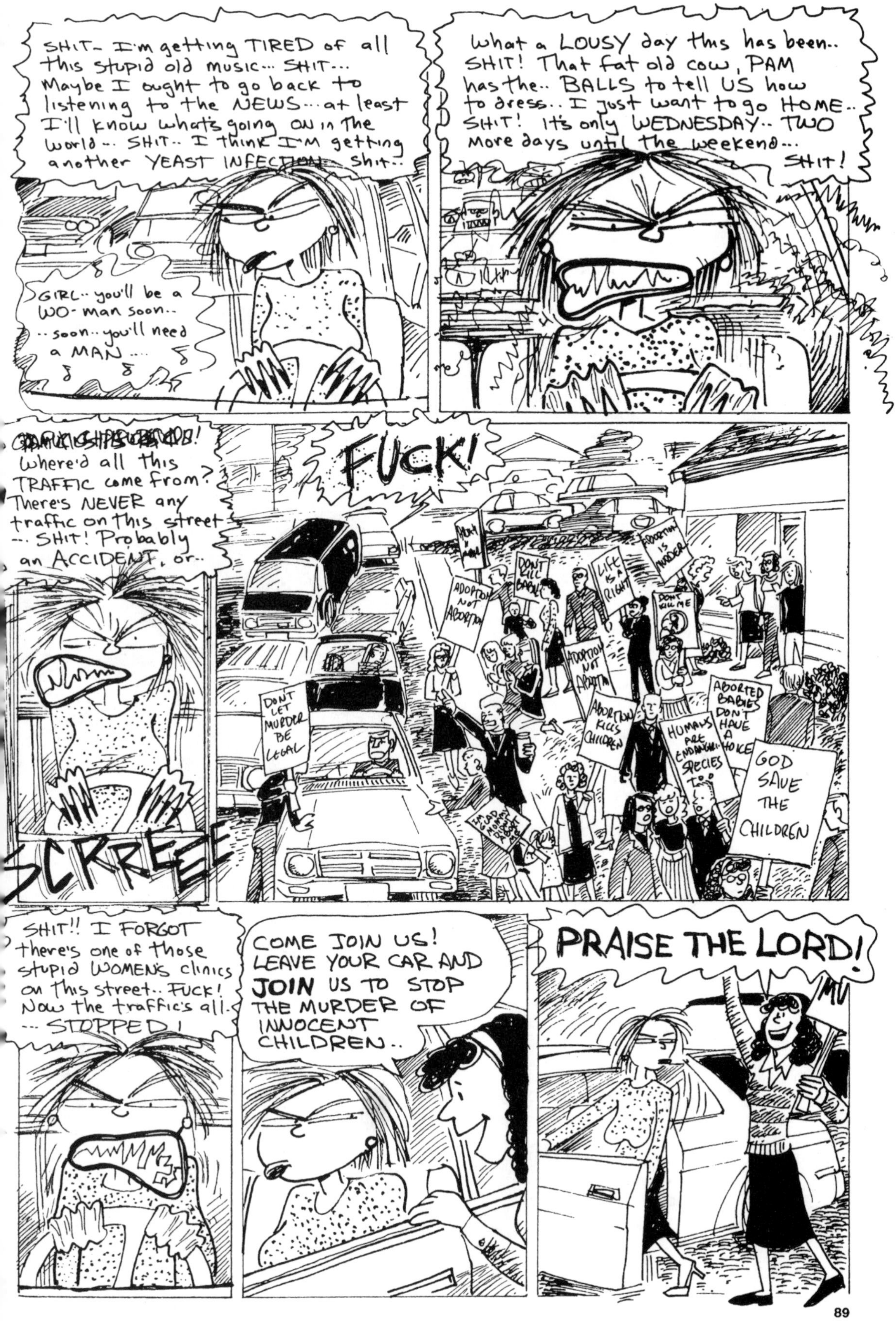
SHIT.. I'm getting TIRED of all this stupid old music... SHIT... Maybe I ought to go back to listening to the NEWS... at least I'll know what's going on in the world... SHIT.. I think I'M getting another YEAST INFECTION... shit..
GIRL.. you'll be a WO-man soon.. ..soon.. you'll need a MAN....
What a LOUSY day this has been.. SHIT! That fat old cow, PAM has the.. BALLS to tell US how to dress.. I just want to go HOME.. SHIT! It's only WEDNESDAY.. TWO more days until the weekend... SHIT!
where'd all this TRAFFIC come from? There's NEVER any traffic on this street.. SHIT! Probably an ACCIDENT, or..
FUCK!
DON'T LET MURDER BE LEGAL
ADOPTION NOT ABORTION
DON'T KILL BABY
LIFE IS A RIGHT
ABORTION IS MURDER
DON'T KILL ME
ADOPTION NOT ABORTION
ABORTION KILLS CHILDREN
HUMANS ARE ENDANGERED SPECIES TOO
ABORTED BABIES DON'T HAVE A CHOICE
GOD SAVE THE CHILDREN
SCRREEE
SHIT!! I FORGOT there's one of those stupid WOMEN'S clinics on this street.. FUCK! Now the traffic's all.. ..STOPPED!
COME JOIN US! LEAVE YOUR CAR AND **JOIN** US TO STOP THE MURDER OF INNOCENT CHILDREN..
PRAISE THE LORD!

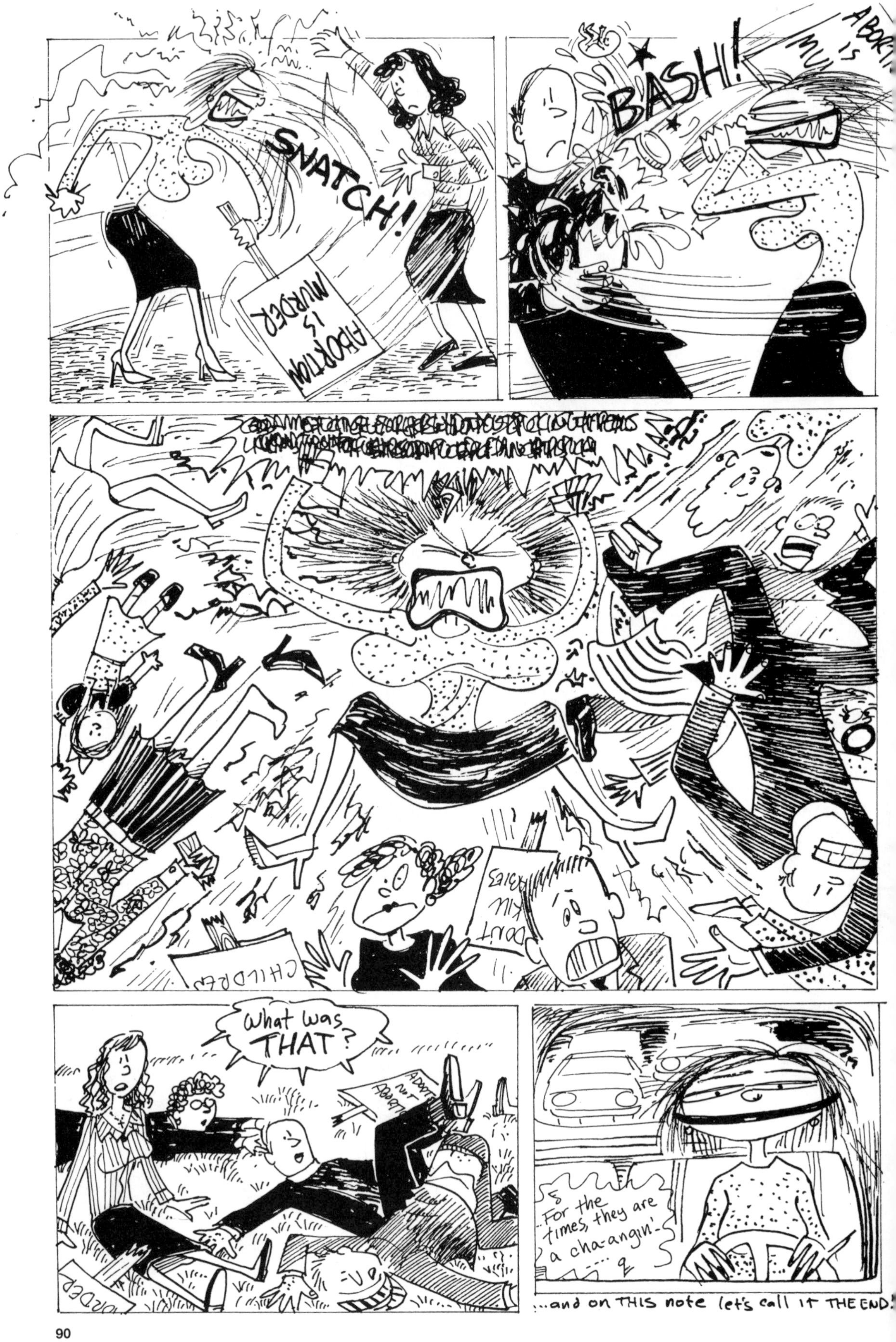
SNATCH!
ABORTION IS MURDER
BASH!
ABORTION IS MU
O
DON'T KILL BABIES
CHILDREN
What was THAT?
ABORTION NOT
MURDER
& For the times, they are a cha-angin'-
...and on THIS note let's call it THE END!

If you enjoyed reading this book, and you're not familiar with *Naughty Bits,* the groundbreaking alternative comic book series that these stories are excerpted from, you've got a lot to catch up on! Twenty issues are out so far, containing not only Bitchy Bitch stories but some very unique backup comics dealing with everything from travels abroad, to doggies in heat to sexual identity to a feminist look at sex comics. Plus a lively letters section filled with discussion of comics as well as current topics (and a long-running search for creative terms for female masturbation) and a cartoon monologue by the artist in every issue! Add to that guest pages introducing comics by lesser-known alternative cartoonists, (particularly women) and a showcase of unique alternative comics that may not be widely available, and you can see why more and more readers are eagerly looking forward to the next issue of this highly acclaimed quarterly series! All back issues are currently available for $3.50 each postpaid, or a six-issue subscription can be had for only $17.50. The series is recommended for Mature Readers. Write to Fantagraphics Books, and while you're at it, ask for their free catalogue of some of the best comics and graphics novels available today!

Fantagraphics Books
7563 Lake City Way, NE
Seattle, WA 98115

Roberta Gregory has literally been a female pioneer in alternative comics, though her work is still not widely known after twenty years of highly-acclaimed creations. She was the first woman to solo self-publish an underground comic in 1976. She appeared in early issues of *Wimmen's Comix* and in practically every issue of *Gay Comix*. She self-published a graphic novel, *Winging It*, in 1988, and a collection of comic strips. Her work covers a broad range of topics: feminism, social and political issues, fantasy, metaphysics and sexual identity. *Naughty Bits* is just the tip of the iceberg! For a free catalogue of her comics, send her a self-addressed stamped envelope, or drop her a line if you liked this book!

Roberta Gregory
P.O. Box 27438
Seattle, WA 98125